D1058485

# LITERATURE THROUGH ART

# LITERATURE THROUGH ART

*A New Approach to French Literature*

HELMUT A. HATZFELD

New York · OXFORD UNIVERSITY PRESS · 1952

The author is indebted to the following publishers for permission to quote material under their copyright:

Appleton-Century-Crofts, Inc.
Charles T. Branford Co., Publishers
Editions de la Maison Française, Inc.
Harcourt, Brace and Company, Inc.
Harper and Brothers
Henry Holt and Company, Inc., Publishers
Hyperion Press, Inc. (Editions Hypérion)
J. B. Lippincott Company, Publishers
Pantheon Books, Inc.
Sheed and Ward, Inc.
Yale University Press

FOR MANY YEARS literary historians, realizing that literature is essentially one of the arts, have believed that the other arts, particularly the arts of design, could give to the art of the word a fundamental, new elucidation and orientation. Unhappily, though recognized in theory, little progress has been made in this direction in practice.

In any event, the art criticism of literati (Fénelon, Diderot) who shared the ideals of contemporary painters has been aptly used as a key to their own literary art. Contemporaneous and later illustrations of works of literature (e.g. La Fontaine's *Fables*) have revealed historically right and historically wrong interpretations respectively. The common spirit in literature and art at a certain epoch became of paramount importance for recent studies in the so-called literary baroque. Here it was evident that sociological-historical links between the arts could be developed to the point where they ultimately help us to understand formal stylistic problems. Many other examples of the relation between the two arts could be enumerated.

The present study, however, will be concerned primarily with the following considerations. A picture may reveal the meaning of a literary text and vice versa. A given poem and picture may illustrate how the same motif is given different artistic incarnation according to the separate domain and medium of poet and painter, the fundamental differences between the two modes of expression having been known since they were discussed in Lessing's *Laocoön*. Again poets may prove to be directly inspired by artists, and painters by *hommes de lettres*; and each may attempt something of a ' transposition of art.' Iconographical problems may hint at unknown literary sources of a painting, and an obscure poem may become clear at once from looking at a picture which the poet had in mind when writing and which the literary critic must rediscover in order to elucidate the poem. A poem divested of its obscurity will often prove to be a simple paraphrase in metaphorical language of something seen or visualized. It is well known that several works of Gustave Flaubert took their inspiration from pictures.

In our attempt to elucidate French literature with the help of pictorial art, however, we have not limited ourselves to the selection of a particular set of possibilities at the exclusion of others, but instead have considered throughout a wide variety of possibilities. The starting point in such comparative studies must always be the cultural pattern of the epoch; the goal, problems of pure form. To separate the two may be 'art appreciation,' but cannot be reconciled with historical scholarship and therefore has no place here. The material itself will dictate the points of contact between the arts, which are different in each century. Therefore we have attempted neither a morphology of the arts nor a history of their exterior relations.

Excluding general speculations and the personal relations between artists and writers, we have put side by side concrete examples of French literature and art as represented by texts and pictures or sculptures from 1100 to 1940 and have drawn such parallels between them as seemed reasonable. This has never been done before. There are, it is true, anthologies of French literature that are excellently illustrated with pictures. These anthologies, however, not only leave to the reader the decisive work of connecting texts and images but also combine the most disparate items without any considerations of epochal boundaries.

To the literary historian, a history of French literature in which art is used as the key to a better and deeper understanding of literature will be of primary concern. The art historian, on the other hand, will take the opposite view wishing to see art elucidated by other forms of expression. To us the paramount problem is the comparative analysis and appreciation of texts and pictures in their *details*. For this purpose the historian must also be a philologist and a critic, i.e. one who can analyze both texts and pictures with correctness and taste. Therefore philologist and critic must be understood here in a double sense; first, factually, in regard to interpretation and iconography and second, formally, in regard to stylistics and formal description.

From a methodological point of view, philology is involved in yet another sense. It is gratifying to see that the text-bound analytical, and stylistic method in literary history as used here, and as opposed to the traditionally vague, synthetic, and persuasive method, finds even on the non-comparative level enthusiastic support from the analysts of literary style. It is they who have called for a change in the way of literary history. The method of *explication de textes* has been used for some years for historical purposes in the sense that the new literary history in the making is considered to be composed of single layers of interpreted texts as encountered in successive epochs. It is this method that is used here on a comparative basis, the *explications de textes* having been supplemented by the *explications de tableaux*.

With regard to the comparative method concerning two arts, it is an encouraging sign that the parallel study of literature and music is also making progress. The only difficulties under which this type of study labors is lack of analytical, specialized work in the field. Souriau's book *La Correspondance des arts* (Paris: Flammarion, 1947) must be mentioned here for the surprising clarity and directness with which the author approaches in a general way a problem that will come up on every page of our book. Souriau formulates the problem in this way: 'What is the extent of resemblances, affinities, and common laws between a statue and a painting, a sonnet and a vase, a cathedral and a symphony, and which are at the same time, their differences which might be called congenital ones? '

The present material has been selected in such a way that even where the stress seems to lie on art rather than on literature the decisive point will be that it is a *literary* scholar who looks at art, i.e. one who of necessity has the works, the problems, and the development of French *literature* in mind when choosing a picture for analysis.

Although this book presupposes some knowledge of the history of French literature as well as of French art, it may well serve as an introduction to the artistic side of literature. The fundamental aids to our purpose are pictures — many pictures — the most important, spontaneous, and correct interpretations of which will come from the contemporaneous literary texts accompanying them. Conversely, the texts themselves and the entire works from which they are taken should be made intelligible in their full meaning and artistic reality precisely by these pictures. Literature and teaching literature make sense in an educational program only if literature is not made subservient to sociological, psychological, and pragmatic considerations — which is decidedly not the role of literature; its very *raison d'être* is refinement and insight into that interior world which Pascal has defined as *esprit de finesse*. I know no better means to give literature, and particularly the leading foreign literature, this rank and importance than to conceive of it as an art to be enriched still further by a systematic comparison with the related pictorial art. This is particularly so for those to whom the eye means more than the ear or discursive thinking.

By systematic analysis of a series of specific works, we have attempted to shed light on six epochs of French literature and art in the course of six chapters. A seventh and final chapter interprets the results of this historical research in terms of their contribution to a critical theory of literary aesthetics. A special bibliography will be found following the notes to each chapter, a general bibliography concerning previous contribution to this theory at the end of the book. The translations, with some few exceptions, are by the author. Modern French has been translated only when it was felt necessary for the convenience of the reader.

While this study has no direct pedagogical aims, it is hoped that it will also satisfy the growing need for the formation of taste through a comparative study of literature and art. The present text has been read by Sister Francis Ellen Riordan and Professor Ernest C. Hassold, for whose friendly competent advice and sacrifice of precious time I am deeply grateful.

*The Catholic University of America*                                    H. H.
*October* 1951

# Table of Contents

# List of Reproductions

# LITERATURE THROUGH ART

1. Tympanum of the Portal of the Abbey Church in Moissac. (Foto Marburg)

# The Romanesque and Gothic Epoch

1000–1350

ROMANESQUE art in France, stemming from the Cluniac reform, coincides chronologically with the first appearance of a literature written in the young vernacular. Old French, carried over from the ninth century in lives of saints, comes of age in the *chansons de geste* of the twelfth century. Joseph Bédier has linked these epics of Charlemagne, Count Guillaume, and Doon de Mayence to the Cluniac sanctuaries and pilgrim roads.[1] He believed that these boldly invented stories, fabricated to explain certain relics, were used to attract pilgrims to these wayside shrines. The epics and the Romanesque cathedrals of the eleventh and twelfth centuries belong closely together anyway, because the epics in their motives and concepts of form are witnesses of the same Romanesque art as are the shrines themselves.

This bond between Romanesque art and literature comes from the fact that in their approach to the Divine they both emphasize the majesty of God, and in their approach to the human they confine themselves to the typical. In addition to these motifs there is, as far as imagination is concerned, a singularly fantastic element that is expressed in an additive or cumulative technique.

## I. The Majestic-Hieratic Approach to Divine and Human Mysteries

Comparing the tympanum of the portal of the Abbey Church in Moissac [2] (1135) (see Fig. 1) with the text of the *Chanson de Roland*, one sees a striking series of corresponding details in this impressive piece of sculpture. This tympanum represents Christ surrounded by the four Evangelists in symbolic fashion. The twenty-four ancients of St. John's Apocalypse appear below them. Christ as the Judge of the world is depicted here in the form that Romanesque art inherited from the Byzantine mosaics, the *Pantocrator* or *Majestas Domini*. The figure is superhuman, a *Christus Rex* bearing the crown, stiff, hieratic, austere, expressing not only the element of the *tremendum* in the concept of the numinous, but also the static, authoritative, absolute element in the concept of power in an archaic society. In other words, one is confronted here with the archaic type of ruler who appears in exactly the same concept in the *chansons de geste*. In these *chansons* the ruler is Charlemagne 'with the white beard'; he is the Emperor who conquers the world after 'having been seven full years in Spain.' One is also reminded of the priest who plays, under the vague name of a Figura, the role of God in the oldest, half-liturgical French play, *Le Mystère d'Adam*. This is significant of the fact that at that time neither in art nor in literature did one dare to impersonate a Christ whose humanity would be overstressed. The ruler king as such has no tradition in literature. He appears to be Charlemagne stereotyped as *Pantocrator*.

As unchangeable and typical as this Christ in glory appears on all the other Romanesque tympana, just as unchangeable appears the epic king in almost all the *chansons de geste*. If there is any variation, it is negligible. It is true that different tympana use slightly different attitudes for Christ; sometimes he is seated, sometimes standing, turned to the right, or turned to the left. The epic king may be called the one 'with the grayish beard' or 'with the snowy beard' instead of 'with the flowery beard,' but the fundamental pattern does not change.

The *Majestas Domini* is, however, reflected in still another way throughout the *chansons de geste*, namely, in the concept of God and expressions that refer to Him. The tympanum alone explains the current locution 'God of the throne,' because on the tympanum Christ is seated on a throne, and *tron* consequently will soon mean in the epics and in Old French in general 'paradise,' 'heaven.' The high judgment seat of Christ at the top of the tympanum accounts furthermore for the expression 'God who is seated high and looking far' (*Berte aux grands pieds*, line 758). The *majestas* idea as such is also responsible for all the current names and epithets of God in the epics, which are indicative of the same spiritual character of the tympanum: *Deus de majesté, omnipotent, alteor, altisme, glorios, posteis, vrais gouvernere, verai justicier, verai droiturier; Pere tot puissant, de gloire, vray pere tout puissant; Damedeus le glorieus poissant, glorieus rois celestes, glorios sire pere; Rois de majesté, roi de tot le monde, rois glorius et forz.*[3] They are like echoes from the most sacred and ancient liturgy: *Hagios ho Theos, Hagios Ischyros, Hagios Athanatos; Sanctus Deus, Sanctus Fortis, Sanctus Immortalis.*

This glorious Divine Majesty, King, Judge, and Sire of the sculpture is surrounded by uncanny, wondrous animals. It would seem that these Oriental, abstract, winged creatures[4] are in the process of becoming the symbols of the Evangelists: the eagle of St. John, the ox of St. Luke, the lion of St. Mark, and the man of St. Matthew. These symbolic animals, purposely unrealistic, are as unfamiliar and extraordinary to modern man as the contemporary *Bestiaire* of Philippe de Thaün. In such bestiaries, symbolic, moral, and anagogic meanings are of such primary concern that mysterious, nonexistent animals are invented, allegedly indicative of man's salvation and of the mysteries of Christ. The monstrous nature of these beasts is apparent. Henri Focillon writes of the symbolic animals, for whose birth Pliny, Oriental idols, old Irish and Germanic animal ornaments, and Christian symbolism are all responsible:

> The romanesque art perceived creatures only through a network of ornamentation and under monstrous appearances. It had multiplied man in the animal and the animal in the fabulous beast. It had hung upon its capitals a whole series of chimeric creatures and marked the tympanum of the churches with the seal of the Apocalypse . . .
> There is in stone a revival of the animal life of the steppes . . . a wild animal, mounted upon his prey, forms with it a compact group. This power of synthesis, which mixes life with life and shapes individuals to make out of them species of double monsters, is at the core of romanesque stylistics.[5]

The lion of the *Bestiaire* is like that of the tympanum: king and judge. He is therefore symbolic of Christ and in particular Christ at the Last Judgment. The different parts of the lion's body are indicative of divinity, justice, and so on:

| | |
|---|---|
| Leüns en mainte guise | [The lion in many a way |
| Multes bestes justise | Judges many animals, |
| Pur ço est reis leüns; | Therefore the lion is king; |
| Or oez ses façuns: | Now listen to what his features are: |
| Il at le vis herdu [hardi] | He has a keen face, |
| Gros le col et kernu | A big neck and a mane around |
| Quaré le piz devant | In front a square breast |
| Hardi et cumbatant; | Daring and ready to fight; |
| Graille at le trait derriere | Slim is his hind part, |
| Cue de grant maniere . . . | A tail of great impressiveness . . . |
| Li leüns signifie | The lion is a symbol |
| Le fiz Sainte Marie . . . | Of the Son of Holy Mary . . . |
| As Judeus s'aparat | To the Jews He will appear |
| Quant il les jugerat . . . | When he will judge them . . . |
| Force de Deité | The power of the Godhead |
| Demustre piz carré, | Is symbolized by the square breast, |
| La cue par nature | The tail naturally |
| Mustre sainte escripture | Is revealed by Holy Scripture |
| U la cue est justise | Where the tail is the justice |
| Ki desur nus est mise.[6] | Which has been set upon us.] |

The Physiologus-bestiary consequently shows better than the Romanesque tympana that the symbols of the Evangelists were originally symbols of Christ Himself. Therefore the eagle is also described as follows:

| | |
|---|---|
| Li Aigle signifie | [The Eagle symbolizes |
| Le fiz Sainte Marie; | The Son of Holy Mary |
| Reis est sur tute gent | He is king over all people |
| Senz nul redutement . . . | Without any doubt.] |

(1251-4)

There are other animals in the *Bestiaire* as mythical as their distorted Greek names: Monosceros (unicorn), Dorcon, Ydrus, Nicticorax, Aptalon, Assidam. They may account for the particular antirealism of the tympanum at Moissac. The Assidam, for instance, is a winged camel:

| | |
|---|---|
| De chameil dous piez at, | [Of the camel he has the two feet, |
| D'oisel dous ailes at | Of the bird he has the two wings |
| E Ysaïas dit | And Isaiah speaks |
| D'iceste en sun escrit. | About this animal in his writings.] |

(2067–70)

The historians of art have not as yet exhausted the study of iconography in bestiaries. One of the latest symbolic animals among the zodiac symbols of Chartres cathedral, namely the he-goat entangled in a bush, generally interpreted realistically as a *drôlerie*, looks very much like the Aptalon of Philippe de Thaün:

| | |
|---|---|
| Puis quiert un buissunet | [Then he looks for a little bush |
| Menu e espesset, | Small and thick, |
| U el se vient jüer | Where he begins to play |
| E ses cornes froter . . . | And to rub his horns . . . |
| Unc ne set mot la beste | No sooner is the animal aware of it |
| Quant prise est par la teste | Than it is taken by the head |
| E qu'ele est enlaciée | And is entangled |
| E el buissun liée. | And captured in the bush.] |

(775–86)

These are the first aspects of literature and art that substantiate Focillon's qualification of this Romanesque epoch as being *épique et tératologique*.

Beyond the conceptual implications, however, there is also a formal principle involved. The juvenile zeal of these first young generations of the Romance-Germanic *Francs de France* shows them as heirs of a misunderstood antiquity. They try to take in with their youthful eyes and unite in an artistic entity as many parts as is psychologically possible. Modern experiments have found that five subunits are the maximum a single glance can catch. This is also the acknowledged, unsymbolic, and formal explanation of the five units on the usual Romanesque tympanum. Christ and the four evangelical animals as nucleus of this principle will soon be paralleled by the five superimposed galleries (*régistres*) of the later tympana.

The number five, as Ernst Robert Curtius has pointed out,[7] is also the basis of the eleventh-century *Chanson de Saint Alexis* (1080). The five parts of the story are: (1) the story of the Saint's parents; (2) his marriage and dramatic separation from the young wife; (3) his penance of seventeen years in Edessa; (4) his penance of seventeen years under his father's staircase in Rome; (5) his death and immediate canonization. This five-act story is told in 125 strophes of five lines each — that is, 625 lines written in ten-syllable lines of five iambic feet each. Anna Granville Hatcher has been able to prove a still closer mathematical principle based on five.

The *Chanson de Roland* may also be subdivided, although written not in strophes but in *laisses*, into five blocks, which include very neatly the so-called Baligant episode: (1) 1–702: Ganelon's mission and his treason; (2) 703–2396: Roland's rear-guard battle; (3) 2397–2608: Marsilie's defeat by Charles; (4) 2609–3547: counterattack of Baligant; (5) 3548–4002: final victory and punishment of Ganelon.

Intriguing is the fact that the psychological principle of five units is counterbalanced by the symbolic principle of three units on the panel as well as in the *Roland*. Thus the five units never make us forget the holy Triad. The tympanum of Moissac strikes us first as the triad of Christ, the Apostles, and the ancients; the poet of the *Chanson de Roland*, as William S. Woods has proved ('The Symbolic Structure of *La Chanson de Roland*,' PMLA, LXV, 1950, pp. 1247–62), groups his *laisses* according to triads of action, psychology, and atmosphere.

The presence of the ancients of the Apocalypse has another implication besides the scriptural one for this young French nation of 1130. As their idea of the Divine is expressed by superhuman proportions, so human dignity is expressed by old age. It is age that makes Charlemagne and Duke Naimes of Bavaria in the *Chanson de Roland* so venerable. Likewise with the pagans, Baligant is of an almost mythical age, judging from the incredible exaggeration of having him outlive Virgil as well as Homer:

2. Tympanum of La Madeleine in Vézelay. (Foto Marburg)

| En Babilonie Baligant ad mandet: | [He sent to Babylon for Baligant; |
|---|---|
| Ço est l'amirail le vieil d'antiquitet, | This is the old admiral of antiquity, |
| Tut survesquiet et Virgilie et Omer. | He outlived Virgil as well as Homer.] |

(2614–16)

## II. Static Presentation of Fantastic Concepts

Another Romanesque sculpture, the tympanum of La Madeleine [8] in Vézelay (see Fig. 2), representing Christ sending forth the Apostles by imparting to them the Holy Spirit, presents new problems. This tympanum of 1130 has been described very pertinently by Marcel Aubert as follows:

> One knows the magnificent representation of the Pentecost, sculptured on the tympanum of the central door with its great figures dressed in cloth that draws concentric folds on breast, hips, and knees, tucked up below . . . but of an infinite nobility. The artist, guided by a scholarly cleric, nourished by the sermons of Honorius Augustodunensis, has represented, together with the Pentecost, the tradition of the keys, and he has figured around the central composition, on the lintel and in the semicircle of the vault . . . the different nations of earth to whom the Apostles are to convey the Gospel, strange and fabulous people whom the people of the Middle Ages knew through the stories of the Ancients: Scythians with dogs' heads, dwarfs with unproportioned ears, pygmies who use ladders to mount on horseback, pagan people whom the Apostles following Christ are to baptize in the Spirit, as Saint John the Baptist (standing upright against the pier) had baptized in the water. And the miracles are worked: The blind see; the deaf hear; the lame walk.[9]

The unequal size of the framings of the groups sculptured in the arch of the vault reminds one of the unequal length of the *laisses* in the *chansons de geste*, which range from five to fifty lines.

Heaping up scenes by a simple addition and juxtaposition is illustrated by the combined emission of the Holy Spirit and the conferring of the keys, as well as the colorful procession of the nations on the lintel, reminiscent of a parallel attempt to describe the battle arrays in the *chansons de geste*. Hero after hero, battle unit after battle unit, helmets, armor, spears, and banners are shown without any subordinating link. Olivier, watching, in the *Roland*, the approach of the pagans, sees in a ' teichoscopy ' a mass of overwhelming details. They are, like those on the Vézelay lintel, brought together by a cumulative technique. Admitting the inadequacy of this technique, both sculptor and author solve their problem relatively skilfully; both evoke masses of people by surface details. As before the reconnoitering eyes of Olivier, so before the visionary eyes of the apostles appear all the pagans of the earth, *la paiennie gent, le paienisme*, who are to be converted to the Faith:

Olivier est desur un pui muntez
Guardet sur destre parmi un val herbus,
Si veit venir cele gent paienur
Sin apelat Rollant sun compaignun:
Devers Espaigne vei venir tel bruur [turmoil],
Tanz blancs osbercs, tanz elmes flambius,
Icist ferunt nos François grant irur . . .
Luisent cil elme ki ad or sunt gemmez
E cil escuz e cil osbercs safrez [brodés d'orfroi]
E cil espiez, cil gunfanun fermez . . .
Tant en i ad que mesure n'en set . . .
Dist Oliviers: Jo ai paiens veüz
Unc mais nuls hom en tere n'en vit plus.

(1017–40 passim) *

[Oliver has mounted a hill,
He looks to the right, down upon a grassy valley,
And sees approaching the pagan people,
Therefore he called Roland his companion:
From Spain I see a big crowd coming,
Many white haubercs, many helmets like flames,
This people will cause us Frenchmen great anger . . .
They sparkle, those helmets which are studded with jewels
And those shields and those haubercs embroidered with golden thread
And these spears, these undisplayed banners . . .
They are so many, that there is no limitation . . .
Says Oliver: I have seen so many pagans
That never anybody on earth has seen more of them.]

The fantastic element of these pagan tribes is also present in the caricatures of the Negroes in the *Chanson de Roland:*

| La contredite gent | [The enemy people |
|---|---|
| Ki plus sunt neir que nen est arremenz | Who are blacker than black ink |
| Ne n'unt de blanc ne mais que suls les denz. | And have of white nothing but the teeth.] |

(1932–4)

Better comparisons, however, are in the Alexander stories, which in endless lines picture the Macedonian hero in India among the most exotic people and situations. These stories begin very early. The *Alexander* fragment of Albéric de Briançon is older even than the *Roland.* The lost parts of this Romanesque epic may be supplied by the somewhat later (1170) rhymed novel by Alexandre de Bernay and Lambert li Tors. Here are not only Pliny's monstrous dwarfs and giants with dogs' heads and pigs' noses, as on the Vézelay tympanum, but still others walking on their heads; there are also nymphs and girl-plants (girls growing in meadows and upon trees), fanciful motifs that the Old French authors probably took from the Archpriest Leo.[10] The following lines describe the monsters with the dogs' heads and those with two heads on a split body:

Quant il viennent als erres que Artus et Liber clost
Coincocifail lor saillent des desers de Rimost,
XXX piez ont de aut, mout sunt lait et empost
Et ont testes de chien si com natural vost . . .

(5452ff.)

D'autre part de la rive a homes apparuz
Que sunt per mei les cors jusqu'as unbils fenduz,
E ot chascuns dos testes e dos piez e dos bus.[11]

(5480ff.)

[When they come to the regions which Artus and Liber enclose
The Coinocifail warriors attack them from the deserts of Rimost,
They are thirty feet high, they are very ugly and treacherous
And have dogs' heads as their natural faces.

On the other side of the river appeared men
Who are split in the middle of the body down to the navel,
And so everybody had two heads and two feet and two trunks.]

In regard to the total form, the figures on the panels of the arch of the
Vézelay tympanum seem at first sight to be independent of one another,
but at second sight they appear to be in a distinct composition. The key
can be found in the composition of the frieze above the lintel. There is
definitely a movement from both sides toward the center. As on the frieze,
so also in the arch of the vault: two slightly dynamic statuary halves are
arranged symmetrically around a middle axis, which is above Christ's head.
The same composition dominates the uppermost panel to the left. This
detail shows further that the group of three persons at the right interrupts
by a contrasting position the dynamic movement of the group at the left
and even of the whole left part of the arch. This contrasting movement
appears everywhere, as in the right of the frieze where the procession of the
nations is interrupted by some people mounting on horseback. Consequently the compositional principle in the whole and in the details is a
'harmony by contrast,' which maintains, in spite of a certain relative movement, the fundamental, static principle of Romanesque sculpture.

Similarly in *Roland*, all the peers are so concentrated around the Emperor Charles, be he absent or present, that scholars have wanted to call
the *Chanson de Roland* the *Chanson de Charles Magnes*. Nonetheless, in
the *Roland* there is also a particular 'poetic panel' with its own center of
gravity, the battle of Ronceval. Charles is far away from the call of the
horn, which reaches him feebly, and the interest focuses on the dying
friends, Roland and Olivier. In the medallion reserved to them by the poet,
they argue, discuss, fight, aid one another, make their mutual excuses,
bleed, weep, pray, swoon, die. This group receives particular treatment,
whereas all the other heroes, Gerin and Gerer, Berenger and Atum (lines
2186–7), even those with very definite features, such as Archbishop Turpin

and Duke Naimes of Bavaria, have their hieratic one-way direction in the poetic sculpture-vault of the battle. They join in ghastly succession the line moving to heroic death in defeat. Hence in both the sculpture and the literature of the Romanesque epoch there is a principle of static, additive composition opposed to a distinctly recognizable trend of dynamic movement and countermovement. This movement gracefully disturbs the rigid static principle. The effect is not achieved through the great and central topics themselves but by harmonizing their opposite elements in detail scenes, which can be more easily arranged and mastered.

The Romanesque sculptor in his first attempt at a dynamic procedure shows each single person, each slightly arranged group, and all of them together in the particular act of marching. This same pseudodynamic technique is found in the *Chanson de Roland*. Relentlessly the poet describes how each baron and all the Francs give blows to and receive blows from the enemies (lines 2066–70). But he cannot depict the movement of a battle, and he cannot invent really individual battle scenes. Instead, he relates in the clumsy language of the frieze of Vézelay:

La bataille est merveilluse e pesant;
Mult ben i *fiert Oliver* et *Rollant*
Li *arcevesques* plus de mil colps i rent
Li *XII per* ne s'en targent nient
Et li *Franceis* i *fierent cumunement*.
(1412–16)

[The battle is marvelous and heavy;
Oliver and Roland are very good fighters
The archbishop lands more than one thousand blows
The twelve peers do not protect themselves with their shields
And the French battle there all together.]

Certain regulating and co-ordinating elements do exist in this type of cumulative technique. There is, for instance, the interruption of the enumerative series by motifs of concentration. On the tympanum this would be, as mentioned above, the dwarfs' difficult mounting on horseback, an operation that interrupts the whole march of the nations. In the *Roland* it is the insertion of atmospheric sketches whose lyricism intrudes into the accumulative battle scenes:

Halt sunt li pui e tenebrus e grant
Li val perfunt et les ewes curant . . .
(1830–31)

[High are the mountains and dark and huge
The valleys are deep and the waters flow . . .]

Or:

Halt sunt li pui et mult halt les arbres,
Quatre perruns i ad luisant de marbre.
(2271–2)

[High are the mountains and very high the trees,
Four shining marble stones are lying there.]

It is not simply an iconographic necessity that, in addition to the fiery tongues figured to the right of Christ, there come from Christ's hands the sevenfold rays of the Holy Ghost. More important than the iconography is the significance of light to the medieval man, for in the matter of art forms he had inherited the resplendent Carolingian *verroterie cloisonnée* and altar statues studded with jewels, and in the matter of concepts the medieval idea of *Gratia divina pulchrificat sicut lux.* Hence there is light everywhere. Christ's *mandorla* and Christ's halo doubly express divine light, as though this Christ with light around the body, light around the head, and light streaming from the hands represents something similar to the light of the Creed, *lumen de lumine,* or the light of the hymn, ' *O Lux, beata Trinitas.'* This light also accompanies the angels who appear to the heroes of the *chansons de geste:*

> Un angre du chiel contreval devala . . .
> Mes de la grant clarté le bon quens aveugla.
>> (*Doone de Mayence,* 1882–3)

> [An angel from Heaven came down to earth . . .
> But blinded the count with his great brightness.]

Dying Roland admires particularly the light and splendor of his sword sparkling under the rays of the sun:

> E Durendal, cum es bele et clere et blanche!
> Cuntre soleil si luises et reflambes.
>> (*Roland,* 2316–17)

> [And Durendal, how beautiful you are and bright and white!
> And under the sun you are shining and full of flames!]

The brilliance of Charlemagne's sword changes thirty times every day:

> Joiuse, unches ne fut sa per
> Ki cascun jur muet trente clartez.
>> (2501–2)

> [Joyeuse never had its equal
> Which every day changes thirty times the kind of brilliancy.]

The army of Charlemagne appears as if bathed in a sea of light:

> Esclargiz est li vespres et li jurz.
> Cuntre soleil reluisent cil adub [armures]
> Osbercs et helmes i getent grant flabur [flammes]
>> (1807–9)

> [Lighted is the evening and the day.
> Under the sun the armors are shining.
> Haubercs and helmets are reflecting a great blaze.]

Such is the intoxication from light in Romanesque literature.

A preserved fragment of the choir screen in the cathedral of Chartres, *The Awakening of the Three Kings*,[12] shows another archaic problem in Old French literature and art — the hieratic patterns or *topoi*. The magi are always characterized by a crown; therefore even if they are sleeping in their beds (as also on one of the capitals of Autun), they must wear this crown. The iconographic rule is: no king without a crown, no apostle without bare feet, no saint without a halo, no figure of the Old Testament without the Jewish hat (*bonnet à côtes*). This is the language of patterns in medieval art.[13] Whatever the situation may be, the attribute of a person is never changed.

In literature, this appears still more striking. A young hero may become a traitor in the course of the plot; he does not thereby lose his epithet ' of the bold heart.' An old king may become a helpless child; he nevertheless remains ' the mighty king.' Protected by Count Guillaume in *Le Couronnement Louis*, Louis, although a puppet, is a ' noble ' king.[14] As on the choir screen the elegant bridle characterizes the noble horse, so in the *chansons de geste* there is the epithet ' running ' (*chevals couranz*). In the same manner, a sword is always polished (*forbi, bruni*), a shield is ' buckled ' (*un escu boucler*), a palace is *de marbre*, a room vaulted (*voultiz*). There are also stereotyped formulas for such events and actions as conversions, prayers, battles, and tournaments, as well as recurring literary types, such as the ' faithful vassal,' the ' treacherous rebel,' the ' unprotected king,' the ' avenger of disgrace,' the ' insolent ambassador.' Descriptions of battles are stereotyped, with only slight variations in their wording, such as to ' give ' or to ' receive' blows, to ' pass ' or to ' throw' the spear, ' the cold iron ' through the ' breast' or through the ' body.' Finally, just as on the sculptures a tree symbolizes Paradise, in the epics ' a pine tree ' signifies a French landscape, ' an olive tree ' a Saracen landscape. Two other stereotyped settings are ' a marble stone ' and ' a brown rock.' [15] This stiffness is both a restricting element and a part of the beauty of the Old French epic as well as of the Romanesque bas-reliefs and statues, which, according to Henri Focillon, ' are doomed to an eternal immobility with their gestures of pressing a book against the body, holding a scepter, or folding the mantle, being always the same.' [16]

## III. Emotional-Dynamic Approach to a Symbolic World

At the end of the twelfth century, art and literature become dynamic, enlivened, graceful, elegant, feminine, more secular. The Gothic cathedrals replace the Romanesque ones as the Cistercians replace the Cluniacs in spiritual leadership. These new Gothic cathedrals, with their elaborate façades, with their choirs and naves, long and high and slim, and with their series of altars for saints, soon turn the Cistercian spirit of *Sursum corda* into a spirit of elegance and svelte forms. In like manner, replacing the *chansons de geste* are the courtly romances with their short meters, rapid narrative rhythm, refined action, aristocratic problems, and alluring plots charged with suspense. The stained-glass windows, the Gothic tympana, and the sculptures of the cathedrals represent the fascinating, attractive, and familiar aspects of Christianity. Together with the life of Christ on earth, the glory of the Blessed Virgin, a host of saints with their curious and variegated legends, and all the secular knowledge of history and astronomy, botany and zoology invade the sanctuaries. These are used deliberately and consciously in order to make the Gothic cathedral a *speculum historiale* and *morale* as well as a *biblia pauperum*.

In secular literature there is a similar transformation. The noble ladies read the *romans antiques* and *courtois*, the Celtic *lais* and lyric poems in the troubadour style for their adventures, casuistic love problems, or stories of passion, such as *Tristan et Yseult* and its counterpart *Cligès* and Fenice, or those of a more smoothed-down pattern that could be decently imitated, such as *Erec et Enide* or *Yvain* and Laudine. *Notre Dame* will be the great patroness of the Gothic cathedrals; *La Dame* will be the prize and goal of any knightly endeavor related in the innumerable rhymed stories. Both Gothic art and literature subsequently add new elements to the medieval heritage that grew out of the Romanesque problems hitherto considered. Further implications in the Gothic period are: the new approach to the still-symbolic representation of the Divine and of human life, which now accents the religious element called *fascinans* (attractive) by Rudolf Otto,[17] as opposed to the *tremendum* (awe-inspiring); the attempt at a physiological-psychological observation, expressed by a subordinating and individualizing technique, and a monumental-global presentation; and finally, the alteration of the symbolic tradition by allegory and caricature.

Because of its element of the religious attitude of the *fascinans*, the figurative exposition bridging the Old and the New Testaments, and its tripartite composition, the sculpture *Resurrection and Coronation of the Virgin* [18] (see Fig. 3) on the western front tympanum of Notre Dame, Paris, first half of the thirteenth century, is significant. This sculpture introduces the Gothic world from three angles at once. First, the old theme of the apocalyptic *Majestas domini* judging the living and the dead or sending the Holy Spirit to strengthen the martyrs-to-be in spreading the Gospel is replaced by the 'fascinating' theme of the glorification of Our Lady. Secondly, this glorification has its scriptural root in the prophets (at the left), who foretold that the Lord would be born of the Blessed Virgin, and in the kings (at the right), who belong to the ancestors of her family; between both groups is the Ark of the Covenant, which prefigures Mary. There is then the double triumph of her resuscitation through Christ after her *dormitio* on earth and finally, in Heaven, through her Assumption and Coronation. The three strata of the tympanum mean something new in formal arrangement: a clear narration of an ancestral story as introduction, and a two-pronged main story with one point of interest focused on earth and one on Heaven, which is a simplification for eye and mind, in spite of the much more elaborate details if compared to the five divisions of the Romanesque sculptures and stories.

Broadly speaking, the literary parallel may be seen in the fact that in Old French literature from the second half of the twelfth century the central religious interest also belongs to Mary, this interest culminating in the legends of Adgar and the more splendid ones of Gautier de Coincy.

As for the details, there are, first, the prefigurative kings and prophets. The tropologic concept fostered by the theologians filters in everywhere and can also be found in the *Ordo prophetarum* and in the *Mystère d'Adam*. In literature, actions are patterned on the actions and gestures of Christ. Vivien in the *Chanson de Guillaume* dies as Christ died. Ganelon, like Judas ' who did the treason,' betrays. The best example is the rhymed hagiography of a contemporaneous martyr, Saint Thomas à Becket, by Guernes de Ste Maxence. This martyr, defending the rights of the Church against the king of England, is described in the typical language applied to Christ's life. The whole story of St. Thomas of Canterbury is presented as a new Passion, as, on the stage, the *Mystère de la passion* itself was grafted upon the prophecies of the *Mystère du Vieil Testament*. The martyr-arch-

3. *Resurrection and Coronation of the Virgin.* West front of Notre Dame, Paris. (Foto Marburg)

bishop of Canterbury is therefore interpreted as an *alter Christus* to such
an extent that he is supposed even to have prophesied his own death, as
did Christ:

> Qu'il murreit en cel an, bien le volt afermer.
> Or n'i out mais de l'an que dous jours a passer . . .
> Ci sui venuz, fait-il, entre vus mort sufrir,
> Or est venuz li jurs quel covint a cumplir
> Et sa vie et sa mort l'unt fait mult halt martir.[19]

> [That he was going to die this very year, that he wanted to state.
> Now, there was not left of the year more than two days to be spent . . .
> I have come here, he says, to suffer death among you,
> Now has come the day when it must be fulfilled,
> And his life and his death have made him a very high martyr.]

The tropologic importance of the Old Testament for the New and the
relation between the ancient promise and the new fulfilment are hall-
marks of the Middle Ages: *Et antiquum documentum novo cedat ritui* (St.
Thomas Aquinas). Not only on Notre Dame of Paris but almost everywhere in northern France, the so-called ' portals of the forerunners ' are
typical of this second principle of formal arrangement: the introduction
of the ancestors as a preface to a new story. This principle can also be
found in the narrative art of Crétien de Troyes, the ancestral story in the
preface being most visible in *Cligès*, which is slightly changed in *Lancelot*
and *Perceval* in order to introduce the two-peaked action.

The work on the Notre Dame tympanum is of the highest artistic quality, the direct result of a composition which, though grandiose, appears
full of an agreeable ease, as described by Marcel Aubert:

> This tympanum appears to us as the master work of art of the thirteenth
> century, due to its grandiose conception, its clear and simple composition,
> its perfect execution. The Blessed Virgin has fallen into a very deep sleep,
> her Son watches her; two angels make preparations to carry her to Para-
> dise; all around her, the kings, her ancestors, the Prophets who have an-
> nounced her divine maternity, the Apostles, witnesses of her sorrows and
> her joys, meditate on this mysterious event. And now the Virgin has en-
> tered Paradise; she is sitting on the throne of God beside Christ who
> blesses her, makes her Queen of Angels and of Men, as says the Psalmist;
> and the Saints of the Old Testament in the concentric circles of the arches
> greet her with acclamations.[20]

Precisely this same, more rare, concept of the Assumption as being not
a resurrection after burial, as seen in most representations, but a *dormitio*
with an awakening in Paradise, is reflected in *The Poem of the Assumption*:

En car, en os le ciel parcer
la fist [Jesus], e puis resusciter,
Plenierement glorifier
La voot, ot lui aluer
e cors e alme au ciel mener.[21]

[In flesh, in bones to pierce Heaven
That is what Jesus granted her, and then to become resuscitated,
He wished her to be fully glorified,
To be placed with Him
And to have body and soul conveyed to Heaven.]

The unparalleled honor bestowed on the Blessed Virgin, crowned Queen of Heaven, reigning with Christ in the Holy Trinity world without end, is likewise seen in certain verses of Li Renclus de Moiliens's *Li Romans de Carité et Miserere*:

CCLIX

O plaine de grace divine
O ame sainte, o cars virgine
O soule mere virginaus
O soule sans pareil voisine . . .

259

[O you, full of Divine Grace
O holy Soul, o virginal Flesh
O only Virgin Mother
O only one without your equal near.

CCLX

O non comparable roine
Ki regnes o Deus sans termine.[22]

260

O incomparable Queen
Who art reigning with God world without end.]

Mary becomes the very center of Gothic piety and in the literature is called: *La sainte mere al Salveur; La mere au roi de paradis; La debonaire Deu amie; La dame de dulçur; La Santisme rien; Nostre Dame Sainte Marie qui fontaine est de courtoisie; La douce mère ki porta sun fiz et sun pere; Tele reine ki si est sainte, sage, et fine; La gloriuse ki li est mere, fille espuse.*[23]

In the concept of Christ, too, there is a change. Instead of the Judge, there is the God-Man, dear to the tender love of the Gothic people — the Brother now, far removed from the *Majestas domini*. His designations in the rhymed legends reveal the same sensibility and spirituality of a generation hungry for a merciful God full of pity. Hence the descriptive names of Christ have become indicative of mercy and pity and love: *Cil qui en croiz a tort fu mis; li fiz Deu ki en croiz pendirent Jueu; li douz roi de misericorde; le beneit cors nostre Seignur; li glorius creatur ki ne vuelt la mort de pecheur; li roi glorieux Qui aus siens n'est pas oublieus.*

Even if the thematic implications are disregarded, there is still a similar handling of the problems of composition and form in the art of Chrétien de Troyes. One hero, or even heroine — Enide in *Erec*, Laudine in *Yvain*, and Guenièvre in *Lancelot* — must be glorified. All events converge toward this final triumph. A series of adventures in which many persons appear comprises the main story from which the climax of the protagonists arises. Both the sculptor's and Chrétien's stories are told in the same way, with gracefulness, rapidity, and ease, without any trace of awkwardness. Dynamic fluidity has replaced hieratic stiffness.

The two-pronged action, whether on a human or on a fanciful level, is also a principle in Chrétien's art: two ways lead into a dangerous land in *Lancelot*; two heroes share in an action in *Perceval*; two lovers, as in *Erec* and *Yvain*, are separated or estranged for the purpose of a final reunion. There is always a steady development of plot. The presentation of Romanesque snapshots is replaced by an attempt at continuity. If there is a break, as during the year when Yvain is entangled in his adventures and Laudine and Lunette wait for him in the castle, a subtle link exists between the two theaters of action by Lunette's imprisonment, from which she is liberated by Yvain. In the very moment that Lunette reinstates Yvain in the eyes of Laudine, then Yvain's last adventure and his final solemn rehabilitation are no longer in the relation of contrasts, but in the relation of a gradation. The combination of contrasts and gradation as a Gothic principle is also visible on the tympanum. On the panel below, Mary is awakened; on the panel above, she is crowned. Mary's awakening implies her final coronation, as Yvain's chivalrous action toward Lunette implies his final reconciliation.

The triumphant ending of any Gothic story is always one of decisive values. If it is not always the coronation of the Virgin, it is at least the finding of the Grail, or the discovery of an abducted earthly queen (*Lancelot*), or the enduring happiness of a loving couple.

As in the middle panel of the tympanum, there are also in the presentation of adventure groups by Chrétien very few protagonists, surrounded by many supernumeraries. Many of the figures provide a lyrical and human touch. On the tympanum this appears in the crossed hands of the second apostle from the right and in the reflective attitudes of the two apostles sitting under trees, their hands supporting their heads — the apostle on the left under an olive tree, the one on the right under an oak.

Two new elements thus make their entrance into medieval art: the individual gesture and the first bashful signs of observed nature. Again, these same elements of psychology and nature characterize the rhymed novels of Chrétien as opposed to the *chansons de geste*. What a fine psychological detail lies in the fact that Enide, because of her protecting love, always discovers the approaching enemies earlier than her husband. Once, when aware of an imminent danger, she even awakens him with one of her tears dropping on his face. And if in Chrétien there are no longer hero types but distinct personalities — Yvain, Gavain, Perceval, Lancelot — so also on the tympanum each prophet has a different kind of beard and dissimilar folds to his garments; each king holds his scepter in a different way. These are people to be treated as individuals:

| Tant con Gauvains, li bien apris | [As much as Gavain the well-bred |
|---|---|
| Par sa cortoisie ot de pris, | Had acquired praise for his courtesy, |
| Autretant ot de blasme Keus | As much had Keus acquired blame |
| Por ce qu'il fu fel et crueus.[24] | For being perfidious and cruel.] |

Similarly, nature is characterized by slight indications of the seasons of the year — May, Pentecost, Easter; or by details of the landscape, such as a mountain, vineyard, wood, valley, heath, orchard, a clear brook, green grass, tilled fields, trees with singing birds in the branches, or even a night bathed in moonlight. These details do not mean much so far as realism is concerned, but they serve as an agreeable accompaniment to this new Gothic art.

Technically, the precursors of Christ and the Virgin are kept neatly in their own Old Testament gallery and are no longer put among figures from the New Testament and from Church history. This is a sign of a sharper historical concept of sacred events, rather than the apocalyptic approach of previous centuries. There is an indirect suggestion of this in the literature also, for authors show a more exact understanding of the tenses and their usage. The past definite becomes the normal, narrative tense in Chrétien, although the historical present had been the tense most widely used in *Roland*.

## IV. Physical and Psychological Observation in Monumental, Global Presentation

To study psychology and nature in Gothic art and literature, one may choose from among the famous Resurrection tympana of Autun (1140), Reims (about 1225), and Rampillon or the tympanum of the Last Judgment [25] (see Fig. 4) on the façade of the cathedral of Bourges. The historians of art stress the ' charming figures of the blessed in the middle part of the tripartite tympanum, a king, a queen, a Franciscan monk, and others who knock at the door of Paradise where Abraham is expecting them and the beautiful figures of the risen bodies that come naked from the tombs and seem to stretch themselves, proud of their beauty, their strength and their youth.' [26] According to medieval theological speculations, none of the resurrected will have a body older than that of a thirty-three-year-old person. This speculation is underscored by the number of the risen. Added to these features is the astonishing turmoil caused by the covers of the caskets having been thrown into all kinds of positions, but still held in the hands of those sitting in the caskets. Other bodies are standing erect, lying down, getting up, moving about, walking, climbing, praying. Finally, there is the drastic popular concept of devils and Hell, as well as that of Heaven conceived as Abraham's bosom.

In the concept of the Last Judgment, the accent is shifted from the

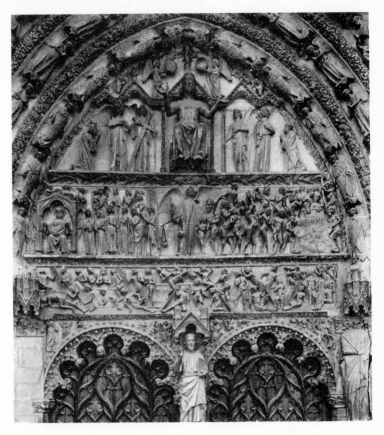

4. Tympanum of the Last Judgment. Façade of the Cathedral in Bourges.
(Foto Marburg)

Judge to the judged ones, from God to man. The monk Helinant began at
the end of the twelfth century to write this idea into his *Vers del juise*, the
verse of judgment, using a particular, new, original strophe and by this
fact alone stressing the high importance of the theme for him: less hope
than fear of the dangerous implications of the *quatuor novissima*. This
concept, with its many ramifications, does not change until, in the fifteenth
century, the accent is again shifted from resurrection and judgment to
death itself.

As to form, dynamic Gothic art certainly comes of age in the turmoil
and movement of these risen bodies. It is not surprising that the contemporary writers, too, are now capable of depicting the collective turmoil of
tournament and battles, and not just an endless succession of single fights,
as was the case in the *chansons de geste*. The short octosyllabic lines con-
tribute their share to the impression of turmoil, as do the condensed groups
of figures between the narrow ' caesuras ' of the coffin covers on the sculpture. The following lines describe a tournament in *Erec and Enide*:

D'armes est tot coverz li chans.
D'anbes deus parz fremist li rans,
An l'estor lieve li escrois [noise]
Des lances est mout granz li frois:
Lances brisent et escus troent,
Li haubere faussent et descloent,
Seles vuident, chevalier tument,
Li cheval süent et escument.
Sor çaus qui chieent a grant bruit,
Là traient les espées tuit.
Li un corent por les forz prandre
Et li autre por le deffandre.[27]

[With arms the whole field is covered.
The battle ranks are trembling on both sides,
At the attack, the noise sets in,
The clashing of the lances is terrible:
Lances are broken and shields are pierced
Haubercs cut and their meshes opened,
Saddles are emptied, knights are killed,
The horses are sweating and foaming.
Around those who are falling, there is great noise.
There, all are drawing the sword
Some are running to attack the fortresses
And the others to take the defensive.]

This same lively rendering of confusion is attempted in another realm by Guillaume de Lorris, who in *Le Roman de la Rose* shows stags, roes, squirrels, and hares frolicking and jumping in ' thirty different ways ' in the rose garden:

Ou vergier ot dains et chevriaus;
Si ot grant plenté d'escuriaus,
Qui par ces arbres gravissoient,
Conins i avoit qui issoient
Toute jor hors de lor tesnieres,
E en plus de trente manieres
Aloient entr'aus torneiant
Sor l'herbe fresche verdeiant.
(1375–82)

[In the garden were stags and roes;
And a great many squirrels,
That jumped around between the trees,
Rabbits were there that went out
The whole day from their dens,
And in more than thirty different ways
Used to gambol among themselves
Upon the fresh green grass.]

This may not be a perfect portrayal of movement, but there is the same feeling of activity as is evident on the tympanum, though with Guillaume de Lorris it is more in the idea than in the rhythm. Closest in effect to this resurrection turmoil, however, is a well-rendered but unfortunately very short scene found in *Partonopeus de Blois*, where Urake unexpectedly enters her sister's palace and surprises the maidens, who are described in the following way:

| | |
|---|---|
| Les puceles sont esperies | [The girls are stirred up |
| Et comme chievres tressalies | And jump around like goats |
| Le unes çà, les autres là | Some here, some there, |
| Si com la peors les mena.[28] | Just as Fear drove them.] |

The tympanum reveals, furthermore, an appreciation of the human body as such — no longer a hieratic pattern, a symbol, or an ornament, but a ' thing of beauty.' France was the first among the Christian nations to re-discover the nude. The nude bodies, particularly the resuscitated woman to the right, like those in the Rampillon tympanum, stress ' the triumph of the human body, masterwork of creation, young, fresh, fondled in its model by a sculptor enamored of the flesh. . . At Bourges, an exquisite young lady comes out of her sarcophagus like a Venus Anadyomene coming out of the pool: her round limbs have the subtlety and elasticity of life.' [29] This feeling for feminine beauty may be considered one of the most distinguishing traits of the *Renaissance du douzième siècle*. Likewise in literature, the slightly dressed damsels who spend curious nights of hospitality with the visiting knights, and the erotic dreams of the troubadours yearning for admission to their ladies' dressing rooms betray this sentiment, though a somewhat clumsy sensuality obscures the issue here. The cult of the feminine body of Yseult and of Queen Guenièvre, and also of Nicolette, whose white limbs have the capacity to heal miraculously, reveals the aesthetic implications of this first Occidental apotheosis of the body.

It is rare, however, to find in literature that sensuality, even though refined and sophisticated, embodies a really classical sensibility, which may be conceded to the tympanum of Bourges. The *Roman de Thèbes* comes closest to such a concept. Its poet describes the splendor coming from the bodies of the Theban women approaching to bury the dead. King Adrastes sees from afar the Theban ladies ' all barefoot and dishevelled ' (line 9813). In drawing the attention of Capaneus to the ladies, he asks if they be a flock of white sheep or a ' ballet ':

Guardez en ces chemins la sus:
Veeir poez une blanchor
Onques mais hon ne vit greignor.
Sont ço oeilles, buens amis,
Dont si reluist toz cist païs?
O son meschines por baler
Que en cel plain vienent joer? [30]

[Look upon those paths up there:
You can see something white
Never was there seen anything whiter.
Are they sheep, good friend,
From whose whiteness the whole country is shining brightly?
Or are they girls ready for a dance
Who come to play in this plain?]

In another instance, three young princesses, rivaling Athena and Diana in beauty, show their future husbands as much of their beauty as is decently possible:

Totes nuz piez, eschevelées,
En la chambre vindrent les fées;
Car monstrer voleient lor cors
As chevaliers qui sont de fors . . .
Onques Pallas ne Diana
La lor beauté ne sormonta.
(939–56)

[All barefooted and disheveled,
The fairies entered the room;
For they wanted to show their bodies
To the knights who came from abroad . . .
Never did Athene or Diana
Surpass them in beauty.]

The body of Enide is evaluated by Erec as in a beauty contest:

De l'esgarder ne pot preu faire,
Quant plus l'esgarde, plus li plest.
Ne püet muer qu'il ne la best . . .
Tot remire jusqu'à la hanche,
Le manton et la gorge blanche,
Flans et costez et bras et mains.
(1487–98)

[He cannot have enough of looking at her,
The more he looks at her, the more she pleases him.
He cannot help kissing her . . .
He views her again entirely down to the hip,
Chin and the white neck,
Flanks and sides and arms and hands.]

Much more important are the psychological subtleties. There are among those who knock at the gate of Paradise a Franciscan in deep reflection, a smiling young king, and a graceful young lady holding her mantle closed. This individual shading of the chosen ones and the protecting gesture of the smiling archangel Michael toward an infant in dangerous vicinity of the master devil are classical and belong to all ages. On the tympanum of Autun, there are visible even surprise, in the figures putting their hands to their chins, and roguishness, in two of the risen who try to find protection at the knees of St. Michael, while an angel sponsors three others with tender brotherliness.

These fine subtleties are not rare in literature. Queen Guenièvre encourages poor Enide to be her friend. She takes her by the hand to introduce her to King Artus:

L'une a l'autre par la main prise,  
Si sont devant le roi venues.  
(1678-9)

[The one has taken the other by the hand  
And so they have come before the king.]

Enide, desperately eager to speak, is inhibited by her promise. So her tongue moves without forming sounds:

Sovant del dire s'aparoille  
Si que la langue se remuet,  
Mes la voiz pas issir n'an puet.  
(3729-31)

[Often she prepares herself to speak  
So that the tongue begins to move,  
But the voice is not able to come forth.]

Erec regains his wife from her would-be seducer, Count de Limors, and rides with her on horseback through the moonlit night, fondling her and calling her ' sweet sister,' as the horse jogs through the woods:

Et Erec qui sa fame anporte  
L'acole et beise et reconforte;  
Antre ses braz contre son cuer  
L'estraint et dit: ' Ma douce suer . . .'  
Et de s'amor la rassëure  
Par nuit s'an vont grant aleüre  
Et ce lor fet grant soatume  
Que la lune cler lor alume.  
(4917-38 *passim*)

[And Erec, who carries his wife along,  
Embraces her, kisses and consoles her;  
He presses her between his arms against his heart  
And says ' My sweet sister . . .'  
And he reassures her of his love.  
Through the night they ride in gentle trot  
And this means great sweetness to them  
That the moon gives them her clear light.]

Soredamors in Chrétien's *Cligès* wants to talk lovingly for the first time to Alexander, she hesitates whether to call him ' friend ' or ' Alexander,' getting greatly excited about this little problem of her heart.

Que dirai je fet ele primes?  
Apelerai je par son nom  
Ou par ami? Je non.  
Comment donc? Par son nom  
l'apele! [31]

[What shall I say first?  
Shall I call him by his name  
Or call him ' friend '? By no means.  
How then? I call him by his name.]

In the *Lai de l'Ombre* by Jean Renart, a lady and a knight have a most charming conversation on love. He swears that if she does not accept his ring he will give it to his second-best choice and throws it into a well so that at least the reflection of his lady may have his ring; whereupon she puts her ring on his finger.

In the greatest contrast to these refinements is the representation of Heaven and Hell on the tympanum of Bourges and likewise in the mystery plays of the medieval stage. Paradise is still symbolically expressed by the ' bosom of Abraham,' who holds on his lap the souls in the form of little children. That this is a Romanesque remnant is indicated by the *casa* with its Romanesque architecture. It is rather disturbing in this Resurrection picture, but it is reminiscent of the medieval stage where Heaven was always a ' mansion.' A more modern treatment, without the framing, is given to Hell, represented as the fiery mouth of Leviathan. Through its wide opening appears a medieval torture chamber. Moreover, this type of representation of Hell is known from the preserved picture of the Valenciennes stage setting for the mystery plays, and from many descriptions in the plays themselves. If there exists a display of medieval sadism, it certainly is here. The knight with the pilgrims in the *Espurgatoire St. Patrice* by Marie de France receives his first impression of the devils at the gate of Hell from their noise, grinning, and bestiality:

| | |
|---|---|
| Après la grant noise et le sun | [Following the great noise and jingle |
| Entrerent tuit en la maisun | All of them entered the house |
| Od hisdus embruissemenz; | With the ugly rumble; |
| Sur lui rechignierent lur denz. | The devils showed him their teeth. |
| Desur tute altre creature | More than that of any other crea- |
| Esteit horrible lur figure. | tures |
| Trestuit issi desfiguré | Their face was horrible. |
| L'unt par grant eschar salüé.[32] | All of the greatly disfigured ones |
| | Have greeted him with great scorn.] |

In the *Mystère de la passion* of Arnoul Greban, three robbers are going to be hanged by their feet on the gallows of Hell; then they are to be plunged into a fiery bath of melted lead and metal. Lucifer gives his instructions to Cerberus for the execution:

> Pren moy ces trois mauvais larrons,
> Puis les traine bas en la cuve
> et là les me plonge et estuve
> Tout tens au gibet estendus,
> les piés encontremont pendu,
> ent grant brasièr et avivé,
> et quand les aras estuvé
> tant qu'ilz tressuent de meshaing
> Fergalus leur fera ung baing
> de beau plonc et de beau metal
> bruyant comme feu infernal.[33]

[Get me these three bad thieves,
Then drag them down into the tub
And therein plunge and bathe them
Whilst they remain hanged on the gallows,
The feet fixed upwards,
In the great furnace always kept burning,
And when you will have bathed them
So much that they are sweating with pain
Fergalus will prepare them another bath
Of beautiful lead and pretty metal
Blustering, as becomes a hellish fire.]

A last Gothic tympanum, the portal of the Vierge Dorée [34] (see Fig. 5) of the cathedral of Amiens, reveals the problem of single scenes united in a monumental composition. There is a collection of apparently miscellaneous scenes: at the bottom, apostles conversing; at the top, Christ crucified, the Blessed Virgin, and Saint John. On the other registers there are scenes from the life of Saint Honoré: his vocation and consecration as a bishop, his offering Mass, his miracles; but most important is the procession of his relics in the second register from the top, filling the whole panel, while each of the other scenes mentioned fills only half a panel.

Nonetheless the apostles in the lower register belong intrinsically to the three parts of the story of St. Honoré. They are his forerunners as bishops; he belongs intimately to them — like them, a *pastor gregis* through apostolic succession and consecrated as such on one of the sculptures. The Crucifixion at the top is the source and *raison d'être* of all the glories and miracles narrated below, particularly of the Mass celebrated by St. Honoré and of his personal sanctity as signified by the procession of his relics.

This intrinsic uniting of apparently isolated scenes is stressed also in the technique. Actually, the greatest surprise of this tympanum is that all these scenes, isolated in themselves, are arranged in a monumental way in conformity with the architecture of the cathedral. Although following the old Romanesque five-partite pattern, these five registers replace the Romanesque principle of one plus four, as seen in Christ and the Evangelists, by the Gothic rhythm of one plus three plus one, as seen in the central nave of the interior to which one exterior aisle is added on each side $(1 + 3 + 1)$. With gradually lesser-stressed horizontals, the Gothic tendency of 'a combination of vertical volumes' is not endangered,[35] and a dynamic surge upwards is stressed in spite of the horizontal panels.

All these scenes, consequently, are as isolated and as linked as are the legends of Gautier de Coincy. These legends are isolated as variegated pictures and stories, but they are linked by the ever-present spirit of the Virgin, just as the sculptures are linked by the spiritual implications concerning St. Honoré. In a language full of difficult and elaborate stylistic devices, sometimes stilted and pompous, Gautier de Coincy aims to build these legends into a monumental work of literature, as does the sculptor with his detailed and complicated work on the life of St. Honoré.

It is not necessary, however, to be dependent on subject matter. The *Lais* of Marie de France are also isolated, entertaining tales. But actually they are, as Leo Spitzer has shown, a meaningful, great composition around a central problem: the tragic aspects of love, illustrated by a cycle of symbolic fairy tales. So the mystery of love is present everywhere and, like a red thread, binds the tales together.[36] Such links make an intrinsic unity out of the parts, guaranteeing that *integritas, perfectio, proportio,* and *consonantia* which were so important to scholastic aesthetics.[37]

The composition of the tympanum, starting with the apostles and ending with Christ, and including the sacred adventures of St. Honoré, thus reveals a monumental but at the same time a cyclic form. This leads to a final consideration of the *Erec* of Chrétien. The older scholars, like W. Foerster and K. Voretzsch, could see in it only a kind of dramatic monumental arrangement in five acts, as stated earlier for the Romanesque composition of *Alexius* and *Roland.* More modern scholars, such as Alfred Adler, see things quite differently. The new principle of composition, global in kind, leads from love lost and misunderstood at the outset to love reconciled and restored at the end. Framed by these fundamental registers,

5. The Portal of La Vierge Dorée in Amiens. (Foto Marburg)

the adventures serving the reconciliation problem progressively develop in nicely visible adventure groups until globally they close the cycle with an episode more important than all the others. In *Erec*, the so-called 'Joy of the Court' is comparable to the role of the relic procession on the tympanum, because it contains the solution of the love motif from which the adventures started, just as the procession underlines the motif of saintliness in a paramount form as a symbol of canonization, embracing the preceding miracles of St. Honoré and his holy life.

The complex details of the sculpture have their exact parallels in literature. The groups of apostles presented as discussing and arguing reveal the interest of the schools in disputations that produced endless theological dialogue. In the secular domain and in the world of knights and ladies, the same endless dialogue exists. Only the subject matter is different. It concerns the subtle questions of love casuistry, as culminating in the *Ars amatoria* of Andreas Cappellanus. The discussion as such, with pros and cons, tricks and gestures, talk and countertalk, belongs to the very greatness of narrative literature in twelfth-century France. In court literature, the discussions take place mostly between the knights and their ladies; but there are others, very charming ones, between mothers and daughters who do not want to take just the husband proposed to them, as is the case with Lavinia and her mother in the romance, *Enéas*. The mother tries to give Lavinia a lesson in love but finds a worthy opponent in Lavinia, who rejects it as far as it concerns the man whom she does not want. Hence she pretends to need an initiation into love:

> ' Turnus est proz, sel deis aimer.'
> ' Ge ne m'i sai pro atorner.'
> ' Et tu l'apren.' — ' Dites le mei,
>    Que est amores? Nel sai, par fei.'
> ' Ge ne te puis neient descrire.'
> ' Qu'en savrai donc, se ne l'oi dire? '
> ' Tes cuers t'aprendra a amer.'
> ' Se n'en orrai altrui parler? '
> ' Comence, assez en savras puis.'
> ' Et ge coment, quant ge ne truis
>    Ki me die que est amors? '
> ' Ge te dirai de ses dolors.' [38]

> [' Turnus is courageous and you must love him.'
> ' I do not know how to turn myself towards love.'
> ' Well, you will learn it.' — ' Tell me then,
>    What is love? I do not know it, honestly.'
> ' I cannot describe it to you at all.'
> ' What shall I know then about it, if I do not
>    hear it spoken of? '
> ' Your heart will teach you to love.'

' Even if I do not hear other people talk about it? '
' Start simply, you will know then enough.'
' How is that, if I do not find someone
  Who may tell me what love actually is? '
' All right, I shall tell you about the pains of love.']

The reproduction of a procession, one of the most common sights in the age of pilgrimages, also attracted Chrétien de Troyes as a topic, and he created his famous, much discussed, and variously explained procession of the Grail. Passing the suffering Grail King, this procession also moves before the eyes of the onlooker:

>Uns vaslez d'une chambre vint,
>Qui une blanche lance tint
>Anpoigniee par le milieu . . .
>Atant dui autre vaslet vindrent,
>Qui chandeliers an lor mains tindrent
>De fin or, ovrez a neel . . .
>An chascun chandelier ardoient
>Dis chandoiles a tot le mains.
>Un graal entre ses deus mains
>Une dameisele tenoit,
>Qui avuec les valez venoit . . .
>Après celi an revint une
>Qui tint un tailleor d'argent.
>Li graaus, qui aloit devant,
>De fin or esméré estoit;
>Pierres precieuses avoit . . .[39]

[A squire came from a room
Who held a shining lance
Clutched by the middle part . . .
Then followed two other squires
Who held candlesticks in their hands,
Of refined gold, worked out with enamel.
Upon each of the candlesticks, there were burning
Ten candles at least.
A Grail was held between her two hands
By a lady
Who came, together with the squires . . .
After her came another one
Who held a silver plate.
The Grail, which preceded her,
Was made of refined gold of the best quality;
It contained precious stones.]

Chrétien, who repeatedly describes the Grail and puts it in the most important place in the procession, uses a technique very similar to that of the sculptor, who places the relic shrine in the center of his composition and underlines its importance by the persons grouped below it and referring to it.

The Virgin of the north transept of Notre Dame de Paris [40] (see Fig. 6), rather than the Virgin under the Cross of Amiens or the Heavenly Queen of Paris, concretizes the twelfth- and thirteenth-century ideal of feminine dignity and nobility in attitude and dress. Our Lady in this Gothic creation is a ' charming young woman who has preserved from her old royal privilege only as much as is necessary for the pride of a noble race in order to surpass the spirit mundane.' [41] Old French literature shows the same interest in woman's dress, hair style, and jewelry as is evident in the sculpture.[42] The coincidence of the details observed is not striking, but what is technically remarkable here is the fact that the great authors use the old Homeric device of showing the act of dressing through successively given details, whereas the painter's and sculptor's description of a dress is necessarily a composite picture. So Enide is presented donning, for her presentation at Arthur's court, the different parts of her court attire that can be seen assembled on the statue, namely: a tunic girded by a gold-fringed belt and covered with a mantle, a golden thread to hold back her hair, a diadem set on her head, and an enameled, gold brooch worn on the breast.

The text from Chrétien:

> Puis vest le bliaut si se çaint,
> D'un orfrois [gold fringe] a un tor s'estraint
> Et le mantel après afuble . . .
> Les deus puceles d'un fil d'or
> Li ont galoné son crin sor . . .
> Un cercelet ovré a flors
> Les puceles el chief li metent . . .
> Deus fermailles d'or neelez
> An une cople anseelez
> Li mist au col une pucele.
> (1646–67 passim)

> [Then she dons the tunic and girds herself,
> It is with a gold fringe that she makes a simple belt
> And then she puts on the mantle . . .
> The two waiting girls with a golden thread
> Have put a ribbon on her brown hair . . .
> A little crown adorned with flowers
> Is put on her head by the girls . . .
> Two clasps of enameled gold
> Worked together as a necklace
> Were put around her neck by one of the maidens.]

From the censorship of the *Poème moral* it is known that a lady also painted her mouth and her eyebrows and liked her sleeves close-fitting and the hips tightly laced:

Anz qu'ele voist à la messe, la covient à mireir
Acemeir lo pipet [mouth], lo sobrecil plomeir
              Si forment lace et loie
Les braz et les costiez k'a grant paine se ploie.[43]

[Before going to Mass, she is used to look in the mirror,
Paint her mouth, varnish her eyebrows.
              So tightly she laces and binds
Arms and hips that she scarcely can bend.]

This picture is verified and supplemented by the description in the
*Roman de la Rose* of Oiseuse, who is admired for her magnificent forehead, her arched eyebrows, the large space between the eyes (*entreiauz*),
her straight nose, her small mouth, full lips, and dimpled chin. This Oiseuse
of the tight-sleeved gown holds a mirror in her white-gloved hands. Her
dress is made of a rich green cloth from Ghent and is delicately sewn
around with fine yarn stitches:

              Front reluisant, sorciz voutiz
              L'entriauz ne fut pas petiz . . .
              Le nes ot bien fait a droiture . . .
              La bouche petite et grossete,

6. The Virgin of the North Transept of Notre Dame, Paris. (Foto Marburg)

S'ot ou menton une fossette . . .
En sa main tint un miroer . . .
Bien et bel et estroitement,
Ot andeus cousues ses manches.
Et por garder que ses mains blanches
Ne halassent, ot uns blans ganz.
Cote ot d'un riche vert de Ganz.
Cousue a lignuel tot entor.

(529–65 *passim*)


[The forehead was resplendent, the eyebrows vaulted,
The space between the two eyes was not small . . .
Her nose was well formed and straight . . .
The mouth small and fresh
And she had a dimple in her chin . . .
In her hand she held a looking glass . . .
Nicely, exactly, and tightly
Both of her sleeves were sewn.
And to prevent her white hands
From becoming sunburned, she wore white gloves,
A gown she wore of a rich green from Ghent
Sewn around with fine yarn stitches.]


Fresne, in *Galeran de Bretagne*, describes in detail her diadem, not very large, but adorned with precious stones and gold and enameled flowers:


D'une cercle non guaires lee
Ouvree a pierres et a flours
D'or et d'asur et de coulours
Tient les cheveux, ce m'est advis,
Qu'il ne lui voisent vers le vis.[44]


[By a not very large circle
Adorned with stones and flowers
Of gold, azur and different colors
She holds her hair together, probably
Lest the strands hang in her face.]


The author completes the picture by describing how the hair falls freely on the shoulders and is covered with a dark veil, which suits the fair hair, and adds as a final detail that her shoes are narrow:


Mais dessus les a sans destresse,
Par les espaules va la tresse
Si les a couvers d'un brun voil

[But else she wears her hair free,
Over the shoulders the tresses are flowing

Qui bien li siet sur le blont poil,     And she has covered them with a
S'est d'uns souliers estroit chaussié.     brown veil
        (2018–22)    Which is becoming to her blond hair,
                  And she has put on a pair of narrow
                  shoes.]

## V. Trends in Allegory and Caricature

Gothic realism in the making is considerably checked by allegory and caricature. The Virtues and Vices [45] (see Fig. 7) on the south porch of Chartres cathedral, together with the *Roman de la Rose*, illlustrate the fact that the once profound symbolism of the Romanesque contained a strong current of artificial allegory. Louise Lefrançois-Pillion has described extensively all the figures of the Virtues and Vices on the pillars of the south porch of Chartres. The Virtues are isolated, seated figures holding shields decorated with their allegorical emblems. Faith is shown with a chalice and Perseverance with a crown. Hope appears with a banner, Charity with the lost sheep, Chastity with a palm, Prudence with a serpent, Humility with a dove, Docility with an ox, Strength with a lion, Temperance with a camel, Harmony with an olive branch. The Vices, however, are much more amusingly depicted in scenes of action. Inconstancy is depicted as a monk who leaves his cloister, Idolatry as a man who kneels before an idol. Despair is a person committing suicide, Avarice someone filling his money box. Luxury is a girl fondled by a young man, Foolishness someone who tries to eat a stone, Pride a person falling from a horse, Wrath someone sitting in an easy chair and pushing back with his foot a kneeling servant. Fear is a knight who flees from a hare, Drunkenness a woman beating her own bishop. Discord is a fighting couple before a jug turned topsy-turvy.

This same method is used in the *Roman de la Rose*, where even the Virtues are shown in action — and they are very secularized Virtues and behave in a very free manner. A Vice, Avarice, is shown in the *Roman de la Rose* as an ugly, dirty, starving woman who hides her well-closed purse so that there will be no temptation to take out even a penny:

> Une autre image i ot assise
> Coste a coste de Covoitise,
> Avarice estoit apelee.
> Laide estoit e sale et folee . . .
> Chose sembloit morte de fain
> Qui vesquist solement de pain.
> Avarice en sa main tenoit . . .
> Une borse qu'ele reponoit [cachait]
> E la nooit si durement
> Qu'el demorast mout longuement
> Ançoist qu'ele en peüst rien traire.
>        (195–231 *passim*)

7. The Virtues and Vices in Chartres. (Archives Photographiques)

[Another image was placed there
Side by side with Covetousness;
It was called Avarice.
She was ugly, dirty and stupid . . .
She seemed, as it were, starved,
Living only on bread.
Avarice held in her hand . . .
A purse which she hid
And knotted so strongly
That a long time was needed
Before she could take anything out of it.]

On the other hand, Largesse gives away everything, even the brooch that,
as a breastpin, closes her dress:

S'ot le vis bel et bien formé
Mais ele ot son col desfermé;
Qu'ele avoit iluec en present [à l'instant]
A une dame fait present,
N'avoit guieres de son fermal,
Mais ce ne li seoit pas mal
Que la cheveçaille iert overte
Et la gorge estoit descoverte.

(1165–72)

[She had a beautiful and well-shaped face,
But she had her collar unclasped,
Because she had there at the very moment

Given a lady as a present
Her brooch.
But this did not suit her badly
That she had opened her collar
And bared her breast.]

The fleeing monk on the sculpture corresponds to such personifications in the *Roman de la Rose* as Jeunesse, the chambermaid of Delit (line 4473), and Fortune, dressed like a queen (line 6123) who, with a turn of her wheel, throws the wealthiest people into the dirt:

E les tombe, au tour de la roe
Dou somet envers en la boe.
(4895–6)

[And she throws them with the turn of her wheel
From the top down below into the dirt.]

The patterns for the statues of the Virtues with emblems reappear in literature in the morality plays. Here the Vices, too, are represented in this stiffer way. In *The Seven Deadly Sins and the Seven Virtues* of the Chantilly Manuscript 617 the stage directions specify that Pride wears a crown and holds a scepter; Wrath holds a sword, Envy a flower and a serpent, Gluttony a piece of cake, Luxury a mirror.[46]

A grotesque of Notre Dame in Paris (see Fig. 8) shows very convincingly that there is a synthesis in the gargoyles between an incipient realism on the one hand and an awkward allegory on the other. This synthesis is caricature, and very clever caricature. All the hidden human passions are portrayed in the glances and gestures of these demons, who are devilish beasts but who are now far removed from the apocalyptic animals. With all their demonic implications they are good-humored monsters, sympathetic, somewhat irritated when they are caught, barking, howling, and shouting, but it would not seem impossible to placate them. They belong to the same family as the humanized, rascally animals of the *Roman de Renard*: Ysengrin, Dame Hersent, and all the others.

The wolf-shaped demon glances as curiously at the streets of Paris below him as the wolf in the *Roman de Renard* spies into Renard's kitchen when the latter's wife is cooking the stolen fish:

Lors apela par un pertuis
' Compere sire, ovrez moi l'uis!
Je vos aport bones noveles ' . . .
E des anguilles covoiteus
Si li a dit: ' Ovrez biau sire! '
E Renarz commença à rire,
Si demande: ' Qui estes vos? '
Et cil respont: ' Ce somes nos.'
' Qui vos? ' — ' Ce est vostre compere.'
' Nos cuidions, ce fust un lerre.' [47]

8. A Grotesque of Notre Dame in Paris. (Foto Marburg)

[Then he called to him through a loophole:
' Sir Godfather, open for me the door
I bring you good news ' . . .
And greedy for the eels
He has told him: ' Open, good lord! '
And the fox began to laugh
And asks: ' Who are you? '
And he answers: ' It is we.'
' Who, we? ' — ' It is your godfather.'
' Oh, we believed it was a thief.']

The grotesques are half-men, like the monster-villain in Chrétien's *Yvain*. He is described as sitting in a curious position and having an over-large head, beastlike hair, a gigantic forehead, elephantlike ears, eyes like those of a screech owl, the nose of a cat, the mouth of a wolf, and the teeth of a boar:

Un vilain, qui ressanblot mor
Grant et hideus et desmesure,

(Einsi tres leide creature) . . .
Vi je seoir sor une çoche,
Une grant maçue en sa main.
Je m'aprochai vers le vilain,
Si vi qu'il ot grosse la teste
Plus que roncins ne autre beste,
Chevos meschiez et front pelé
S'ot plus de deus espanz de le,
Oroilles mossues et granz
Autés come a uns olifanz
Les sorciz granz et le vis plat
Iaus de çuete et nes de chat
Boche fandue come los,
Danz de sangler, aguz et ros,
Barbe noire, grenous tortiz
Et le manton aers au piz
Longue eschine, torte et boçue
Apoiiez fu sor sa maçue.[48]

[A churl who looked like a moor,
Huge and ugly and unproportioned
(Consequently a very ugly creature) . . .
Was seen by me sitting upon a trunk,
A big club in his hand.
I drew nearer to the churl
And saw that he had a big head,
Bigger than that of a horse or any other animal,
Enmeshed hair and a hairy forehead,
It was broader than two hands together,
His ears were mossy and large
As large as those of an elephant.
His eyebrows were big and his face flat,
His eyes were owl-like and his nose catlike.
His mouth was slit like that of a wolf,
His boarlike teeth were sharp and rough,
His beard was black, his moustache twisted
And his chin close to the breast,
His long spine was twisted and hunchbacked.
He leaned upon his club.]

But the more such monsters remain animals, the more sympathetic they become. So there are Yvain's lion (*frans et debonaire*, line 3393); Marie de France's werewolf, Bisclaveret; and Bucephalus, the horse of Alexander the Great, nodding his head to greet his master.[49] On the other hand, the gargoyles, as E. Roy [50] has seen, are also reminiscent of all the superstitious, dangerous, medieval fictions and monstrous legends that led to the burning of the witches and to the persecution of the Jews. Some legends, particularly those of Adgar, also tend toward superstition.

# The Flamboyant and Renaissance Epochs

## 1350–1600

A T THE end of the Gothic period — owing somewhat to the flair for the pompous on the part of the Dukes of Burgundy and in some measure to the lack of great ideas — new, playful forms are lavished on ornaments and decorations by the artists of the flamboyant school and the *rhétoriqueurs* who precede the humanists. The first bourgeois, appropriating these exuberant forms, interpret in a most unrefined and crudely realistic way everything that still bears traces of symbolism. The symbol becomes a fetish. They also create simpler, realistic forms to imitate everyday life and to express their enjoyment and fears. The period has found a competent interpreter in Johan Huizinga, to whom it may suffice to refer for the ideological points involved.[1]

As far as technique, skill, and presentation are concerned, art in general seems ahead of literature. The painter's full-fledged realism, on the other hand, proves less rich in details in a single picture than does a single poem or a single chapter from a story, for the details of a picture are confined to dress in portraits, furniture in interiors, and trees and flowers in landscapes. Consequently many pictures sometimes seem necessary in order to elucidate a single literary text with its successive details of different kinds, including even psychological and philosophical considerations. It would go too far, however, to say that pictures now serve to elucidate literary texts rather than that the texts serve to interpret the pictures. The issues to be discussed may be classified according to metaphysical, sociological, psychological, aesthetic, and cultural categories.

## I. Devotional Trend in Religiosity and the Expression of Awe by the People

The implications and repercussions in the devotional approach to the Divine and the consequent expression of awe in the manner of the people are seen in the famous *Ballade que Villon feit à la requeste de sa mère pour prier Nostre Dame.* Four paintings illustrate this ballad: Enguerrand Charonton's *Le Couronnement de la Vierge,* Jean Miraillet's *La Vierge de Miséricorde,* Justus of Ghent's *The Last Supper,* and Nicolas Froment's *Le Buisson ardent.*

The complete text of Villon's poem is as follows:

1        Dame des cieulx, regente terrienne,
         Emperiere des infernaux paluz,
         Recevez moy, vostre humble chrestienne,
         Que comprinse soye entre vos esleuz,
5        Ce non obstant qu'oncques rien ne valuz.
         Les biens de vous, ma dame et ma maistresse,
         Sont trop plus grans que ne suis pecheresse,
         Sans lesquelz biens ame ne peut merir
         N'avoir les cieulx, je n'en suis jangleresse.
10       En ceste foy je vueil vivre et mourir.

         A vostre Filz dictes que je suis sienne;
         De luy soyent mes pechiez aboluz:
         Pardonne moy comme à l'Egipcienne,
         Ou comme il feist au clerc Théophilus,
15       Lequel par vous fut quitte et absoluz
         Combien qu'il eust au deable fait promesse.
         Preservez moy, que ne face jamais ce,
         Vierge portant, sans rompure encourir,
         Le sacrement qu'on celebre à la messe.
20       En ceste foy je vueil vivre et mourir.

         Femme je suis povrette et ancienne,
         Qui riens ne sçay; oncques lettre ne leuz;
         Au moustier voy dont suis paroissienne
         Paradis paint, où sont harpes et luz,
25       Et ung enfer où dampnez sont boulluz:
         L'ung me fait paour, l'autre joye et liesse.
         La joye avoir me fay, haulte Deesse,
         A qui pecheurs doivent tous recourir,
         Comblez de foy, sans fainte ne paresse.
30       En ceste foy je vueil vivre et mourir.

                        ENVOI
         Vous portastes, digne Vierge, princesse,
         Iesus regnant, qui n'a ne fin ne cesse.
         Le Tout-Puissant, prenant nostre foiblesse,
         Laissa les cieulx et nous vint secourir,
35       Offrit à mort sa tres chiere jeunesse.
         Nostre Seigneur tel est, tel le confesse,
         En ceste foy je vueil vivre et mourir.

9. Charonton, *Le Couronnement de la Vierge*. (Archives Photographiques)

Lines 1–4, 18–19, and 27–8 are striking in their unusual concepts. First, Mary is not only the Heavenly Lady and the Queen of the Earth but also the 'Empress of the infernal ponds'; secondly, without reference to Christ, Mary has her own elected ones and is a 'goddess' to whose protection the sinners must rush; thirdly, the Divine Child in His mother's womb is called the sacrament celebrated at Mass — that is, the Eucharist. Villon shows himself a great poet by grading, for instance, the designations of Mary: *dame — regente — emperiere — vierge — déesse*. The last expression has a double meaning: first it embodies his mother's psychology of a simple woman; secondly it represents his own prehumanistic trend in the sense in which Dante calls God *Sommo Giove*. It would be difficult to find in literature many parallels to Mary as 'Empress of Hell.'[2] Furthermore, does *infernaux paluz* mean Hell or Purgatory? Or both? The question is answered by a glance at the painting *Le Couronnement de la Vierge* (see Fig. 9), in the Musée de l'Hospice de Villeneuve-lès-Avignon, by Villon's contemporary, Enguerrand Charonton. Here *La Vierge* fits all the titles by which Villon addresses her: *dame des cieulx* in her brilliant damask robe with jewels and ornaments, honored by the Father, the Son, and the Holy Spirit, venerated by angels and saints; *dame* in the natural gracefulness and simplicity of her grandeur, with her sweet, beautifully shaped white hands; *regente terrienne*, in that 'the middle section represents the world . . . the beautiful panorama of Avignon';[3] and *emperiere des infernaux paluz*, for the lower part represents two trenches separated by a rock, in which the souls on the left are being liberated by angels, whereas those on the right representing the seven cardinal sins, remain. Consequently, Villon in his ballad uses a motif from contemporary painting. Even more specifically, he has his mother say that Heaven as painted in her parish church gives her hope and the painted Hell arouses her terror, a peculiarly fifteenth-century note, as murals in small churches are an innovation of that century.

The *haulte Déesse, a qui pecheurs doivent tous recourir* (27–8), is similarly explained by the contemporary pictures of the Madonna of the Cloak, or Cope (*Schutzmantelmadonna*), the *Mater omnium* sponsored by the Mendicant Orders. She is shown isolated, without Christ or the Trinity, covering kings, bishops, and all types of people with her mantle, ' protecting a devout family as a hen protects her little chickens.' [4] So she is *La Vierge de Miséricorde* (see Fig. 10), as seen on the altarpiece by Jean Miraillet (1425).

Villon's *Vierge portant . . . le sacrement qu'on celebre à la messe* (line 19) poses other problems concerning the extension and identification of the Incarnation with the Eucharist. This type of mystical anachronism is, in vernacular literature, extremely rare. There is one other example in the Spaniard, Juan de los Angeles (1536–1609), who compares Mary being with Child and visiting her cousin Elisabeth to the first Corpus Christi procession. But in art things are different. Villon may have witnessed the first tabernacles in the form of Mary statues, or may have seen pictures of

10. Miraillet, *La Vierge de Miséricorde*. (Archives Photographiques)

11. Justus of Ghent, *The Last Supper*. (Photo Alinari)

the type of *The Last Supper* (see Fig. 11) by Justus of Ghent (b. 1410), where the room of the Last Supper is a church and Christ as the priest is giving Communion to the kneeling apostles. The details of the picture are as follows:

> The scene is in a church. In the middle of the choir, decorated with columns of green and red marble with gilded capitals, the table, covered with a white tablecloth, is set for the Last Supper. All the guests have left their places to receive Communion from the hand of Christ. It is he who occupies the center of the painting: his lengthened face is framed by a thin beard and by long, stiff, red hair. Three of the apostles, kneeling behind Him, have already received the sacrament and are steeped in deep reflection. Jesus offers the bread to another apostle while at a certain distance five more apostles, making a genuflection, await their turn with folded hands.[5]

The decisive point is that in art the mystical anachronism is *not* exceptional in the fifteenth century. When Nicolas Froment represents *The Burning Bush* [6], in St. Sauveur of Aix, it is not God the Father who appears to Moses in the bush, but the Blessed Virgin with the Child. Thus the art parallels of the period explain the unusual concepts of Villon's text, which have all the elements of a new, realistic, and naïve religiosity.

## II. Spirit of Minuteness and Its Expression in Genre Scenes and Interiors

This touching religiosity exists not only in the poor and naïve mother of Villon, but also in the upper, well-to-do bourgeois classes. Here it is stifled, however, by the practical spirit of enjoying the earthly paradise of a home with all the conveniences of a wealthy leisure class. This materialistic spirit, though unconscious of its implications, announces itself in the numerous details and lengthy enumerations in literature, giving the impression of a parvenu who counts his money publicly and with satisfaction. For instance, there are the preparations of an abbot for the reception at dinner of a great lady, *la dame des Belles Cousines, patronne et fondresse* of his monastery:

> And he then had loaded one of his carts with great quarters of bucks, with boars' heads and sides, with hares, conies, pheasants, partridges, fat capons, poultry and pigeons . . .
>
> The lord Abbot brings her into the lower hall, well tapestried and having a good fire; wherein a dresser and tables were set, all bespread with salads, cress in vinegar, great platters whereon were roast lampreys, in pasties, in their sauce; great soles broiled, fried, and roasted in orange sauce; mullets, barbels, salmons roasted, boiled or in pasties, great plaice and carp; dishes of crawfish, great fat eels in gelatine; dishes of sundry sorts of corn covered with jelly, white, red and golden; Bourbon tarts, talmouses and almond cream flans, etc.[7]

Now since there are in a fifteenth-century early French prose work, such as *Le Petit Jehan de Saintré* by Antoine de la Sale, just quoted, whole pages of such enumerations of meat and fish dishes, cakes and pies, served on fine tablecloths in rooms with clear windows and warm fires, one is confronted with two different art motifs: (1) the endless listing of objects as an expression of the joy of direct observation; and (2) the coziness of a well-to-do *intérieur* expressed by the abundance of a well-set table.

The first principle, the joy of observation, is independent of the kind of object observed. This is easily seen in a contemporary portrait by Jan van Eyck (1382–1440), *Canon van der Paele* (see Fig. 12), in the famous Madonna picture in the Musée Municipal in Bruges. The painter has portrayed the Canon with breviary and eyeglasses in his hands; he has stressed each wrinkle and wart, each fold and button, each vein of his head, the pouches under his eyes, the double chin, and the few remaining strands of hair. All this discloses clearly the painter's delight in the enumeration of details.

The second principle concerns, however, the kind of details generally preferred: man and intimate life, coziness and homeliness, *intérieurs* with carpets and tapestries, chests of drawers, vessels and dishes. Such a selection is the legitimate forerunner of the genre. For the flamboyant epoch this new type of intimate room with its enumerated details of the kitchen utensils and the menu is significant.[8]

The advanced Flemish painting of the epoch reflects the virtual achievements in literature. It should never be forgotten, however, that this worldliness developed slowly from the religious sphere. Interiors in miniatures,

12. Jan van Eyck, *Canon van der Paele*. (Photo Alinari)

such as the *Birth of John the Baptist* [9] in a fifteenth-century Flemish manuscript, preserved in the Trivulzio Library, Milan, belong to those scenes of which Arnold Goffin has said: 'Everything is sweet intimacy, homely cordiality . . . a warm, colorful interior where glints from furniture and tin, copper and the curtains with their deep red, pour into the light sifted through the window panes a tone of peaceful happiness.' [10] It is but a short step from this kind of realistic setting of the sacred stories into the secularized interiors or into literary ones such as this by Antoine de la Sale: 'The elegant little dining room was like a drawing room richly hung with tapestries, covered with large and smaller carpets, with glass windows, and a pretty fire in the stove; and there were also three tables, with very beautiful linen, artistically set, and the sideboard splendidly covered with beautiful plates and dishes.' [11] The scenes of people eating and drinking at a table carefully set, as in *Le Petit Jehan de Saintré*, or sitting around a fire in a cozy room, as is the case in the fifteenth of the *Quinze joies de mariage* or in the *Grand Testament* (v. 1473ff.) of Villon, are clearly *intérieurs* of bourgeois worldliness.

These entirely worldly *intérieurs* surreptitiously crept into a famous prayerbook, *Les Très Riches Heures du Duc de Berry*,[12] in the form of the miniatures of the Frères de Limbourg. Such a secularized *intérieur* is found in the picture of *Janvier* (see Fig. 13), showing the duke at dinner. It reveals what the table and dinner descriptions in *Le Petit Jehan de Saintré* were striving for, mentioning all the names of the banqueters: Dame Jeanne, Catherine, le Seigneur de Geary, Dame Isabel, Sir Geoffroy de Saint Amant, and so on (ch. 69). The aim is to achieve by motley and varied grouping a close imitation of reality. As Henri Malo has pointed out,[13] there is evident here not only the very genuine portrait of the duke himself but even the particular friends, clerical and lay, of his court. All these courtiers can be identified. The objects on the table are also highly particularized. There are the famous *salière* (salt-box) *du pavillon* and a saucer in the form of a ship from the duke's collection of precious household goods. Furthermore, the motifs of the tapestries on the wall are distinctly recognizable, and even the pet dog of the duke is present and fed in front of the table. While almost identical details are found in the work of the author Antoine de la Sale, the details as found in the picture of the Duke of Berry had to be identified by art historians.

Literature does even more in the way of minuteness and genre scenes because of the possibility of a successive, cinema-like presentation of in-

13. Frères de Limbourg, *Janvier*, Musée Condé, Chantilly. (Foto Marburg)

dividual, realistic scenes, as in some descriptions from the short stories, framed and unframed, of the *Cent Nouvelles nouvelles*, the *Quinze Joies de mariage*, and the *Arrêts d'amour* by Martial d'Auvergne. There is the spoiled, lazy woman traveling with her husband and complaining at each moment about the discomfort of a journey on horseback: 'Now she says that one of the stirrups is too long and the other too short; now she wants to have her coat, then she takes it off again; now she remarks that the horse has too hard a gait and that she becomes ill; now she wants to alight and one must help her into the saddle again, and when a bridge is to be crossed, her husband has to lead the horse by the bridle.' [14]

In the twenty-third of the *Cent Nouvelles* (1461), a young silly woman, wife of a notary and in love with the notary's clerk, tries to tease him by throwing little stones on his writing paper. In the fifth, another wanton lady throws a cushion from her window at the head of a coachman. The coachman tumbles and falls on his face. Scarcely on his legs again, he gets a second cushion on his head, and this time he falls backward while the lady laughs foolishly.

Such scenes may be widened to a great tableau, as is the case in novel 81 of the *Cent Nouvelles* in which a hunting party, soaked from rain, knocks at the door of a rich lady's country house during the night. She arouses the servants, comes downstairs with a girl bearing a torch, and invites all the hunters to a splendid meal.

Can painting vie with such scenes? The above-mentioned Flemish scene of the woman in childbed, representing either St. Anne giving birth to the Virgin Mary or Elisabeth to St. John the Baptist, is not strong enough to cope with that literary French naturalism *avant la lettre*. But again in this respect the Frères de Limbourg challenge literature, particularly in another miniature from the breviary of the Duke of Berry, *Février* (see Fig. 14). The scene of the interior in this picture shows garments drying indoors after a snowy day. It is viewed from the outside snowy landscape, which enhances the coziness and naturalism of the *intérieur*. As the rich peasant woman warms herself at the fire in the kitchen, it can be seen that she is wearing a petticoat similar to the one hanging over a pole, a garment visibly lacking to her servants, who also are warming themselves. The husband, well-protected against the snow by a white overcoat, yet shivering in the cold, goes to join those in the house. The warmth of the heated room is almost felt in contrast to the heavy gray outdoors, where one man is shown cutting a tree and another leading a donkey carrying a load. The cottage is characterized by the pigeon house (*pigeonnier*), beehive, and sheep fold (*bergerie*) in the yard.[15]

With all this taken into consideration, it may be stated that in the literature and art of the fifteenth century an early dedication to this-worldliness, an abandonment of high-flown Gothic idealism, and a flight from metaphysics and symbolism into details of everyday life come drastically to the fore. These traits are also found in the proverbs of the time, full of gluttony (*gourmandise*), drinking (*beuverie*), gossip (*bavardage*), back-biting (*médisance*), and greediness (*avarice*) [16] proverbs that will even be painted later by Breughel. The mean and petty genre scenes flourish, together with the 'amorous and sometimes obscene stories of stupid or cunning girls, reckless wives, cheated husbands, and sensual monks.' [17] Meanness, pleasure, and shamelessness give rise to intimate and indiscreet scenes viewed through keyholes, as in the *Grand Testament* of Villon, where the author spies on the wanton Canon carousing with Dame Sidoine (lines 1473ff.). A husband accuses his wife of wearing an indecent dress, 'trop ouverte par devant, et que la languette du collet va trop bas' (*Les Arrêts d'amour*, no. 27). [18] It becomes quite usual to show couples in their bedrooms, she beseeching him for a new gown, or playing the sick woman to hide a guilt. [19] The Old French *fabliau* has reached the prose status with full literary rights. The naturalism of *Février* has been outdone in literature.

14. Frères de Limbourg, *Février*, Musée Condé, Chantilly. (Archives Photographiques)

## III. Nature Seen through Civilization

Nature, appealing in its primeval immediateness to Germanic and Anglo-Saxon pantheism, is acceptable to the Latin sensibility of the French only in a form refined by art and cultivated by man. When this typically French way of always showing the cultural implications in nature appeared for the first time at the end of the Middle Ages in some of the famous miniatures of the Frères de Limbourg, the accent on human interest is not so self-evident; the fact that they observe any details in nature whatsoever has deceived some critics. This fact gives additional value to the statement of Arnold Goffin:

> Nature, in the works of the Frères de Limbourg, is more animated and more living than it had ever been before in the graphic arts, but it is a chosen nature made for the eyes of the princes to serve as a noble decoration to their sovereign existence. The Frères de Limbourg painted the same way as Froissart wrote in order to procure entertainment and pleasure to their royal sponsors, those Valois so fond of luxury, knowledge, and refined beauty. The seasons of the year which they unfold in the calendar of the Chantilly Hours is no longer the laborious year of the peasant as it was sculptured in the cycles of the doorhalls of the cathedrals; it is rather the year of the lord and the courtier with its succession of variegated pleasures, festivities, excursions, games, hunting parties, eternal enjoyment. . . And in the background of every picture, in its perspective, is visible the haughty silhouette of a royal castle as a token of power and sovereignty. . . This French feudalism attempted elegancy and refinement of spirit.

Whereas the penetrating endeavor of a modern historian of art is needed to unmask the interest in nature of the Frères de Limbourg as being primarily an interest in civilization, the verses of a contemporary of these painters,[20] the poet Charles d'Orléans, do the same service spontaneously and therefore still more reliably by self-evident literary parallels. When Charles d'Orléans sings the coming of spring, he finds no direct approach to nature but only metaphors of court and military life. Nature has dropped her winter cloak of ice and a new, embroidered gown of sun is her livery now; the quartermasters of summer have arrived to decorate her future lodging with flowery carpets and tapestry:

*Rondeau I*

Le temps a laissé son manteau
De vent, de froidure et de pluye
Et s'est vestu de broderie
De soleil luyant, cler et beau

. . .

Rivière, fontaine et ruisseau
Portent, en livrée jolie,
Gouttes d'argent d'orfaverie.
Chascun s'abille de nouveau.

*Rondeau II*

Les fourriers d'Esté sont venus
Pour appareillier son logis,
Et ont fait tendre ses tapis
De fleurs et verdure tissus.

*Rondeau I*

[The time has laid his mantle by
Of wind and rain and icy chill,
And dons a rich embroidery
Of sun-light poured on lake and hill

. . .

River and fountain, brook and rill,
Bespangled over with livery gay
Of silver droplets, wind their way
So all their new apparel vie;
The time hath laid his mantle by.] [21]

*Rondeau II*

[The quartermasters of Summer have arrived
To prepare his lodgings
And have laid out his carpets
Woven of flowers and verdure.]

One of the seasonal miniatures of Pol de Limbourg, *Avril* (see Fig. 15), from the *Très Riches Heures du Duc de Berry*, shows a group of courtiers and beautiful ladies gossiping on an April day in a meadow covered with new grass, interspersed with tender young trees. But the talking seems less concerned with their preferences among the pretty flowers than with the choice of the prettiest flower among the girls. This prevailing sentiment of courtship amidst the beauties of nature, despite the little scene of *cueillette de fleurs*, is also expressed, only more eloquently, in the poetic homage of Jean Froissart (1337–1410). The compliment, elegant in spite of its verbal clumsiness, states that the poet's Lady Love, Marguerite, is the prettiest flower of all:

Sus toutes flours tient-on la rose à belle,
Et, en après, je croi, la violette.
La flour de lys est belle, et la perselle;
La flour de glay est plaisant et parfette . . .
Chascune flour a par li son merite.
Mès je vous di, tant que pour ma partie:
Sus toutes flours j'aime la Margherite.[22]

The statement of J. Huizinga that painting precedes literature in nature description because it does not remain entangled in symbolical and allegorical implications needs careful reconsideration. It is true that François Rabelais' detailed description of the Abbey of Thélème portrays Fran-

15. Frères de Limbourg, *Avril*. (Archives Photographiques)

çois I's pseudo-castle of Chambord on the Loire, but his is not the first description of this kind in literature. Before the Frères de Limbourg were painting into the background of their miniatures exact reproductions of the different castles of the Duke of Berry, the writer Guillaume de Machaut (1300–1377) [23] was describing in detail in *Le Jugement du Roi de Behaigne* the castle of Durbuy belonging to his master Jean de Luxembourg, King of Bohemia, and this as early as 1346. Furthermore, in the midst of his allegory *Remède de Fortune*, he realistically describes the park of Hesdin (v. 3889–4018) and a whole day of castle life, with Mass in the morning, dinner at noon, concert in the afternoon, and *coucher* at night.

## IV. Awareness of Beauty, Joy, Sorrow, Decay

Considering anew the topic of feminine beauty, after the Gothic clichés of Chrétien de Troyes, the attributes of the Blessed Virgin, and the resuscitated bodies, one is now confronted with jubilation over the wonder of natural youthful gracefulness, combined with the feminine elegance of furs, silks, and jewels. Eustache Deschamps (1340–1410) has expressed this jubilation with unprecedented enthusiasm in the 'self-portrait' of a fifteen-year-old girl:

*Portrait d'une pucelle par elle-même*

Il me semble, a mon avis,
Que j'ay beau front et doulz viz
Et la bouche vermeillette;
Dites moy se je suis belle?

J'ay vers yeux, petits sourcis,
Le chief blont, le nez traitis,
Ront menton, blance gorgette;
Sui-je, sui-je, sui-je belle?
· · ·
J'ay mantiaux fourrez de gris,
J'ay chapiaux, j'ay biaux proffis
Et d'argent mainte espinglette;
Sui-je, sui-je, sui-je belle?

J'ay draps de soye et tabis [moiré]
J'ay draps d'or et blancs et bis,
J'ay mainte bonne chosette;
Dites moy se je suis belle.

Que quinze ans n'ay, je vous dis;
Moult est mes tresors jolys,
S'en garderay la clavette;
Sui-je, sui-je, sui-je belle? [24]

The early painters try in vain to express this kind of jubilant beauty. Incomprehensible as it may seem, they even paint the king's mistresses under the title of the Virgin, as did Jean Fouquet in the *Madonna de Melun* [25] (1452), using Agnès Sorel as a model. But this beauty is technically depicted according to theoretical standards of aesthetics and does not spring at all from the spontaneous jubilation of a painter's heart. This Madonna lacks expression; she is a puppet. The painter treats in a merely technical manner the elements of beauty enumerated in the poem of Deschamps. Since the promoter of the use of Agnès Sorel as model was one of her great admirers, Etienne Chevalier, the king's treasurer, the whole thing strikes Huizinga as sacrilegious. This mental attitude, he adds, has another parallel in literature, namely, in the already mentioned *Quinze Joies de mariage,* where the fifteen joys of Our Lady are used as a pattern for fifteen disastrous aspects of marriage, sarcastically called *joies.* The word play, too, on *saint* (holy) and *sein* (bosom) in the contemporary *Cent Nouvelles nouvelles* is an almost exact reflection of the same blasphemous, erotic spirit that presumes to 'honor' Our Lady with the beautiful breasts of Agnès Sorel.[26] In other words, in the fifteenth century, when beauty seemed bound either to holiness or obscenity, the painters could not solve the problem by combining these two exclusive extremes. They failed to see

16. Clouet, *Elisabeth d'Autriche*. (Photo Alinari)

that charming, secular, jubilant beauty that Eustache Deschamps sketched in his poem.

This dignified and jubilant feminine beauty appears in painting with François Clouet (1510–72) in the beautiful portrait of *Elisabeth d'Autriche* (1570). (See Fig. 16.) The picture, representing the seventeen-year-old queen of Charles IX and daughter of Maximilian II, expresses youthful charm in the same way Eustache Deschamps had expressed it poetically. Clouet, however, as Samuel Rocheblave has pointed out,[27] puts much more psychology into his portrait, a psychology that springs from the silence of the lips and the mystery of the gaze, so gentle and fine, preserving the grace of youth with the gravity of a young wife. The childlike, charming, irregular face is unaffected rather than sophisticated and less concerned with elegance than with probity, the eyes gently observing and kind beneath a still undeveloped shrewdness under the very high, pure, and almost imposing arch of the brows. The gown is magnificent, but all the while the eyes reflect a purity and modesty serenely undisturbed by the rich setting of brocade, laces, pearls, rubies, and other precious stones.

Flamboyant art can, however, express grief and sorrow. The great sorrow experienced in the long period of the Hundred Years War and the plague, the lack of security, and the loss of stability in religious matters, though combined with the ancient tradition of Christian dignity and righteousness, can best be read in the famous panel by Pierre Villatte, *La Pietà de Villeneuve-lès-Avignon* (see Fig. 17), so 'classical' by comparison with the contemporary Pietà of the German Hans Baldung Grien (1475–1545). This picture represents the grandiose figures of Christ, the Blessed Virgin, Saint Mary Magdalen, and the donor, an old priest. The priest proves by his expression that he understands sorrowfully the suffering he witnesses. Georges Lafenestre in *L'Exposition des primitifs français* refers to these figures 'of a powerful solemnity, pathetic, of a majestic sincerity, real types of the French soil, enhanced and idealized by their sorrow . . . the Virgin of a concentrated sorrow, but quiet and silent, and therefore all the more poignant, without a sigh, without a gesture, with the dignity of resignation, submissive and pious, representing the dignity of a mother who folds her hands and closes her eyes.'

Such a sorrowful mother, drawn from the realities of life and without leaning on the tradition of the Pietà motif, has also been created by Antoine de la Sale in his *Réconfort de Madame du Fresne*. The author, to comfort a woman who has lost a child, tells her the story of a boy-hostage who could not be released by his father for reasons of military honor. The night before the execution, the parents of the boy, M. and Mme Du Chastel, are discussing the unavoidable situation, and it is the dignified, heartbroken mother herself who advises her husband not to surrender and not to save the little boy's life.[28]

> The lady's great grief consisted in seeing that her husband had to lose his honor or that she had to lose her beautiful and gentle son. Then she said to her husband: 'Because such is the will of God, He wills and orders that of the bad choices the less bad has to be taken. With folded hands I beseech you therefore, milord, and two counsels I want to give you. . .

17. Villatte, *La Pietà de Villeneuve-lès-Avignon*. (Foto Marburg)

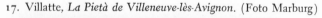

The first is that you forget about all your sorrows . . . and that we put all
of them into the hands of our true God. . . The second is that it is self-
evident that children are more the sons or daughters of their mothers who
have carried them in their womb than those of their husbands. . . Therefore he is particularly my son whom it has cost me so much to carry . . .
and about whom I have suffered so many pangs. . . None the less, now
and forever, I abandon him into the hands of God . . . without any con-
straint, force, violence whatsoever . . . in order to maintain your honor
only, which otherwise would be lost forever. . . God has given him to
you in order to redeem your honor.'

When the general heard milady speak in such a high manner, he thanked
Jesus Christ with a contemplative sigh. . . Then he answered her in a
few words: ' My darling . . . I thank you for the very high and woeful
gift which you have made me now. . . I have just heard the watchman
blowing his horn announcing the day . . . and I have to get up; but you
must still rest a little.' — ' Rest,' said she, ' alas, milord, I have no heart,
eye or other limb of the body which would be able to rest. But I shall get
up, too, and we shall go to Mass, both of us, to thank Our Lord for everything.' [29]

This dignity in sorrow is a more secularized but worthy counterpart of the
Pietà in Avignon; both express silence, renunciation, piety.

The sorrow expressed by Christine de Pisan (1363–1440) did not reach
this majestic dignity. In her tears and sighs of early widowhood: ' I am so
lonely; lonely I wish to be ' (' Seulette suis, seulette vueil estre '), or in her
desperate consolations: ' My friend, weep no more ' (' Mon ami, ne
plourez plus '), she shows a delicate, spontaneous femininity and the capacity of rhyming one strophe on a single sentiment, which takes shape
without the aid of thought but then deteriorates into poor rhetoric.[30]

Besides dignified feelings, art and literature after 1400 are concerned
with human decay, not only in the famous topic of the ' Dance of Death,'
with its literary verse accompanying the murals in churches and church-
yards, but even in the portraiture of human persons. Villon's Jean Cot-
tard, the notorious drunkard stumbling into the corner of a butcher shop
and getting a terrific bump, is mitigated by witty lines on Noah's fine
legacy of having planted the vine. But the ' implacable sincerity ' with
which Girard d'Orléans (1360) paints the ' heart-rending stupidity, desperate resignation and abased and downcast physiognomy ' [31] of King
John [32] betrays the art of a disintegrating age. The portrait of Charles
VII [33] by Fouquet would make one hesitate to approve of Villon's song
to the planter of wine (Père Noë qui plantastes la vigne), for wine seems
to have destroyed this king with the copper colored nose, congested, un-
dermined . . . half hidden between the small curtains of his box from
which he hears mass in the Holy Chapel of Bourges . . . covered by thick
and heavy garments.[34] This king experiences the sad humiliation that has
never been expressed more to the point than in Villon's motif of les ta-

*vernes et les filles.* The king's profound melancholy, on the other hand, is voiced by the royal prince and poet Charles d'Orléans (1394–1465), nephew of Charles VI and father of Louis XII. While a prisoner in England, he became the singer of melancholy. In his *Ballade XVIII* he sighs: 'Je suis celui au coeur vêtu de noir'; and he tries this eternal melody of grief also in the language of his captors: 'In blake mournying is clothyd my corage.'

## V. Struggle for a Modern Perspective

The solution of perspective presented difficulties for literature and art alike. A painter like Henri Bellechose in the fifteenth century uses practically the same technique as does a prose writer like Joinville at the beginning of the fourteenth. In both there is the simultaneous, illogical presentation of events taking place at different times. This is a 'false perspective' in so far as it means a surface presentation without any depth of space or time. This wrong perspective is accompanied by a fancy shaping and grouping of figures according to psychological rather than logical principles. Jean de Joinville tells in his *Histoire de Saint Louis* that he was once summoned to Paris for an oath of allegiance. On his way he found three men who had been murdered. He heard that the king wanted to have the crime investigated, with all the details preceding the murder. Telling this story, Joinville makes no difference between primary and incidental, present and more remote events. He juxtaposes everything without any logical arrangement:

> Li roys *manda* tous ses barons a Paris et lour fist faire sairement. . . Il *le me demanda*. . . Je *trouvai* trois hommes morz sur une charette . . . et *conta mes escuiers* que li rois *ala* au perron pour veoir les morts . . . et li prevoz li *conta* que li mort estoient troi de ses serjanz . . . et *dist* au roy que il *trouverent* ce clerc que vous veez ci, et lui *tollirent* toute sa robe. Li clerc s'en *alla en pure sa chemise* . . . et *prist* s'arbaleste . . . il les *escrie* . . . que il y *mourroient*. Li clers *tendi* l'arbaleste et *trait* et en *feri* l'un par le cuer . . . *fist* li prevoz au roy. 'Sire,' *fist*-il, 'li clers . . . s'*en vint mettre* en vostre prison . . . et je le vous amein.' 'Sire clers,' *fist* li roys, 'je vous retieing i mes gaiges ' . . . Après ces choses je *reving*.[35]

This juxtaposition of events taking place at different times is effected by the use of the tenses: there is practically only the past definite (*passé défini*) — no pluperfect for remote actions, no imperfect for incidental or more picturesque action (except for indirect speech), no perfect (*indéfini*) for action related to the storyteller. Nyrop writes: 'The older language uses the simple past and the perfect tense indiscriminately. . . The simple past was also used to indicate a past event in connection with the present . . . In the Middle Ages the simple past was used sometimes in the sense

18. Bellechose, *La Dernière Communion et le martyre de Saint Denis*, Louvre.
(Archives Photographiques)

of a pluperfect.' [36] Finally, the psychologically important word precedes
in rank the psychologically less important word: for example, *et conta mes
escuiers* (modern: *et mon écuyer raconta*); *en pure sa chemise* (modern:
*en sa chemise seulement*). Here the importance of the report and the surprise of seeing a man without any clothes but his shirt overstresses the
verb 'report' and the striking adjective (*pure*) that accents the unusual
dress.

It is not necessary to decide the famous question whether all this is a
lack of technical skill, as it certainly appears to the modern, rational point
of view, or is rather a willed expression of a more childlike glance at a
world where values and time and emotions play a different part than they
do in the modern world. A picture by Henri Bellechose, representative of
many others, as is the text of Joinville, illustrates this problem. In *La
Dernière Communion et le martyre de Saint Denis* (see Fig. 18) there are
juxtaposed the last mystical communion of the saint behind the prison
grill and his decapitation outside the prison. In the language of the gram-
marian, here are joined two incompatible tenses, incompatible because the
precedence of one action over the other is ignored. The executioner who
swings his axe to behead the blindfolded saint, crowned with the mitre,
is aggrandized to the point where he appears superior to his victim. This
is certainly wrong in perspective as well as in psychology. The painting
thus makes the usage of the tenses more understandable and arouses the
same questions: Is the Crucifixus between the two illogically juxtaposed
scenes simply a means of separating the two non-simultaneous actions on
the same panel? That is, has He only formal or ornamental importance?
Or rather, is the Calvary the typically medieval, timeless link between the
Eucharistic scene of Christ as the high priest on the left and the martyrs
on the right, shedding their blood for Christ as He did for them? Although

this may not be decided with certainty, the lack of perspective in the art of Bellechose hints at the same solutions and also at the same unsolved problems concerning the meaning of techniques as those found in the co-ordination of Joinville and in his use of tenses and word order, all baffling to the modern critic.

But the new perspective also comes to the fore during the age of flamboyant art. Earlier than the Spanish *Don Quijote* of Cervantes, the above-mentioned *Petit Jehan de Saintré* of Antoine de la Sale, sometimes called the pre-*Don Quijote,* had solved the perspective problem in literature. His story as such seems to be a short novel, with occurrences taking place on the surface rather than in strata, which give depth and perspective. Petit Jean de Saintré becomes the plaything-lover of the much older *Dame des Belles Cousines,* but during the absence of Petit Jean she betrays him, giving her love to a young bourgeois abbot. Petit Jean, upon returning, challenges the abbot to a duel and makes the lady's situation impossible at court. Now Antoine de la Sale, the author, has tried desperately to give depth to his novel by placing it against a cultural-historical background. He thus introduces the appointment of Petit Jean as a leader in an expedition of the Teutonic knights against Prussia and the Eastern pagan states. The description of the army and its officers fills more pages than the love

19. Jan van Eyck, *La Vierge du Chancelier Rollin,* Louvre. (Archives Photographiques)

story; although it makes the novel clumsy, it gives it an added importance. Furthermore, the elaborate opposition between the aristocratic young knight and the rich bourgeois abbot introduces the whole problem of the crisis of the nobility and the uprising of the young *bourgeoisie*, whose new bankers (like Jacques Cœur) can provide prebends for their sons. Thus it becomes truly a modern novel, with depth and perspective from both a historical and a social point of view.

In painting, the problem of perspective is solved with similar virtuosity, as can be seen in *La Vierge du Chancelier Rollin* (see Fig. 19) by Jan van Eyck. E. Durand Gréville describes the details of its striking depth:

> If one looks through the empty space between the head of the Divine Child and the Virgin, one discovers, graded to the depth, a town full of beautiful steeples and towers, a broad place with living figures, a bridge in the form of a donkey's back, crowded with people, a river winding through the landscape and furrowed by microscopically small boats, and in the center is an island with a magnificent castle surrounded by trees, and finally in the far distance a line of snowy mountains disappearing in the sky.[37]

The first modern prose novel and the first modern painting with background arise simultaneously in the same French-Flemish realm of the Dukes of Burgundy and have absolutely the same artistic meaning. They show the extent of the northern pre-Renaissance even without Italian influence.


## VI. Forms of a Rampant Paganism

The clumsy outward efforts to achieve a Renaissance under François I consist of an embryonic humanism, handicapped, however, by an embryonic pietism, which did not too deeply affect French civilization, John Calvin having emigrated to Geneva. Calvin's own teachings of predestination are clad in the splendid, oratorical prose rhythms of the *Institution chrétienne*. Clément Marot's scarcely visible leanings toward Italy, appearing here and there in a sonnet, are counterbalanced by his translations of the Psalms. Rabelais, in his ill-digested humanism, is burdened by his eternal *moniage* on his shoulders. The Greek studies together with the Hebrew at the new Collège de France continue to serve the Scriptures more than Homer. In short, the half-hearted attempts at a Renaissance in France hover between the Epicureanism of a Louise Labé and the Platonism of a Maurice Scève in Lyon on the one hand, and the Biblical reformation tried first by Lefèvre d'Etaples and his friends in Meaux on the other.

For an understanding of this pietistically encumbered paganism, there is no better example than the picture *Eva Prima Pandora* (see Fig. 20) by Jean Cousin, painted about 1538. Here is the same half-heartedness.

A Venus, influenced by Giorgione and Titian, is called Eve, under the impact of the teachings of Calvin. But she is also called Pandora. It is like
a Rabelaisian glance at beauty with a bad conscience, like Calvin's concept of original sin poisoning the beauty of life in principle. This Eve-
Pandora is as distorted as Rabelais' concepts of life — hedonism grafted
on a misunderstood asceticism — for there is distortion not only in the
idea but even in the forms. The face of the woman is much too small.
The more regular features and forms are clearly not those of a model but
those of pedantic, theoretical canons of Greek beauty handed down to
Cousin by the Italian masters. There is no spontaneity, no simplicity, just
a compromise: pietistic humanism; Cicero's period serves Protestant pes-
simism.

In literature also the full pagan approach to feminine beauty is not
visible in the first half of the sixteenth century. The feeling still prevails
that beauty must be counterbalanced by ugliness, youth by age, life by
death. As Villon in the fifteenth century drew a double portrait of the
young and the old *belle heaulmière*, described with an amazing, anatomi-
cal completeness, melancholy, and sarcasm, so Clément Marot in the
sixteenth would not dare his *blason du beau tétin* without contrasting it
with the *blason du laid tétin*.

It is only in the second half of the sixteenth century that French painting under the guidance of Italian traditions overcomes the painfulness of
the sexual implications and even goes to a certain extreme by overrealisti-
cally stressing the elements of beauty. This stage is reached in a picture
from the School of Fontainebleau, *Gabrielle d'Estrée dans son bain.*[38] This
painting hints at a neopagan carelessness in exhibiting the body in a rea-

20. Cousin, *Eva Prima Pandora*, Louvre. (Archives Photographiques)

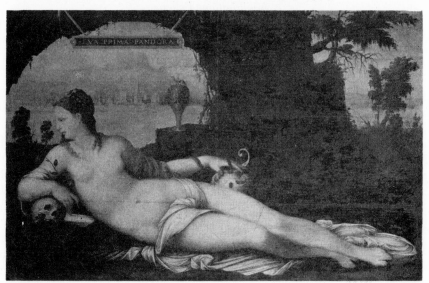

listic scene, unmitigated by mythology. To paint the king's mistress not as Diana bathing in the woods but as her very self in a bathtub is something so unheard of immediately after the Christian medieval centuries that Etienne Moreau-Nelaton describes the picture as follows:

> A beauty, proud of the carnal advantages with which nature has endowed her, has exposed to the painter's brush a bust entirely deprived of veils. The lady is standing in a bathtub. Near her, a wet nurse with a country coif [*bonnet de campagne*] offers her breast to a newborn babe, whereas a child, wide awake, stretches out his hand towards a refreshment [*collation*] of fruits prepared beside the bather. The scene has as theatre a small [*cosu*] apartment, in the background of which a chambermaid with a jar [*ai-guière*] in her arms is waiting for the moment when the elegant lady needs her assistance for dressing.[39]

It is a fact that the realism surrounding this beauty, almost a foreboding of *Bain Turc* of Ingres or even the *Olympia* and *Déjeuner sur l'herbe* of Manet, is as bewildering in the sixteenth century as is Marguerite de Navarre's crudeness, scarcely veiled by moralism, in her *Heptaméron*,[40] in which this pietistic woman proves to be an excellent pupil of Boccaccio. The atmosphere of this picture, as typical of the French reaction to neopaganism, comes closest, however, to that of the love poetry of Ronsard and the Latin poetry of Du Bellay.

Ronsard has the sentiment of the ancients, and the source of his sensual love poems, which correspond in spirit to the picture, is evidently mythology, which also combines love and nature to a high dègree. Spontaneously he sees dryads and naiads everywhere, and his Greek studies only help him to see better, as evidenced in his ode:

### A la Fontaine Bellerie

O Fontaine Bellerie,
Belle Fontaine chérie,
De nos nymphes quand ton eau
Les cache au creux de ta source
Fuyantes le Satyreau,
Qui les pourchasse à la course
Jusqu'au bord de ton ruisseau.

Water, evoking and veiling nymphs, is also the Renaissance dream of Jean Goujon in his *Fontaine des Innocents* [41] in the Louvre (1568). These water-nymphs have been described as symbolizing the rivers of France. Their flowing, semi-transparent draperies suggest the fluidity of water with a sensuous charm. The nymphs of Goujon are truly Ronsardian nymphs.

With the first School of Fontainebleau and the minor poets of the Pléiade, Goujon's and Ronsard's classical assimilation deteriorates into something trifling. But to a greater extent than in the Fontainebleau

School and in the Gabrielle d'Estrée portrait, Ronsard's innate sense of beauty overcomes to a certain degree the erotic atmosphere of a picture by graceful embellishments which mitigate and reduce the objectionable elements. Therefore he draws a different picture of his sweetheart from that of Gabrielle d'Estrée. His picture extends to beautiful spring and summer mornings and the lover's license to wake up his sweetheart. One day Marie had promised him to be in the garden early, and as she does not appear, the poet enters her room:

> Marie, levez-vous, ma jeune paresseuse
> Ja la gaye alouette au ciel a fredonné
> Et ja le rossignol doucement jargonné,
> Dessus l'espine assis sa complainte amoureuse.

How can the maiden oversleep on such a glorious day? Ronsard feigns to be shocked. He is the seigneur; she the beautiful but poor Marie Dupin of Bourgueil. He kisses triumphantly the beauty that slept too long:

> Harsoir en vous couchant vous jurastes vos yeux
> D'estre plutost que moy ce matin esveillée,
> Mais le dormir de l'aube aux filles gracieux
>
> Vous tient d'un doux sommeil encor les yeux sillée.
> Ça, ça que je les baise et votre beau tétin
> Cent fois pour vous apprendre à vous lever matin.

It is worth mentioning that Ronsard, in his enthusiasm for feminine beauty, once called on François Clouet, whom the Pléiade used to call 'Dieu Janet,' to paint his lady love:

> Pein-moy, Janet, pein-moy, je t'en supplie,
> Sur ce tableau les beautés de m'amie.[42]

At the end of the sixteenth century, the half-Italian School of Fontainebleau created a graceful group called *Amor Disarmed*.[43] Cupid has fallen asleep, after having become dangerous to mankind. The Muses and the Graces surround him and take away his arrows and quiver, his mother, Venus, standing by without hindering this disarming. This group illustrates the frivolous spirit of the then-discovered Greek anthology and is trifling in general, but it is also somewhat stilted, because the primary concern of the painter is to imitate the beauty of the different women in the style of Primaticcio. To understand the sportiveness of the picture, it is helpful to keep in mind the contemporary poetic variations of similar themes. Remy Belleau (1528–77) depicts a Cupid stung by a bee and complaining bitterly about it to Venus. She, however, answers in a charming scolding that those wounded by his, Cupid's, arrows would have reason to complain much more:

> Mignon, dist Venus, si la pointe
> D'une mouche à miel telle atteinte
> Droit au cœur (comme tu dis) fait,
> Combien sont navrés davantage
> Ceux qui sont espoints de ta rage
> Et qui sont blessés de ton trait! [44]

The element of jest, which gives the picture its hidden charm, is stressed even more by Jean Antoine de Baïf (1532–89), who deals with the same topic of Cupid stung by a bee and scolded by his mother in trifling, short, five-syllable lines fraught with sulky diminutives:

> CUPID: Vois, dit il, l'atteinte
> Qu'une mouche fait;
> Vois, combien méfait
> Une bestelette
> Qui si mingrelette
> Fait un mal si grand.

> VENUS: De toi même il t'en prend
> (Venus lui vint dire
> Se prenant à rire);
> Bien qu'enfantelet
> Tu sois mingrelet,
> Tu ne vaux pas mieux:
> Vois quelle blessure
> Tu fais qu'on endure
> En terre et aux cieux.

Thus it can be understood that it is, indeed, the playful spirit of the Fontainebleau School and of the minor poets of the Pléiade that distinguishes the classical themes of the sixteenth century from the austere and serious classical topics as developed mainly in the seventeenth by Poussin and Racine.

# *The Baroque Classicism of the Seventeenth Century*

## 1600–1715

BY ONE of the most striking processes of history, France reaches her understanding of all the elements of classical antiquity — reason, restraint, decency, proportion, and measure — at a moment when the rest of Europe under the influence of Spain and the Counter-Reformation had developed the Renaissance style in art and literature into something exuberant, which is usually called baroque. The classical tendencies of France cannot escape, however, this general European trend. Theoretically she opposes it; practically the French works of this century absorb this baroque spirit to such an extent that Henri Peyre can state that no Greek would have recognized a tragedy of Racine as something belonging to the Hellenic spirit.[1]

Nevertheless, the general interest in the unchangeable and eternal values of human dignity, in the soul of man, in his moral and heroic actions, in his passions and virtues, enables Catholic, monarchic, and absolutist France to imitate an antiquity that was interested in the same values in a pre-Christian way. The sentiment of heroism coming from the foreign wars fought under Louis XIII and Louis XIV could well be assimilated to the heroic topics of antiquity. This sentiment overflows into every type of art, tragedy, novel, sermon, and landscape. The human personality, however, is more important than anything else. The portrait will be a dominating feature in literature and art with Molière and La Bruyère, Pascal and Mme. de Sévigné, Philippe de Champaigne and Rigaud, Largillière and Coyzevox. The reason and *esprit géométrique* of Descartes, the *raison du cœur* and *esprit de finesse* of Pascal in their classical-baroque fusion will also be found in the geometrical *châteaux* and in the immense vistas of their gardens, as well as in the paradoxical logic of the Racinian plots. Free will and grace with the Jesuitic and the Jansenistic accentuation will mark the difference between Corneille and Racine no less than that between Le Sueur and Philippe de Champaigne. The discovery of the eternal man in the contingencies of contemporaneous personalities takes place independently in Bossuet and the Brothers Le Nain. The *bienséance* stressed

21. Poussin, *Shepherds of Arcadia*, Louvre. (Foto Marburg)

by the *Précieuses* in the salon of the Marquise de Rambouillet will be a welcome, sweet tyranny to Poussin and Racine and will aid them to artistic perfection.

## I. The Assimilative Imitation of Antiquity

The pastoral novel *L'Astrée*, by Honoré d'Urfé, opens the seventeenth century with a still falsified expression of antiquity, and describes goddesses and shepherdesses with, as Milton would say, their 'lovely hands,' 'tinsel-slippered feet,' and 'golden comb' (*Comus*, 875ff.). In the novel the shepherdess Astrée represents the ideal of beauty of the Spanish pastoral novels, where the baroque-classical compromise appears in the most obvious form. The aim is a maximum of sensuality that is still compatible with Christian morality: 'Her hair was covered with only a wreath . . . You would have seen a bare arm and a leg as white as alabaster, round and smooth so that there was no trace of a bone, the leg long and straight and the foot small and delicate, the envy of Thetis.' [2]

Pastoral painting as represented by Nicolas Poussin (1594–1665) avoided this languishing type of pastoral well known from Italian pictures. As a kind of Christian humanist, Poussin understands that the attitudes of mind expressed by dignified classical attitudes of the body convey the most serious lessons on life and death. The story of his picture *Shepherds of Arcadia* [3] (see Fig. 21) is that of young country people who have spent many happy days with their flocks in the fields and pastures. On a certain day, however, they find a tombstone with the inscription: '*Et in Arcadia ego*' (I, too, was born in Arcadia), which reminds them that the shepherd who lies buried here had once frolicked like themselves. Thus they become melancholy and silent and think of their own death.

These moods are not lacking in *L'Astrée*. Diane, another shepherdess, ponders in a similar way, on the banks of the Lignon, on the futility of life:

> Après s'y être assise, et que sans mot dire elle eut longuement tenu l'œil sur le courant de la rivière . . . ' Ainsi,' dit-elle, ' vont courant dans le sein de l'oubly toutes les choses mortelles! . . . O que celuy-là estoit bien véritable, qui disoit que jamais une mesme personne ne passa deux fois une mesme rivière. . . Le temps par une puissance à laquelle rien ne peut résister, va poussant et chassant toutes choses devant lui.

This classical melancholy resignation is not the *carpe diem* cry of the Renaissance. The Greek concept of restraint becomes a mitigated baroque resignation, because the French understand the parallel between man and nature. This is voiced by Malherbe when he consoles M. du Perrier upon the death of his daughter:

> Et Rose, elle a vécu ce que vivent les roses
> L'espace d'un matin.

More than that, there is Christian resignation particularly expressed in the face of the shepherdess on the right in Poussin's picture. It is as though she would stress Malherbe's lines of resignation:

> Vouloir ce que Dieu veut est la seule science
> Qui nous met en repos.

Poussin's presentation is also reminiscent of the melancholy resignation in the presence of death so typical of Bossuet. It is the practice of Bossuet in his *Oraisons funèbres* to introduce death first from a natural, human, pagan, and classical point of view, and to deal with the Christian eschatalogical implications only in a second development. His first classical ' provisional ' exposition of the theme reminds the reader of Poussin's painting:

22. Poussin, *The Legend of the Renunciation of Diogenes*, Louvre.
    (Archives Photographiques)

Vanité! ô néant! ô mortels ignorants de leur destinées! . . . Elle devait périr si tôt. . . Madame . . . a passé du matin au soir ainsi que l'herbe des champs. Le matin elle fleurissait; avec quelles grâces! vous le savez: le soir, nous la vîmes séchée. . . La voilà, malgré ce grand cœur, cette princesse si admirée et si chérie! la voilà telle que la mort nous l'a faite.[4]

The ancients themselves had still another concern about death: the whereabouts of the other world and the impossibility of release from ' the land from whose bourne no traveler returns.' The meaning of the ancient legend is illustrated by Poussin's picture of *Orpheus Asking the Way to Hades*.[5] The interest of Orpheus in recovering his wife Eurydice from Hades is voiced in a general way by a *pensée* of Blaise Pascal:

L'immortalité de l'âme cest une chose qui nous importe si fort, qui nous touche si profondément qu'il faut avoir perdu tout sentiment pour être dans l'indifférence de savoir ce qui en est.[6]

Poussin, through the somber cloudy darkness of a rocky landscape with the gaping mouth of Hades in the background, expresses all the anxiety surrounding this obsession with the afterlife. Exactly the same impression that comes from this landscape is found in the *Bergeries* of Racan:

Ces antres ténébreux ne sont point sans danger:
Je ne vois dans ces champs ni troupeau ni berger.
J'ai perdu mon chemin, je ne trouve personne;
La frayeur me saisit, toute chose m'étonne.

(v. iii)

The gay La Fontaine is also impressed by the lugubrious aspect of a landscape, the Val de Thréson, he writes about in his *Voyage au Limousin:*

C'est un passage dangereux,
Un lieu pour les voleurs, d'embûche et de retraite,
A gauche un bois, une montagne à droite,
Entre les deux
Un chemin creux.
La montagne est toute pleine
De rochers faits comme ceux
De notre petit domaine.

The seventeenth century is a century of renunciation, taught in the highest degree of practice by the Abbé de Rancé, founder of the Trappists. *Renoncement* is extolled in the *Cid* of Corneille, where Don Rodrigue and Chimène renounce love for honor; in Racine's Emperor Titus in *Bérénice*, who renounces marriage for a duty of state; in Mme de La Fayette's *Princesse de Clèves*, who renounces happiness for dignity. Poussin's picture of *The Legend of the Renunciation of Diogenes* (see Fig. 22), which typifies the motif of renunciation found in literature, shows the philosopher throwing away one of the last things he had kept, his cup, when he sees a shepherd drinking water in the hollow of his hands. For the painter Poussin this gesture is a classical symbol of the ascetic Catholic, French ideals of 1650 and earlier, as found in the *Peintures morales* (1643) of P. Lemoyne, considered as Racinian sources.[7] It is not obvious at first sight that the painter also tells what Diogenes had renounced before throwing his cup away — namely, the whole of civilization, which, in this picture, as writes Jeanne Magnin, ' has transformed nature. Imposing structures show their terraces on the top of the hills with cupolas and porches. The towers of a castle dominate the woods around [left]. A farm aligns its barns and stables along the river [right]. Diogenes condemns such conquests which subdue man and handicap his liberty.' [8]

Antiquity, or rather Greco-Roman mythology, is still used to symbolize certain aspects of nature that painters are not able to express directly as yet. ' Morning dawn following the dark night ' is for Poussin the time when *Selene Leaves Endymion,*[9] the beautiful youth whom she, Selene, the moon goddess, is used to visit every night until Aurora would appear, followed by the sun horses of Helios coming from the sea, the realm of Thetis. Thus the language of Poussin is an aid to understanding the Homeric language of Fénelon:

> Demain, quand l'Aurore avec ses doigts de roses entr'ouvrira les portes dorées de l'orient, et que les chevaux du soleil, sortant de l'onde amère, répandront les flammes du jour pour chasser devant eux toutes les étoiles du ciel, nous reprendrons, mon cher Télémaque, l'histoire de vos malheurs.
> (*Télémaque*, iv, ' Calypso ')

Even Boileau still believes that mythological language is the primary condition of poetry:

> Ce n'est plus la vapeur qui produit le tonnerre,
> C'est Jupiter armé pour effrayer la terre. . .
> Sans tous ces ornements le vers tombe en langueur,
> La poésie est morte ou rampe sans vigueur.
> (*L'Art poétique*, chant iii)

Le Bossu in his *Traité du poème épique* (1675) thinks the same about narrative poetry. La Fontaine's irony, however, uses the mythological setting to kill it, namely in his fable of the lazy kitchenmaids, aroused every morning by the cock's crowing:

> Dès que Téthys chassait Phébus aux crins dorés,
> Tourets entraient en jeu, fuseaux étaient tirés . . .
> Dès que l'Aurore, dis-je, en son char remontait,
> Un misérable coq à point nommé chantait.
> (*Fables*, v, 6)

23. Poussin, *Landscape with Fauns and Nymphs*. (Courtesy of the Metropolitan Museum of Art)

Even when Poussin paints a landscape, there is at issue a mythological *Landscape with Fauns and Nymphs* [10] (see Fig. 23). The sentiment of nature in France at this time still needs animation by man, as was the case at the time of the Frères de Limbourg. But now the not fully understood heroic-pantheistic mythology of the ancients must fill the breach. The third book of *L'Astrée* by d'Urfé, when sketching a Lignon landscape, offers the same preoccupation with

> belles Dryades et Nappées qui . . . se plaisent . . . à danser parmi les prés qui emaillent le rivage d'un perpétuel printemps de fleurs.
>
> (Op. cit. p. 45)

Corneille avows that a nature without mythological beings does not appeal to him at all:

> Moi, si je peins jamais Saint-Germain ou Versailles,
> Les nymphes, malgré vous, danseront tout autour;
> Cent demi-dieux follets leur parleront d'amour;
> Du satyre caché les brusques échappées
> Dans les bras des sylvains feront fuir les Nappées
>
> . . .
>
> Otez Pan et sa flûte, adieu les pâturages;
> Otez Pomone et Flore, adieu les jardinages! [11]

## II. The New Feeling for Nature and Landscape

There are, however, moments in French art and literature when a direct sentiment of nature breaks through. In the seascape *Acis and Galatea* [12] of

Claude Lorrain (1600–1682), the mythological love story is negligible. It is the beautiful landscape that is important here:

> the ideal beauty of the ruddy sea and the sky where a golden mist enwraps the pine trees bathed by the waves . . . some trees extend over the soil a velvet-like shade and a little honeysuckle which escaped from the neighboring wood is nestling there.[13]

What Claude Lorrain actually conveys with this painting is certainly what Louis Tristan l'Hermite in his poem *La Mer* expresses as his own ideal:

> Sur le gazon d'une falaise
> . . . rêver à mon aise
> Sur la majesté de la mer.

It is indeed Tristan l'Hermite who knows how to evoke mythological, idealized, dream landscapes exactly like those of Claude. In his works the presence of mythological beings is replaced by the very character of nature, with the water itself becoming a nymph because it seems capable of dreaming of flowers, whilst far-off echoes from the woods seem to come from Diana's horn. This hovering between a Greco-Roman polytheism and an unconscious pantheism still keeps the classical French mind from a radical, direct contact with nature.

> L'ombre de cette fleur vermeille
> Et celle de ces joncs pendans
> Paroissent estre là dedans
> Les songes de l'eau qui sommeille.
>
> Dans ce bois ni dans ces montagnes
> Jamais chasseur ne vint encor;
> Si quelqu'un y sonne du cor,
> C'est Diane avec ses compagnes
> (*Le Promenoir de deux amants*)

Painter and poet, in spite of achieving a greater directness, still dream of a so-called classical scene, where only settings of beauty in formal arrangement occur and where *raison* excludes every possible realistic ugliness, as it does in classical tragedy. The Frenchman with his sense of Greco-Roman beauty refuses to reproduce the haphazardous elements in nature which later will be the delight of the romantics; instead, he rearranges nature to conform to order and beauty, adding structures, fashioning trees, paths, and flower beds according to a plan of ideal abstraction. Of the greatest importance, then, are the noble buildings such as are seen in *Disembarkation of Cleopatra at Tarsis* [14] by Claude Lorrain. The feeling for nature is prevalent, however:

24. Lorrain, *The Embarkation of the Queen of Sheba.* (From the original in the National Gallery, London, by permission)

A mist is rising above the sea which in her calm has trembled during the whole day under the heat of the sun. The shades become longer on the flagstones of the pier, where . . . Cleopatra advances with her escort. The procession has just left the royal galley, a somber purple mass which displays in the sunset its rosy flags, and walks towards the palace, whose marble façade retains a reminder of clarity.[15]

On the one hand, there is the baroque ideal expressed by Malherbe, which ' makes nature give way to the wonders of art ' in those

> Beaux et grands bâtiments d'éternelle structure,
> Superbes de matière et d'ouvrages divers.
> (*Sonnet à Charlotte Jouvenel*, ' Caliste ')

On the other hand, there is the ideal of Racine — to sketch the unchanging substance of the world in a neutral scenery, where all actions from courtship to the severance of diplomatic relations can take place. ' This drawing,' writes Courthion, ' which outlines the temples, the boats and the smooth hills, without daring to be precise, without pretending to describe, never loses its force.' Implying the forgetfulness of space and time, as Racine does with his own particular handling in a psychological way, of the unities of time, place, and action, Courthion continues: ' Without seeing on the ruins anything else but the illumination of the hours of the days, that flight of time, wherefrom he draws his melody, Claude writes his painting into time as a musician does his fugue or his sonata.' [16]

It is indeed an exact comparison to state that Racine with his eternal expressions, ' these places, banks, or shores ' (*ces lieux, ces bords, ce rivage*), a little tinged with the light and shade of his epithets ' peaceful,' ' charming,' ' feared,' ' fatal ' (*ces paisibles lieux, ces bords heureux, ces lieux charmants, ces bords redoutés, un rivage funeste*), evokes landscapes as does

Claude Lorrain, only it is with a poet's sensibility. He gives them a time-less patina with the bewitching music of his verse:

> Depuis que sur ces bords les Dieux ont envoyé
> La fille de Minos et de Pasiphaé
>
> (*Phèdre*, I. 1)

or

> Ariane, ma sœur de quel amour blessée
> Vous mourûtes aux bords où vous fûtes laissée
>
> (*Phèdre*, I. 3)

As Racine simply changes the musical key for his locations of landscape, so with slight variations Claude Lorrain repeats his *marines* continuously as, for example, in *The Embarkation of the Queen of Sheba* [17] (see Fig. 24).

Looking only at the setting, one may easily confuse the *Embarkation of the Queen of Sheba* and the *Disembarkation of Cleopatra*, for there are no 'individual specific forms of space,' but only 'formal relations of phenomena'; there is no sun that 'shines from the vault of Heaven, but it always radiates towards the spectator from a flat backdrop, and this backdrop serves to indicate one of the four delimitations of imagined space symbolized by the picture.' [18] Through the suggestion of light or dusk, noon, or dawn and 'the color which tends to dissolve the forms into an unmeasured but infinite space' [19] the spectator perceives a truly individual climate; it is the individual climate with which Racine surrounds his equally suffering victims: Andromaque, Monime, and Junie.

In Racine's plays the place of action is always the unchangeable terrace of the palace, whereas the dialogues evoke the sea crossed by Andromaque, by Bérénice, and by Iphigénie, pushing the imagination to vague extensions of endless water and an atmospheric fluidity. A descriptive prose writer like Fénelon does not fail to stress the same impressions of details with which Claude Lorrain was absorbed:

25. Lorrain, *The Flight into Egypt*, Munich. (Courtesy of Franz Hanfstaengl)

J'aperçus comme une forêt de mâts de vaisseaux. La mer était couverte de voiles que les vents enflaient; l'onde était écumante sous les coups des rames. . . J'entendais de toutes parts des cris confus, j'apercevais sur le rivage une partie des Egyptiens . . . qui semblaient aller au-devant de cette flotte qu'on voyait arriver.

(*Télémaque*, ii)

Claude Lorrain's feeling for the atmospheric light of day and night, for sun and moon, has still other literary parallels. Racine has his psychological sunset in Phèdre's words: ' Soleil, je te salue, pour la dernière fois.' Corneille has his starlight impression in the Cid's words: ' Cette obscure clarté qui tombe des étoiles.'

Now one can ask, what is the particular interest of the stage setting in the classical pictures and dramas? When Claude Lorrain, in the manner of Poussin, puts stories of Holy Writ for the sake of animation into a landscape, such as in *The Marriage of Isaac and Rebecca*,[20] the temptation is to ask with Leonardo da Vinci in Fénelon's fifty-third *Dialogue des morts*: ' Est-ce une histoire? . . . C'est plutôt un caprice.' And Claude Lorrain will give the same answer that is given there to Leonardo by Poussin: ' C'est un caprice. Ce genre d'ouvrage nous sied fort bien pourvu que le caprice soit réglé et qu'il ne s'écarte en rien de la vraie nature.' Nature as painted by Claude Lorrain corresponds exactly to Fénelon's ideal:

De là, on découvrait la mer . . . claire et unie comme une glace. . .
On apercevait de loin des collines et des montagnes qui se perdaient dans les nues et dont la figure bizarre formait un horizon à souhait, pour le plaisir des yeux.
Le figuier, l'olivier, le grenadier et tous les autres arbres couronnaient la campagne et en faisaient un grand jardin.

(*Télémaque*, i)

The landscapes of Claude Lorrain reveal a particular taste for miniature men and women in a more grandiose than idyllic setting, where water and trees are preponderant. These features are visible in the preceding picture as well as in another called *The Flight into Egypt* [21] (see Fig. 25), a *bergerie* with the Holy Family in the background, a pretext and not a theme, as in the pictures of the Middle Ages.

The miniature human creatures in the grandiose landscape suggest something of the feelings of Pascal:

Que l'homme contemple donc la nature entière dans sa haute et pleine majesté; qu'il éloigne sa vue des objets bas qui l'environnent . . . qu'il se regarde comme égaré . . . et qu'il apprenne à estimer la terre . . . et soi-même. . . Qu'est-ce qu'un homme dans l'infini? . . . qu'est-ce que l'homme dans la nature? Un néant à l'égard de l'infini, un tout à l'égard du néant . . .[22]

As to the preference for trees and water, a letter of Guez de Balzac to M. de la Motte-Aigron is revealing:

> C'est un pays à souhaiter et à peindre, que j'ai choisi pour vaquer à mes plus chères occupations et passer les plus douces heures de ma vie. L'eau et les arbres ne le laissent jamais manquer de frais et de vert. . . . Cette belle eau aime tellement la belle terre qu'elle se divise en mille branches, et fait une infinité d'îles et de détours, afin de s'y amuser davantage; et quand elle se déborde, ce n'est que pour rendre l'année plus riche.[23]

It is not surprising, then, that Claude Lorrain selects such an unfamiliar scene from the Acts of the Apostles as *Philip Baptizing the Eunuch* [24]. Here is a pretext for water and a type of landscape where ' crystalline brooks . . . murmur between their verdant banks . . . spreading into lovely pools.' [25] Such a Golden Age landscape, where everything is beautiful and idealized, also appeals to a dramatist like Jean Mairet in *La Sylvie*, v. 1, where, as in the picture, the fertile fields and hills vie in beauty:

> Ces guérets semblent dire à ces côteaux voisins:
> Vous voyez nos épis, montrez-nous vos raisins.

With all these discussions, the problem of the meaning of nature for the seventeenth century is still far from being solved. This becomes particularly evident in the case of La Fontaine. Scholars still discuss the meaning of La Fontaine's fables. In comparing them to the awkwardly handled treatment of animals by his predecessors, they declare La Fontaine's more highly developed art to result from his more highly developed sentiment of nature, which, since Taine, has been explained as an outcome of La Fontaine's living in the open air and in the woods in his function as *maître des eaux et des forêts*. Considering, however, the wording of certain fables, La Fontaine's interest seems to be of a quite different kind. Why does he compare the fox in wolf's skin to Patroclus carrying the arms of Achilles?

> Le renard, ayant pris la peau [du loup] court
> Et répand la terreur dans les lieux d'alentour.
> Tel vêtu des armes d'Achille,
> Patrocle mit l'alarme au camp et dans la ville.
> (*Fables*, XII, 9)

In describing two goats, *nos aventurières*, stubbornly blocking each other's way on a small footbridge, why does he compare them to two proud contemporary monarchs vying for *préséance?*

> Je m'imagine voir, avec Louis le Grand,
> Philippe Quatre qui s'avance
> Dans l'île de la Conférence.
> Ainsi s'avançaient pas à pas
> Nez à nez nos aventurières?
> (IV, 4)

Is it just fun? Is it social satire? Neither. Depicting animal behavior is a means, a caricatural means, of picturing a deeper human psychology. One is still on very general ground in contending that this attitude is most in conformity with the psychology of the century — that of La Rochefoucauld, Mme de Sévigné, and La Bruyère. It is much safer to check with the painter Charles Le Brun's (1619–90) sketchbook of animal heads.[26] Here, beyond any doubt, the expressions of sheep, cats, camels, oxen, and cows are studied as parallels of sheeplike, catlike, camel-like, oxlike, and cowlike human faces in order to discover traits in man which might correspond to fundamental attitudes of the respective animals. Le Brun really solves the problem of the meaning of La Fontaine's fables. Again nature has served their interests in problems of human behavior.

For those who, adhering to the 'old' interpretation of La Fontaine, find the theory above still debatable, it may be fitting to quote Charles Du Bos. Although he did not have the foregoing parallels at hand he wrote: 'As far as La Fontaine is concerned . . . it is less exact to say that his animals are men than it would be correct to state that his men are animals, not, of course, in the sense of beasts and of the brutality of instinct, but rather in a sense of mere visual picturesqueness of contours and silhouettes.'[27]

### III. Predominant Interest in Human Personality: the Psychological Portrait

When one considers the paramount psychological interest in man which produced this flood of memoirs, letters, maxims, portraits, and *caractères* and which reduced the action of a tragedy to its psychological crisis and the *dramatis personae* to some few protagonists, only then can one understand such a picture as Charles Le Brun's *Alexander Entering Babylon*.[28] Instead of the expected pageant with innumerable horses, soldiers, and prisoners, Alexander appears practically alone on his elephant-drawn battle wagon. His is the attitude of the victor in splendid isolation. Hence the triumph of Alexander is not portrayed in the concept of a Shakespeare or a Rubens but in the concept of Racine: there is at issue not the victory but the victor, not the interest of the eye but the interest of the soul.

A classical demonstration of soldiership and heroism is effected in another contemporary form by Hyacinthe Rigaud (1659–1743) with his *Augustus III, Prince of Saxony*,[29] who, challenging the world with his youthful, almost feminine face and curly wig, his elegant, triumphant attitude and polished armor, is posing as a courtier and a warrior. La Bruyère, in the chapter 'Du mérite personnel' in his *Caractères*, speaking about the military hero in general, gives the best interpretation of this picture:

> Dans la guerre, la distinction entre le héros et le grand homme est délicate; toutes les vertus militaires font l'un et l'autre. Il semble néanmoins que le premier soit jeune, entreprenant, d'une haute valeur, ferme dans les périls, intrépide . . .[30]

Alexander and Augustus III are heroes of the same cut as the young Cid and the young Britannicus.

Painters and writers reveal their interest in military grandeur as such in the portraits of Louis XIV's great generals. The sober Philippe de Champaigne (1602–74), painting the *Viscount de Turenne* [31] (see Fig. 26), portrays his energy, vigor, impassibility, honesty, incorruptibility, nay, the fabulous indestructibility he enjoyed in the minds of his admirers. Thus this picture explains Mme de Sévigné's outcry at the news of his death: 'Le Roi en a été affligé comme on doit l'être de la perte du plus grand capitaine et du plus honnête homme du monde.' [32] When Fléchier gave his *oraison funèbre*, he praised Turenne as a pillar of force, cut off in the prime of life. He was killed on a reconnoitering mission by a stray bullet, and now the security of France, which had been entrusted to him, was endangered: 'Je me trouble, Messieurs, Turenne meurt, tout se confond; la fortune chancelle, la victoire se lasse, la paix s'éloigne.'

26. Champaigne, *Viscount de Turenne*, Munich. (Courtesy of Franz Hanfstaengl).

27. Coysevox, *The Grand Condé*, Louvre. (Archives Photographiques)

The sculptured bust of *The Grand Condé* [33] (see Fig. 27) was done by the artist Antoine Coysevox (1640–1720). Condé's features reveal a particularly critical intelligence, a remarkable perspicacity, and that *esprit de finesse* which adapted the tactics and strategy of Gustavus Adolphus to the battle of Rocroi, where Condé defeated the Spaniards. When Bossuet stood in the pulpit in front of Condé's bier, he sculptured his portrait in words as Coysevox had done in stone.

> Montrons dans un prince admiré de tout l'univers . . . ce qui fait les héros, ce qui porte la gloire du monde jusqu'au comble, valeur, magnanimité, bonté naturelle, voilà pour le cœur; vivacité, pénétration, grandeur et sublimité du génie, voilà pour l'esprit.[34]

La Bruyère said of him: ' Un homme incapable de céder à l'ennemi . . . qui était rempli de gloire et de modestie . . . sincère pour Dieu et pour hommes, un homme vrai, simple, magnanime.'

The grandeur of the statesman and diplomat is caught in a marvelous manner by Philippe de Champaigne in his painting of *Cardinal Richelieu* [35] (see Fig. 28). He has given him, it is true, a certain theatrical gesture of sublimity. The Cardinal seems to walk through the royal palace conversing with and looking toward an invisible partner. His attentive listening is underscored by the intelligent and elegant gesture of his hand, which precedes the answer. His nimble haughtiness seems to ask Clytemnestre's question in Racine's *Iphigénie*:

> Dans quel palais superbe et plein de ma grandeur
> Puis-je jamais paraître avec plus de splendeur?
>
> (III, 1, 807–8)

The nobility of *Bossuet, Bishop of Meaux* (see Fig. 29), by Hyacinthe Rigaud (1659–1743), is of another kind. This is a pastoral and inherent splendor. Here is the incomparable Eagle of Meaux in his full episcopal dignity — bishop, apologist, preacher, scholarly authority — shown with his books and manuscripts, and the thinker with the clear eyes and the pure forehead, the spiritual hero who recalls Sarazin's lines:

> Car il est des héros d'une douce manière,
> Il en est de justice, il en est de bréviaire.

Hyacinthe Rigaud, who worked out the pontifical dignity of Bossuet, also concretized the royal éclat of *Louis XIV* (see Fig. 30). He made him truly *le Roi Soleil* in the Roman, heroic conception of his kingship. The pompous pride of this new Augustus spreads from the king's features over

28. Champaigne, *Cardinal Richelieu*, Louvre. (Photo Giraudon)

29. Rigaud, *Bossuet, Bishop of Meaux*, Louvre. (Archives Photographiques)

the magnificent folds of the ermine-lined mantle of velvet cloth, whose fundamental color is a deep blue, trimmed with the lilies of France in orange. The throne, in the blue also, is protected by a ruddy canopy with yellow trimmings. The king with his rich, dark locks, declaring with his sovereign glance, ' L'Etat c'est moi,' is leisurely leaning on his scepter, the crown resting beside it; he is the half-god, and so understood by Benserade (1613–91)in his sonnet:

> Quelle taille, quel port a ce fier conquérant!
> Sa personne éblouit quiconque l'examine,
> Et quoique par son port il soit déjà si grand,
> Quelque chose de plus éclate dans sa mine.

Saint-Simon, who did not like the king, notes the same fact in his *Mémoires* — namely, that the king expanded his personal pride and power into his policy: ' L'orgueil du Roi voulut étonner l'Europe par la montre de sa puissance . . . et l'étonna en effet.' [36]

The morganatic queen of Louis XIV, *Madame de Maintenon* (see Fig. 31), was painted by Pierre Mignard (1610–1695) as the pseudo-queen with her ermine mantle bashfully displayed, almost nunlike with her hair half veiled, the highest schoolmistress of the country, chaperoning Saint

Cyr. Mignard portrays her with intelligent eyes and plump face and tender hands, theatrically expressing modesty and learning. She has no real grandeur, an explanation of which may be found in La Bruyère's *Caractères*, 'Des Femmes':

> Il y a dans quelques femmes une grandeur artificielle attachée au mouvement des yeux, à un air de tête, aux façons de marcher, et qui ne va pas plus loin; un esprit éblouissant qui impose, et que l'on n'estime que parce qu'il n'est pas approfondi.
>
> (III, 2)

Bossuet's portrait of the coquettish Yezabel recalls Mme. de Maintenon's portrait also:

> Voyez-moi cette femme dans sa superbe beauté, dans son ostentation, dans sa parure! Elle veut vaincre, elle veut estre adorée . . . elle veut tout soumettre à son empire.[37]

Henri Bremond even suspects the pious Madame de Maintenon of doubtful intrigues against Mme Guyon and Fénelon in the affair of Quietism.[38] If this is true, the inner and psychological portrait of this widow of the realistic writer Scarron, this former educator of the illegitimate children of Louis XIV, who finally forced the king to marry her, would come close to

30. Rigaud, *Louis XIV*, Louvre. (Foto Marburg)

31. Mignard, *Madame de Maintenon*, Versailles. (Archives Photographiques)

the prototype of all literary portraits of the seventeenth century. It is the one Célimène draws of Arsinoé in the *Misanthrope* of Molière. The poisonous exaggerations involved in such portraits cannot be overlooked:

> Dans l'âme elle est du monde, et ses soins tentent tout
> Pour accrocher quelqu'un sans en venir à bout.
> Elle ne saurait voir qu'avec un œil d'envie
> Les amants déclarés dont une autre est suivie;
> Et son triste mérite, abandonné de tous,
> Contre le siècle aveugle est toujours en courroux.
> Elle tâche à couvrir d'un faux voile de prude
> Ce que chez elle on voit d'affreuse solitude . . .
>
> (III, 855–62)

This portrait is later continued in a direct speech to Arsinoé by Célimène:

> Cette affectation d'un grave extérieur,
> Vos discours éternels de sagesse et d'honneur,
> Vos mines et vos cris aux ombres d'indécence
> Que d'un mot ambigu peut avoir l'innocence,
> Cette hauteur d'estime où vous êtes de vous,
> Et ces yeux de pitié que vous jetez sur tous,
> Vos fréquentes leçons et vos aigres censures

Sur des choses qui sont innocentes et pures,
Tout cela, si je puis vous parler franchement,
Madame, fut blâmé d'un commun sentiment.
A quoi bon, disaient-ils, cette mine modeste,
Et ce sage dehors que dément tout le reste?
Elle est à bien prier exacte au dernier point;
Mais elle bat ses gens, et ne les paye point.
Dans tous les lieux dévots elle étale un grand zèle;
Mais elle met du blanc, et veut paraître belle.

(III, 927–42)

The elegant painter Nicolas de Largillière (1656–1746), on the other hand, showed in all the exterior splendor of her lace-trimmed silk dress the interior simplicity of *Madame de Thorigny*,[39] expressed in the noble face and decent bearing in spite of the artificial pose, concession to the taste of the time. La Bruyère again elaborates on the meaning of such traits:

> Il y a dans quelques autres [femmes] une grandeur simple, naturelle, indépendante du geste et de la démarche, qui a sa source dans le cœur et qui est comme une suite de leur haute naissance; un mérite paisible, mais solide accompagné de mille vertus qu'elles ne peuvent couvrir de toute leur modestie, qui échappent et qui se montrent à ceux qui ont des yeux.
>
> (Op. cit. III, 2)

## IV. The Harmonious Fusion of Reason and Sentiment, *Géométrie* and *Finesse*

Passing from the problem of subject matter to that of form, we must first consider that René Descartes (1596–1650), the great philosopher of

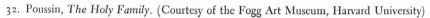

32. Poussin, *The Holy Family*. (Courtesy of the Fogg Art Museum, Harvard University)

the seventeenth century, tries to reduce everything to geometrical proportions and calculation, but Pascal's answer is that in certain domains, such as art, music, religion, and life itself, nothing can be understood without quite another spirit, not that of the brain, but that of the heart: *l'esprit de finesse*. In modern phraseology, this would mean that the classical and rational abstraction of Descartes is vitalized by the existential baroque of Pascal, who found fault with Montaigne for confusing mysteries with problems.

These considerations should be kept in mind when looking at a picture like *The Holy Family* (see Fig. 32) by Poussin. In front of a flat, antique, marble pilaster there is a harmonious Raphael-like grouping, with Mary and Joseph balanced by a group of angels at the left and the Divine Child, St. John, and St. Elisabeth at the right. But this geometry is agreeably disturbed by the idyllic landscape in the background and the dynamic action of the angels helping to bathe the Child. The angels also perform that formal function of filling empty spaces, which in contemporary drama is called ' *liaison des scènes*.' How the classical spirit of geometry and the baroque spirit of finesse are particularly joined in this picture is pointed out by David M. Robb and J. J. Garrison:

> To a casual observer the painting looks not unlike a Raphael . . . but . . . the group, while organized internally in a left-to-right orientation (Classic order) has also its regular space-in-depth movement (Baroque order). The landscape has the measured cadence of the figures with a transparent film of air softening and enveloping its cubes and planes.[40]

Fénelon was certainly conscious of this classicism modified by French baroque when, in one of his *Dialogues des morts*, he makes Poussin himself the mouthpiece of this ideal and has him tell the pure, radically classic Parhasius, famous Greek painter, the following:

> J'ai évité la confusion et la symétrie. J'ai fait beaucoup de bâtiments irréguliers, mais ils ne laissent pas de faire un assemblage gracieux, où chaque chose a sa place la plus naturelle. Tout se démêle et se distingue sans peine; tout s'unit et fait corps; ainsi il y a une confusion apparente, et un ordre véritable quand on l'observe de près.[41]

Heinrich Wölfflin could have used these words to oppose his definition of baroque, as ' parts subdued to a unity,' against the Renaissance ideal of ' isolated parts not subdued to a unity.' The *beau désordre* in the seventeenth-century French pictures, as opposed to those of the other European countries, is so moderate, however, that:

> Tous les historiens du baroque reconnaissent, non pas qu'il s'est arrêté aux frontières de la France, mais que ces barrières ont ralenti son élan . . . pour former . . . cet amalgame classico-baroque, qui est le style de la vie française sous Louis XIV.[42]

Molière declares as his own the same classic-baroque ideal of a *beau désordre:*

> La beauté des contours observés avec soin,
> Point durement traités, amples, tirés de loin,
> Inégaux, ondoyants, et tenant de la flamme,
> Afin de conserver plus d'action et d'âme.[43]

This is the key to Versailles and all that concerns it.

The Chapel of Versailles,[44] planned by J. H. Mansart (1646–1708), is in its architecture as cool as a dignified, belated, Renaissance church can be, just as Bossuet's *Oraisons funèbres* appear at first sight masterworks of classic rhetoric, the many metaphorical spots not being evident. Yet in the chapel, sweetness and tenderness break into the marble austerity with the colorful, warm, open heaven of its cupola, with the angels and the saints. It is the same with the metaphors of Bossuet. It is, beyond any doubt, the pattern according to which Fénelon interprets the old Greek temple, ir- remissibly bound as he is to the baroque understanding of ancient classi- cism:

> Le temple est tout de marbre. C'est un parfait péristyle; les colonnes sont d'une grosseur et d'une hauteur qui rendent cet édifice très majestueux; mais au-dessus de l'architrave . . . on voit en bas-reliefs toutes les plus agréables aventures de la déesse.
>
> (*Télémaque*, IV)

In the Galerie des Glaces,[45] also designed by Mansart, there is again a severe geometrical arrangement of symmetrical pilasters, mirrors, doors, can- dlesticks, benches, and ornaments. Yet all this is set ablaze by bewitching reflections coming from the walls of mirrors and from the color carnival of the painting by Charles Le Brun on the vaulted ceiling. Lines by Molière may describe the elegance of this candlelit salon:

> Les distributions et d'ombre et de lumière
> Sur chacun des objets et sur la masse entière;
> Leur dégradation dans l'espace de l'air
> Par les tons différents de l'obscur et du clair!
> (Op. cit. 469)

In general the French artists reject the Italian baroque chiaroscuro as a mere technical means, although when they do use it, it certainly has a meaning that can be made clear by literature. The most striking case is the *clair-obscur* in the paintings of Georges de la Tour (1600–1652). His *St. Sebastian Mourned by Women* (see Fig. 33) is dramatized by the torch- light effects that underscore the mourned one and the mourning women. The figures are very sharply cut in classical mode despite the painterly presentation. Exactly this kind of spiritual *tenebroso* is found in the dramas of Racine, who delights in wrapping in torchlight and *clair-obscur*

33. De la Tour, *St. Sebastian Mourned by Women*, Staatliches Museum, Berlin.
(Foto Marburg)

the past remembrances of his heroes. Andromaque declares to her *confidente* that she will never be able to marry Pyrrhus after having seen him in the light of burning Troy, raging against the Greeks:

> Songe, songe, Céphise, à cette nuit cruelle
> Qui fut pour tout un peuple une nuit éternelle,
> Figure-toi, Pyrrhus, les yeux étincelants
> Entrant à la lueur de nos palais brûlants.
> (III, viii, 997–1000)

It is during the night, in the light of the torches, that Nero sees his victim Junie kidnapped by his soldiers and falls in love with her:

> Cette nuit, je l'ai vue arriver en ces lieux,
> Triste, levant au ciel ses yeux mouillés de larmes,
> Qui brillaient au travers des flambeaux et des armes.
> (*Britannicus*, II, ii, 386–8)

Bérénice cannot separate the grandeur of Titus from the *clair-obscur* effects of a nocturnal parade:

> De cette nuit, Phénice, as-tu vu la splendeur?
> Tes yeux ne sont-ils pas tous pleins de sa grandeur?
> Ces flambeaux, ce bûcher, cette nuit enflammée,
> Ces aigles, ces faisceaux, ce peuple, cette armée . . .
> <div align="right">(<i>Bérénice</i> I, v, 301–4)</div>

Madame de Sévignè in her letter of Friday, 20 February 1671, to Mme de Grignan is also under the spell of the *clair-obscur* when describing the outbreak of a fire in her neighborhood during the night — a real, personally experienced, and tragic *notturno*:

> A trois heures après minuit j'entendis crier . . . au feu . . . Je me levai dans cette crainte, *sans lumière*, avec un tremblement qui m'empêchait quasi de me soutenir. . . Je vis la maison de Guitaut *toute en feu*; les *flammes* passaient pardessus la maison de Mme de Vauvineux. On voyait dans nos cours, et surtout chez M. de Guitaut une *clarté* qui faisait horreur. . .

There is an architectural parallel to the *clair-obscur* that invades classical pictures and scenes in the intentional disturbing of the well-ordered Renaissance fronts to bring some shades into their bright clarity. These baroque implications of French classicism may be understood first from an outside view of Versailles from the east [46] — that is, from the town. The *beau désordre* seems due particularly to the presence of the high chapel on the right side, with nothing corresponding to it on the left.

What is still more striking is the immense space in front of the castle, and the space behind the castle seems almost limitless, as may be seen from the picture of the *Palace of Versailles from the Gardens* (see Fig. 34). Here is the baroque feeling of immensity in space and time, unknown to the ancients but well known to French classical tragedy, where, when the curtain drops after a catastrophe, there supposedly follows a long, psychological agony of the hero, which takes place in the imagination of the

34. Palace of Versailles from the Gardens. (Archives Photographiques)

audience. What monster will Nero become after his first murder, the as-sassination of Britannicus? What a world of longing and nostalgia Bérénice will have to experience after having been forsaken by Titus! This psycho-logical prolongation, these spiritual spaces, are the Versailles gardens of the soul.

The Abbé Longhaye has written an acute comment on Pascal's frag-ment: ' Le silence éternel de ces espaces infinis m'effraie . . . ' He under-lines Pascal's psychology of the prolongated, limitless space as a source of awe. The thought is made vibrant by the rhythm and melody of the sen-tence. The abbé writes:

> Pascal makes a meditation on the empty space which expands beyond the world. Due to a combined effort of reason and imagination, he experiences the same . . . horror which we feel, when, at nightfall, at the turn of a way, on the top of a last hill, we discover suddenly an immense panorama, deserted, mute, feebly lighted . . . Of the three rhythmical groups to which Pascal's short sentences have been reduced, the first two groups represent rather well the object itself. The last one, however, is entirely psychological. Detached, dragging along as if out of breath, it seems to stress the inertia, the torpor, the action interrupted by a sudden impo-tence. Effect of melody without any doubt, but still more of rhythm.[47]

Pascal, no doubt, shared the interior rhythm and the feeling for space of the architect, Le Nôtre.

The baroque architectural arrangement of Versailles means, in Pascal's language, that the king's apartment is the *infiniment petit* center of an *infiniment grand château*, including the town of Versailles and Le Nôtre's extensive gardens. For all its implied classicism, the principle adopted here is the same as that which impelled the great abbots of the seventeenth cen-tury to arrange around their monastery-church, or rather around the taber-nacle of these churches, as the center, all the buildings, gardens, fields, and woods, just as they arranged above the tabernacle, beginning with stucco and ending in painting with virtuoso perspectives, the vaulted cupola with its infinite prospect into infinite heavens.

A particular example of this baroque concept is the Parisian abbey church of Val de Grâce (see Fig. 35), the cupola of which was painted by Mignard and praised, as quoted above, by Molière. This cupola crowned a tabernacle enhanced by four twisted columns in the style of St. Peter's. According to the original plan, the Eucharistic center of this church had a distant echo in crescent streets surrounding the sanctuary in elegant curves, as though they were distant worshippers of the *Panis angelicus*.

To understand the boundlessness of the baroque interior of Val de Grâce or any similar structure, one must envision the church during an *oraison funèbre*, with the supplementary decorations around the bier.[48] A descrip-tion of the funeral service of the Chancellor Séguier may illustrate the point. It is Mme de Sévigné who describes it to her daughter in a letter dated 6 May 1672:

I was yesterday at a service performed in honour of the Chancellor. . . Painting, sculpture, music, rhetoric, in a word, the four liberal arts were at the expense of it. Nothing could exceed the beauty of the decorations: they were finely imagined, and designed by Le Brun. The mausoleum reached to the top of the dome, adorned with a thousand lamps, and a variety of figures characteristic of him in whose honour it was erected. Beneath were four figures of Death, bearing the marks of his several dignities. . . One of them held his helmet, another his ducal coronet, another the ensigns of his order, another his Chancellor's mace. The four sister arts, painting, music, eloquence, and sculpture, were represented in deep distress, bewailing the loss of their protector. The first representation was supported by the four virtues, fortitude, temperance, justice, and religion. Above these, four angels, or genii, received the soul of the deceased. . . The mausoleum was adorned with a variety of little seraphs, who supported an illuminated shrine, which was fixed to the top of the cupola. Nothing so magnificent or so well imagined was ever seen; it is Le Brun's masterpiece. . . As for the music, it was fine beyond all description. Baptiste [Lulli] exerted himself to the utmost. . . I do not think the music in heaven could excel it.[49]

Such were the baroque settings invented with all possible *raffinement* for the illimitable rhetorical flights of the Eagle of Meaux.

35. Val de Grâce, Paris. (Foto Marburg)

The impression of boundlessness and infinity in church interiors is thus stressed by the high catafalques that scarcely fill a small portion of the vertical space; in the Park of Versailles the infinite is symbolized by endless perspectives of avenues, series of lanes, lawns, trees, and rows of statues, all forcing the eye to the central point far away. The visitor, overwhelmed by such an impression, is likely to realize Pascal's cosmic experience quoted above: ' Le silence éternel des espaces infinis m'effraie.'

This art of the infinite corresponds to the view of a type of man whom modern sociologists call, in Bergson's phrase, *homme ouvert*, because he is open to the infinite and to the divine; whereas the designation of his counterpart, the Renaissant and the modern man, is *homme clos*, because he is closed to the transcendental and restricted to the narrow boundaries of the human. Corneille, Pascal, Bossuet, and Racine are *hommes ouverts*.

It is possible, however, to overstress the geometrical classicism and take out the grandeur of the infinite. This is the worm of enlightenment in the French baroque, the *hommes clos* working underground, and their efforts are visible in the miniature work of La Rochefoucauld, Saint-Evrémond, Mme de Sévigné, Mme de La Fayette, La Fontaine, as well as in De Brosse's Luxembourg Palace.[50] The French roofs, chimneys, towers, and the elegant, slight fluctuation of the front are elements too small to change fundamentally the character of an Italian Renaissance *palazzo*. Here the symmetry is so complete that Pascal's words apply no less to the Luxembourg Palace than to the *Maximes* of La Rochefoucauld:

> Ceux qui font les antithèses en forçant les mots sont comme ceux qui font de fausses fenêtres pour la symétrie.
>
> (*Pensées*, ' Rhétorique ')

Here are the center and wings, with *fenêtres* and *fausses fenêtres*, of the word-*palazzo* of La Rochefoucauld:

Les vertus se perdent dans l'intérêt
comme
les fleuves se perdent dans la mer.
(M. 171)
Les vices entrent dans la composition des vertus
comme
les poisons entrent dans la composition des remèdes.
(182)
L'intérêt
qui aveugle les uns        fait la lumière des autres.
(40)
On peut être
plus fin qu'un autre        plus fin que tous les autres
mais non pas.
(394)

Furthermore, to change unnecessarily a *palazzo* into a *château* corresponds exactly to Molière's method of extending a slight subject matter, like that of *Tartuffe* or *Les Femmes savantes*, to the so-called *longue carrière de cinq actes*, the *château*-form of the tragedy; whereas the *palazzo*-form of a three- or even one-act play would have been the correct thing for a comedy, as proved by *Les Précieuses ridicules*.

Baroque finesse, on the other hand, characterizes again the works of sculpture, such as the *Milo of Croton* [51] by Pierre Puget (1622–94). This athletic man attacked by a lioness betrays, in expression and movement, all the terrors of extreme pain — a modern Laocoön. Movement and contortion are as complicated and entangled as Racinian or Pascalian psychology, but all this complication does not prevent the silhouette of the man and lion itself from being simple and clear, just as the actions of a passion-torn dramatic hero of the seventeenth century follow the most clear and icy logic. It is the way in which Corneille's young Horace kills his sister:

> C'est trop, ma patience à la raison fait place,
> Va dedans les enfers plaindre ton Curiace.
>
> (IV, V, 1319–20)

Puget's artistic ideal coincides with that of Fénelon, as is evident from a passage describing a Rhodesian with whom Télémaque will wrestle. This Rhodesian is a literary Milo:

> Il était encore dans toute la vigueur de la jeunesse; ses bras étaient nerveux et bien nourris; au moindre mouvement qu'il faisait on voyait tous ses muscles; il était également souple et fort.
>
> (*Télémaque*, v)

The common ideal is indeed baroque flexibility combined with classical thought.

## V. Jesuitism and Jansenism in the Arts

It has become a cliché to state that Corneille is the dramatist of will power and heroism, with his pattern of tragicomedies in which the martyr, the saint, and the hero overcome all difficulties, and that Racine is the dramatist of weakness and defeat, with his pattern of tragedies in which the will, seemingly unaided by grace, is bound to succumb before difficulties taking shape relentlessly, like fate. Corneille is indeed the representative of Jesuitic and Racine the representative of Jansenistic values in the seventeenth century. Art can elucidate on a larger scale what this means.

The picture by Poussin, *Awakening of a Dead Girl by St. Francis Xavier* (see Fig. 36), is typical of Jesuitic religious art (such as *Polyeuctes*) first created in Spain and Italy and simply imitated in France. Three features

36. Poussin, *Awakening of a Dead Girl by St. Francis Xavier*, Louvre. (Photo Alinari)

are characteristic: first, the praying saint-hero as the promoter of super-human aid; second, the visible aid of Heaven, shown in a majestic Christ, accompanied by angels, blessing His Church with a miracle by returning the soul to the dead girl; third, the gestures of gratitude and admiration of the baffled bystanders — that is, a projection of the story into the psychological effect, a principle of this art discovered by Emile Mâle. The picture preaches the triumph of that sanctity and devotion which Molière felt obliged to praise through the mouth of Cléante, though it be only in order to get permission to stage his *Tartuffe:*

> Et comme je ne vois nul genre de héros
> Qui soient plus à priser que les parfaits dévots,
> Aucune chose au monde est plus noble et plus belle
> Que la sainte ferveur d'un véritable zèle . . .
>
> (ɪ, vi)

The conception of Christ as being majestic is in keeping with the baroque conscience of the European artists and poets of the time. This Christ can best be described by Cornelian verses, which express the same intrusion of the heroic into the devotional:

Bien qu'il soit Dieu de paix, le foudre est en ses mains,
Et tout bon qu'il veut être, il sait venger l'injure
Et qu'on fait à sa gloire et qu'on fait à ses saints.[52]

Another French inheritance from general European post-Tridentine
Jesuit art is the painting of ecstasy and mystical rapture. In Poussin's *The
Death of St. Bruno* [53] the monks are overwhelmed at being present while
the soul of a saint is entering Paradise. One falls down in humble self-
effacement; another worships on his knees in rapture; a third speaks to his
companions out of the fullness of his heart. This ' Carthusian of a more
mature age,' says F. E. Toulongeau, ' holds a crucifix in his right hand.
This character has something greater and nobler than all the others. . .
He admires the death of St. Bruno even more than he deplores the loss.' [54]

St. Francis of Sales, throughout his mystical *Traité de l'amour de Dieu*,
and even Boileau in secular verse tell us St. Bruno's secret, discovered and
followed by his companion at the saint's bier — saintly wisdom:

Qu'est-ce que la sagesse? Une égalité d'âme
Que rien ne peut troubler, qu'aucun désir n'enflamme.
(Boileau, *Satire*, VIII)

37. Champaigne, *La Madeleine pénitente*, Louvre. (Photo Giraudon)

The balanced taste of France has, except in the case of Mme Guyon, avoided that spurious mysticism called quietism, which, lacking the ascetic training, deteriorates into a spiritual sensuality. The non-French art of the time is full of such quietist Magdalens as Franceschini's *Magdalena*.[55] She swoons, believing she has had a vision after her self-scourging, but is prevented by her companions from falling to the floor in her ecstasy. This concept of a spurious mysticism is not entirely absent from French painting. There are traces in the older Simon Vouet (*La Madeleine repentante*, Musée de Besançon), as well as in French poetry. Even Bossuet, the notorious adversary of conscious quietism, has composed verse that could actually be placed under Franceschini's *Magdalena*:


En regardant au ciel, mes yeux fondus en pleurs
De langueurs accablés vous disent: Je me meurs.
                    (*Les trois amantes*)


The genuinely French Magdalen of a true spirit of penance, dignity, and restraint will prove, however, to be a Jansenistic Magdalen: *La Madeleine pénitente*[56] (see Fig. 37) by Philippe de Champaigne. She is the converted sinner, dignified by her conversion, just as Mlle Eve de la Vallière, famous mistress of Louis XIV, became, as Sœur Louise de la Miséricorde, an exemplary Carmelite nun, as testified by Bossuet's sermon at her profession. That the sin was atoned for by the most austere penance is evident in her noble face and in a humility that invites the Lord to take her as a holocaust, although the sadness for having sinned will never leave her. That is exactly the spirit of Port Royal and of *La Fréquente Communion*, by Antoine Arnauld, which asks an almost impossible form of penitential preparation for approaching the Table of the Lord, so the result is the sadness of having to abstain from the sacrament for lack of worthiness.

Jansenism also meant stressing the subjects of the Old Testament. Non-Jansenistic artists treated these themes also, but with the added gracefulness of Greek art, finding particular human elements in both cultures. Nicolas Poussin's *Moses Saved from the Waters*[57] (see Fig. 38) is done in the Italian style. Poussin painted a group of graceful young women surrounding their princess and, in the background, the Nile under the symbol of the River God; but the center of the foreground is the little foundling Moses, who was destined to give mankind the law of the Lord.

The classical-baroque character of Poussin's picture results from the combination of elements of beauty and of tenderness as well as of exaggeration and pompousness, of which latter there is nothing in the source (Exodus ii. 5–10). This combination is also found in Saint-Amant's epic poem *Moyse sauvé*, which expresses essentially the same sentiment but by the use of different details:

Si tost que la princesse eut veu l'heure arrivée
Que pour jouir des champs elle avoit réservée . . .
Malgré ses tristes soins, elle ne laissoit pas
De ravir tous les cœurs avec ses doux appas.
Cent visages divins brilloyent à l'entour d'elle
Cent vierges aux beaux yeux, qui suivaient ce modelle
De sagesse, d'honneur, de grâce et de vertu . . .
Le long et droit canal que ce beau pré renferme
S'ornoit de deux beaux ponts qui de la terre ferme
Aboutissoyent à l'isle, et l'art y faisoit voir
Des plus rares ouvriers l'industrieux sçavoir.
Quand il [Moyse] voguait ainsi sur la coulante plaine
Tous les vents suspendus retenoyent leur haleine . . .
Dès que l'illustre nymphe [the princess] eut contemplé ses charmes,
Qu'elle entendit sa voix, qu'elle aperceut ses larmes . . .
Une vive, une triste et pronte esmotion
Faite d'estonnement et de compassion,
Tira de ses beaux yeux deux torrents pitoyables . . .
' Je veux que cet enfant trouve une mère en moi,
Qu'il se voye eslever en digne fils de roi.' [58]

A close psychological and esthetic parallel is Racine's *Esther*, where another Biblical scene is beautified by the presence of a company of young girls:

> Ciel, quel nombreux essaim d'innocentes beautés
> S'offre à mes yeux en foule et sort de tous côtés.
>
> (I, ii, 122–3)

Also the theme of the story of Esther and her people's salvation is essentially the same as that in Poussin's picture — the preservation of faith in the true God:

> Ce Dieu, maître absolu de la terre et des cieux . . .
> L'Eternel est son nom. Le monde est son ouvrage,
> Il entend le soupir de l'humble qu'on outrage,
> Juge tous les mortels avec d'égales lois
> Et du haut de son trône interroge les rois.
>
> (III, iv, 1050–55)

Under the influence of austerity, which characterizes, in addition to the Jansenists, other spiritual groups such as the *Oratoire* and the Sulpicians, France changed the religious-art pattern of Europe, for example, by giving a new accent to the Crucifixion. In *Christ on the Cross with Angels* (see Fig. 39) by Charles Le Brun (1619–90), no human being, no Virgin, no Saint John tries to console or to be consoled by Christ dying on a historical, Biblical, Roman cross. There are only angels to adore the Divine Sacrifice according to the famous seventeenth-century hymn, *Ecce Christus intrat sacerdos et hostia;* Christ is humanly alone. It is Pascal who gives the key to this austere picture:

38. Attributed to Poussin, *Moses Saved from the Waters*. (Courtesy of the Museum of Fine Arts, Boston)

Jésus souffre dans sa passion les tourments que lui font les hommes; mais dans l'agonie il souffre les tourments qu'il se donne à lui-même: *turbare semetipsum*. C'est un supplice d'une main non humaine, mais toute-puissante, car il faut être tout-puissant pour le soutenir.

Jésus est seul dans la terre, non seulement qui ressente et partage sa peine, mais qui la sache: le ciel et lui sont seuls dans cette connaissance.[59]

It is the same severe and dignified spirit that translates mysterious passages of the New Testament into a new language. Pierre Mignard's dialogue between *Christ and the Woman of Samaria* [60] shows the moment that Christ (John iv. 10) tells the Samaritan woman: ' If thou knewest the gift of God, and who he is that saith to thee, Give me to drink; thou perhaps wouldest have asked of him, and he would have given thee living water.' But the sinner in deep thought before the Lord seems to hear the more penitential message from Pascal's *Mystère de Jésus* and to have a still more serious dialogue with Him — the timeless sinner's colloquy with the timeless Redeemer:

— Si tu connaissais tes péchés, tu perdrais cœur.

— Je le perdrai donc, Seigneur, car je crois leur malice à votre assurance.

— Non, car moi par qui tu l'apprends, t'en peux guérir et ce que je te le dis, c'est un signe que je te veux guérir. A mesure que tu les expieras, tu les connaîtras, et il te sera dit: ' Vois les péchés qui te sont remis! ' Fais donc pénitence pour tes péchés cachés et pour la malice occulte de ceux que tu connais.

— Seigneur, je vous donne tout.

(Op. cit. p. 73)

Considering that the other nations were stressing the modern saints, it may seem strange that France dedicated a new church to St. Paul with pictures such as *St. Paul Preaching at Ephesus*,[61] by Le Sueur (1617–55). The *Pensées* of Pascal again explain clearly the importance of the subject for the French seventeenth century:

> Il était prédit que le Messie convertirait les nations. Comment cette prophétie se fût-elle accomplie sans la conversion des nations? Et comment les nations se fussent-elles converties au Messie, ne voyant pas ce dernier effet des prophéties qui le prouvent? Avant donc qu'il ait été mort, ressuscité, et converti les nations, tout n'était pas accompli.
>
> (Op. cit. p. 80)

A picture that is Jansenistic in a narrower and more rational sense of the word is one painted for Port Royal and in the spirit of Port Royal by Philippe de Champaigne: *Ex voto: Mother Agnès Arnauld and Sister Catherine of St. Suzanne* (see Fig. 40). The picture portrays a miracle, but the conception is diametrically opposed to that of *Awakening of a Dead Girl* by Poussin. The painter's daughter, Sister Catherine, was stricken with paralysis. Mother Agnès Arnauld only reluctantly consented to a novena for her. Finally, however, she prays so fervently with the nun that at a certain moment she declares she has felt the favorable answer of

39. Le Brun, *Christ on the Cross with Angels*, Louvre. (Archives Photographiques)

40. Champaigne, *Ex voto: Mother Agnès Arnauld and Sister Catherine of St. Suzanne,*
Louvre. (Archives Photographiques)

Heaven. Exactly this moment is represented in the picture. The miracle to
be worked must be guessed from the confidence expressed in the Superior's
face and from a little ray of light illuminating the picture. Pascal's niece
once had been touched with the same relic of the Holy Thorn that Sister
Catherine holds on her lap and, like her, had been healed.

Pascal, with the same restraint as Philippe de Champaigne, yet more
eager to discover the blessings received by the Jansenists, writes:

> Voici une relique sacrée. Voici une épine de la couronne du Sauveur du
> monde . . . qui fait des miracles par la propre puissance de ce sang
> répandu pour nous. Voici que Dieu choisit lui-même cette maison pour y
> faire éclater sa puissance.
>
> (Op. cit. p. 81)

### VI. Inwardness of Everyday Life

The ideals of a culture formerly were reflected in every sector of life,
consequently also in everyday life as conceived by realistic artists such as
the Frères Le Nain and authors such as Scarron, Sorel, Furetière, La Fontaine, and La Bruyère. The particular French feature of seventeenth-century realism appears to be inwardness.[62] A picture such as *Peasant Family*
( see Fig. 41) by Louis Le Nain is not like the so-called genre pictures the
contemporary Dutch and Spaniards were painting; rather it shows the
peasants in a portrait-like isolation. It is not a scene of fighting, drinking,
or gambling; it is a meditation on childhood, youth, and mature age as
represented by the peasants. Louis Le Nain remains classical in that he
generalizes individual persons and happenings, just as Bossuet wanted to
show in the death of Henriette d'Angleterre the tragedy of death itself:

'Je veux dans un seul malheur déplorer toutes les calamités du genre hu-
main et dans une seule mort faire voir la mort et le néant de toutes les gran-
deurs humaines.' One who knows only Flemish pictures would be inclined
to ask at once: What actually are these peasants doing? Le Nain would
give the Cartesian answer: 'Ils pensent, donc ils sont.' This capacity for
reflective thinking is underscored to such an extent in these intelligent
faces that they seem to convey Pascal's message:

> L'homme est visiblement fait pour penser; c'est toute sa dignité et tout
> son mérite . . . Toute la dignité de l'homme consiste en la pensée . . .
> C'est de là qu'il faut nous relever et non de l'espace et de la durée que
> nous ne saurions remplir.
>
> (Op. cit. p. 42, 43)

The correctness of this interpretation is attested to by Fierens, the leading
Le Nain scholar: 'The peasants of Louis Le Nain, sparing in gestures and
in words . . . conscious of the dignity of their condition, appear in groups
not to act but to affirm that they are men and have a right to our respect.'[63]

The philosophical *Repas de paysans*[64] of Louis Le Nain proves again
that these peasants do not sit down at table, as do the Flemish ones, to
struggle for the choice pieces of meat. As to this particular picture, Werner
Weisbach thinks the well-to-do peasant in the middle has invited the poor
barefoot beggar-peasant at the right and is trying to explain the philosophy
of the wealthy to the poor, unconvincingly, as the beggar's physiognomy
betrays. The bashful peasant to the left, a hired farmhand, as it seems,
drowns the problem in a glass of good French red wine. This is indeed a
realistic philosophy lesson, and one that La Rochefoucauld did not fail
to express in an abstract way:

41. Louis Le Nain, *Peasant Family*, Louvre. (Foto Marburg)

Il est plus aisé d'être sage pour les autres que de l'être pour soi-même
. . . La philosophie triomphe aisément des maux passés et des maux à
venir; mais les maux présents triomphent d'elle.

(Maximes, 132)

The *roman bourgeois* called *Travelers at an Inn* [65] by Mathieu Le Nain,
is merely anecdotic and cannot vie with that of his brother. Rather it recalls the beginning of the third chapter of the first book of *Le Roman
comique* of Paul Scarron:

> Dans toutes les villes subalternes du royaume, il y a d'ordinaire un tripot
> où s'assemblent tous les jours les fainéants de la ville, les uns pour jouer,
> les autres pour regarder ceux qui jouent; c'est là que l'on rime richement
> en Dieu, que l'on épargne fort le prochain.

These generalities of the literary text appear in the picture, of course
without the literary irony but much more detailed, as described in the
Catalogue of the Burlington Fine Arts Club:

> A group of nine figures, five men seated at table, two with scarlet cloaks;
> on the left, two youths standing; on the right, a boy and a girl, the latter
> blowing a soap bubble. Two of the men at table are playing cards; a third
> is pouring wine from a straw-covered bottle into a glass; the other two are
> apparently amusing themselves by playing some game which involves clos-
> ing the eye. One holds a hurdy-gurdy under his left arm, the other a roll
> of paper in his right hand.[66]

The literary parallel to the symbolical *La Halte du Cavalier* [67] (see Fig.
42) of Louis Le Nain is made by the art historian Paul Fierens: This
peasant girl, 'upright like a caryatide supporting the vault of Heaven — ro-
bust with a frank, silly smile — has put on her head a great copper vessel.'
She is 'bare footed . . . fat-faced . . . has sculptural forms down to the
vertical folds of her skirt.' She is almost La Fontaine's Perrette:

> Perrette, sur sa tête ayant un pot au lait,
> Bien posé sur un coussinet,
> Prétendait arriver sans encombre à la ville.
> Légère et court vêtue, elle allait à grands pas . . .
> (Fables vii, 8)

These girls of La Fontaine and Le Nain do not consider, in their notorious
silliness, what dangers they risk of spilling the milk and breaking the vessel
or of falling into the trap of a flattering cavalier resting beside his horse —
a perilous eclogue in the making, Fierens adds, the accompaniment being
played on a rustic flute by one of the lads, unaware of his role. La Fontaine's symbolic realism derives a symbolic light from Le Nain. Also in the
*Repas* the farmhand in front of the free beggar is comparable to the dog
with the collar in front of the free wolf in La Fontaine's fable. The implications of inwardness and psychology in Louis Le Nain and in La Fon-

taine are considerable. Do they not preach the value of personal dignity and individual liberty?

> . . . dit le loup: vous ne courez donc pas
> Où vous voulez? — Pas toujours; mais qu'importe?
> — Il importe si bien que *de tous vos repas*
> *Je ne veux en aucune sorte,*
> Et ne voudrais pas même à ce prix d'un trésor.
> Cela dit, maître loup s'enfuit, et court encor.
> (*Fables*, 1, 5)

The subject matter of Le Nain's *The Mendicants* [68] is not attractive pictorially but it is from a 'moral' point of view. To an eye sensitive to this inwardness it shows wealth and poverty in seventeenth-century harmony, where there is not as yet a social question and one accepts, as Bossuet phrases it, ' toutes les extrémités des choses humaines: la félicité sans bornes aussi bien que les misères.' [69] It also illustrates La Bruyère's views: ' Il y a du plaisir à rencontrer les yeux de celui à qui l'on vient de donner,' and ' La libéralité consiste moins à donner beaucoup qu'à donner à propos.' [70] At the same time, this stressed poverty contains the accusation found in La Bruyère's famous description of the peasants as animals hunting for food in the deserted fields. The brothers Le Nain are moralists on the same level as La Bruyère.

## VII. Artistic Expression of ' Bienséance '

Whoever discusses French classicism must finally mention its great ideal of combining morals and taste: *la bienséance* — an ideal St. Francis de Sales introduces even into the spiritual life, and an ideal that makes this

42. Louis Le Nain, *La Halte du Cavalier*. Victoria and Albert Museum.
   (Crown copyright)

literature so noble and sublime. It had been exaggerated by the *Précieuses* and consequently ridiculed by Molière. The problem involved here may be illustrated by Nicolas Poussin's *Les Philistins frappés de la peste*.[71] Ostensibly the picture purports to show the ravages of the pest in Asdod, but there are no disfigured bodies, as, for example, the Spanish baroque artists would have shown with pleasure. There are only people dying from this terrible disease, a man who holds his nose, thus hinting at the presence of corpses, and another who takes a baby from the breast of the dead mother. So the attention is drawn from the horrible aspects to this little creature, resembling, as Gilles de la Tourette puts it, in its expression of helplessness one of ' those birds whose mother has been killed and which are too young to fly away to find food.' [72] Obviously the painter's technique is parallel to that of the dramatist who merely suggests terrible events rather than actually representing them. The duel in Corneille's *Cid*, the murders of Camilla (*Horace*) and Pyrrhus (*Andromaque*), the suicide of Hermione (*Andromaque*), and the death of Hippolytus (*Phèdre*) all take place behind the scenes. Nothing gruesome is tolerable to the classical eye. Messengers must report the horrors in decent words.

Classicism is likewise bound to decency in the realm of the passions. Racine can analyze the greatest crimes of love and perversion, but his characters use only urbane, polite, modest language; the poet never becomes graphic. To guarantee this, certain words are forbidden and declared not noble, such as: *barbe, cerveau, dent, épaule, foie, mollet, peau, poumon*, et cetera. Even some animals are thought to be lacking in the requirements of *bienséance: bouc, âne, vache, cochon, chameau* cannot be mentioned on the stage or shown in a picture. This has a charming consequence in Poussin's *Eliézer and Rebecca*.[73] Eliézer arrives at the fountain to sue Rebecca for Isaac, and God grants him a sign: He will sue the one who will say, ' Drink, and I will give thy camels drink also ' (Genesis xxiv. 24). In the French painting, however, for reasons of *bienséance*, instead of camels a wreath of *jeunes filles en fleur*, Rebecca's confidantes, fills the whole space. And, writes Marthe de Fels: ' Eliézer appears as though he were in a ballet of Rameau, the charming prince who comes to elect his shepherdess. One thinks of Perrault who dresses with marvels the modest events of everyday life. And Poussin is not less ethereal [*aérien*].' [74]

In the final analysis, Poussin does not act differently from the *arbiter elegantiae*, P. Bouhours, S.J., who in a Biblical translation replaces *Abraham engendra Isaac* by *Abraham fut le père d'Isaac*. He, also, acts according to the counsel of Boileau: ' N'offrez rien au lecteur que ce qui peut lui plaire.' Le Brun, too, reproaches Caravaggio for having painted *de vils objets* at the crib, meaning the traditional ass and ox.[75] There is a *Discours sur la bienséance* by Jean Pic, which appeared in Paris in 1688, where *bienséance* is differentiated from *honnêteté, modestie, civilité* and defined as ' une vertu morale, avec laquelle non seulement ce que nous faisons nous sied toujours bien, mais encore la manière, dont nous le faisons.'

With these examples from art and literature, it must be clear that France, in mitigating the baroque exuberance of Europe by a well-digested study of classical *mesure*, created a civilization which, in all its features, maintained the classical spirit of reason and taste without losing thereby the outlook on the infinite and eternal, the reason of the heart, and the great Christian values, which are particularly responsible for the sublime, heroic, moral aspects of this civilization called the *classicisme français*.

# The Rococo of the Eighteenth Century

## 1715–1789

THE literary studies concerned with the French Enlightenment tend to be so occupied with its intellectual problems as to forget about its forms, whereas art historians tend to see there nothing but elegant forms. Critics, however, spontaneously use the same qualifying terms for a comedy of Marivaux, a lyrical poem of Gresset, a novel of Crébillon, or a letter of Voltaire as they use for a painting of Watteau, a wash-and-chalk sketch of Fragonard, a panel decorated by Boucher, or an easel canvas of Lancret. Referring to both spirit and form, they speak of voluptuous and rascally drawings, exquisite miniatures, fragile marvels, *opuscules fugitifs*, *mignardise* and *marivaudage*, works of facility, *galanterie*, luxury, softness, capricious taste (*goût voltigeant*), of *jolies bagatelles*, impromptus, intellectual flirtation, pleasing delicacy, veiled indecency, of an art of giving wings to the coarse, nobility to the cheap, a certain naïveté to the daring. They speak of an art of polished, pretty trifles, of *gamineries folles*, of corruption covered by intelligence and politeness, of a playful destruction, of repressed dreams — in short, of a moral anarchy clad in a melancholy irony, a carnival of bad desires inflamed by reason itself and changed into something sparkling, charming, bewitching, light, idyllic, insolent, insinuating, contagious, electrifying, dangerous.

Gracefulness combined with *esprit*, or, as Elie Faure sees it, ' the rationalist passion,' [1] is the distinctive mark of art and literature in eighteenth-century France. This rococo spirit is embodied in particular aspects of the mind, mood, and life of the Frenchman between 1700 and 1800 and is reflected in many striking examples from literature and art.

## I. Love, Flirtation, Eroticism

The principal topic of rococo is the gamut of flirtation and love from idyl to lasciviousness. The *Music Lesson* (see Fig. 43) by Nicolas Lancret (1690–1743) is a sequel to similar paintings by Watteau — *The Concert, The Enchanter, Teaching of Love* [2] — and a single glance discovers a score of implications of rococo art in literature. There are the park landscape that plays the role of a salon in the open air and the park corner that corresponds to a boudoir. It is, according to Erika Hübener, the same frame of action that is found in all the rococo novels, where girls contrive to be invited to the homes of friends or relatives in the country in order to give their lovers an opportunity to spin their intrigues.[3] There are the young women themselves, eager to study anything — music, literature, art — on condition that these subjects be offered in an agreeable form. These young ladies have been called *liseuses Newtoniennes* and *belles Wolfiennes* because they liked to read only a *Newtonianism for Ladies,* as presented by Algarotti to the Marquise de Chatelet, or to be instructed in the philosophy of J. Ch. Wolff or the astronomy of Copernicus in the way in which Fontenelle explained it to a fictitious marquise. Then there is the famous music teacher who can assume the role of a lover or a pander at wish, like the *Neveu de Rameau* of Diderot or Bazile in Beaumarchais's *Le Barbier de Séville.* Thus these young women represent the phase of awakening love so often shown in the youthful heroines of Marivaux — subtle, intelligent, and reticent. In their charming bashfulness they appear more like *figurines* of the *commedia dell'arte* or of Dancourt's *vaudevilles* than real persons.

43. Lancret, *Music Lesson,* Louvre. (Archives Photographiques)

44. Watteau, *La Danse dans un pavillon*. (Courtesy of the Cleveland Museum of Art, Gift of Commodore Louis D. Beaumont)

Another picture, *La Danse dans un pavillon* [4] (see Fig. 44) by Jean Antoine Watteau (1684–1721), shows the century's ironical, cynical view of chastity and its yearnings for sensuous enjoyment. ' It is funny that people have made a virtue out of the vice of chastity,' says Voltaire.[5] The amorous couple in the background is an illustration of these forces. As rococo cynicism is never without a certain melancholy, however, the country dance of the couple in the center takes over this role.

In both examples the preoccupation with love reveals what in rococo literature is called *les égarements du cœur et de l'esprit*, after the title of the well-known novel of Crébillon *fils* (1736). Meilcour, the hero of this novel, refuses to let his reason guide the passions of his heart and is ' absorbed by this confusion of ideas and sentiments.' [6] At the end of his love experiences, Meilcour has to confess: ' The work of my senses seemed to me the work of my heart.' This *égarement*, which Marivaux would call ' *les effets surprenants de la sympathie*,' is decidedly evident in Watteau's dance: teasing, birdlike advance, feigned retreat, elusive escape. The sensuous love scene in the background has the stronger accents, similar to those of Marivaux's seducer in *Les Sincères* (sc. iv): ' He would say to the mistresses of others: " Where would be your fidelity, if I only wished "; to the indifferent one: " You don't stick to your opinion; I arouse you, don't I? "; to the prudish one: "But you ogle me! "; to the virtuous one: " You resist the temptation of looking at me "; to the young girl: " Confess, your heart is stirred." ' The petting and the dancing scene together combine both the rougher and more refined aspects of rococo sensuality as formulated by Diderot:

> Je ne méprise pas les plaisirs des sens, . . . j'aime à voir une jolie femme, j'aime à sentir sous ma main la fermeté et la rondeur de sa gorge, mais il m'est infiniment plus doux encore d'avoir dit à celle que j'aime quelques choses tendres et douces.[7]

Watteau's picture is thus representative of two shades of love, *tendresse* and *sensualité*, which are dealt with by Marivaux in two novels: *La Vie de Marianne* and *Le Paysan parvenu*.[8]

While the love scene in Watteau's picture represents a kind of counterpoint to the leading voice of the dancing scene, it becomes the first voice in Pater's picture, *Reunion of Comedians in a Park*.[9] During a garden party in the midst of a merry company, an actress in a beautiful silk dress feigns to repel the advances of a cavalier, which she herself, however, has invited in the boldest way. An actress was not expected to obey the moral laws to the same degree as the nobles and the commoners. She represents the woman unhampered in her love-making, as praised by Claude Adrian Helvétius in *De l'esprit*, not under the disguise of an actress but of a woman of Madagascar:

> What can we expect from a constant declamation against the falsehood of women, if this vice is the necessary effect of a contradiction between the desires of nature and the feelings which women, due to the laws and to decency, are forced to feign? If in Malabar on Madagascar all the women are sincere, the reason is that they satisfy there without scandal all their fancies, they have a thousand lovers.[10]

Pater's actress displays the same mixture of wickedness and charm that is typical of Prévost's *Manon Lescaut* and all these rococo types — the innocent coquettish one, the harmless corrupt one, the prudish seduced one, the unsatisfied genuine one, the touching seducing one, and so on. The fact that Pater's scene pleases, however, is owing to the extreme gracefulness of this elegant actress. She has indeed that *art de plaire* which Voltaire defines under *grâce* in his *Dictionnaire philosophique:* ' That secret charm which invites one to look on, which attracts, which fills the soul with a sweet sentiment.'

The borderline between piquancy and eroticism is reached with *The Swing (Escarpolette)* (see Fig. 45) by Jean Honoré Fragonard (1732–1806), the final phase of a long series of more moderate garden-swing motifs. In Fragonard's case, the figure of the ogler and the title of the picture, ' *The Fortunate Chances of the Swing*,' underline the obscene implications

45. Fragonard, *The Swing*. (From the original in the Wallace Collection, by permission)

of this rococo *si spirituellement encanaillée*, as Gustave Lanson phrases it, but even here a strong ingredient of *esprit* keeps the subject in the line of a relative decency. His 'Latin sense of moderation,' says Alfred Leroy,[11] 'turned Fragonard away from vulgarity; he never stresses; he skims risky subjects; he alone can make them acceptable; he masters the difficulties like a virtuoso; he suggests; he does not state.' This is the same trait that the Abbé Caylus, in discussing the aesthetics of the Régence, believes to have discovered in the *Contes* of La Fontaine and even in the old French *fabliaux — un goût exquis*.

The spirit of *The Swing* is representative of the indiscretion of the piquant motifs of *tête-à-têtes, levers, couchers, bains,* and *toilettes* — endless themes not only of Fragonard and Boucher but also of novelists, such as the Marquis de Pezay in *Félis au bain* (1763) or Chevrier in *Le Quart d'heure d'une jolie femme ou Les amusements de la toilette* (1753). The indiscreet ogler appears in such novels as an invisible sprite who reveals all the secrets of the couch or the bathtub, as in Crébillon's *Sopha* and Voisenon's *Misapouf*. Diderot, less decent than Fragonard, writes to Sophie Volland from Langres on 10 August 1759 about Mme Aine's being assaulted in a dark corridor by M. Le Roy, *jeune homme insolent et lascif*.

She loses her slippers, as does the lady in the swing, and her coif, and Diderot calls this scene more pleasing than any from the *Iliad*. Nowhere is Diderot more rococo than when he writes to Sophie Volland 'with the ease and freedom of . . . conversation passing from one idea to another with an unflagging zest,' as Eric M. Steel says.[12] It is as though he were waggishly inviting Sophie to a seesaw, swing, or rocking party.

## II. Nature as a Setting for Voluptuous Enjoyment

In this rococo civilization, eroticism is inseparable even from nature. Watteau's picture *Fête d'amour*,[13] with the great statue of an almost living Venus, shows the more serious obsessions of rococo sensuality — a dream of beauty that sees in all nature aspects of the female body. Even the statues, never lacking in the *fêtes champêtres*, assume a kind of life and seem ready at any moment to descend from their pedestals to mix with the flirting couples. For the statue of Antiope in his painting *Les Champs Elysées* [14] Watteau even uses the same model from his picture *Jupiter et Antiope*. Nothing is more striking than the fact that Diderot and Buffon betray the same obsession even when treating scientific matters. In the famous *Entretien entre D'Alembert et Diderot*, D'Alembert asks: ' What is the difference between a human being and a statue, between marble and flesh? ' Diderot answers: ' Very little. Marble is made from flesh, and flesh from marble.' Trees and flowers are seen by Diderot as women: ' Who has not noticed the flexibility of the willow . . . the stiffness of the hemlock tree . . . the *coquetterie* of the rose, the bashfulness of the bud, the pride of the lily, the listlessness *(nonchalance)* of the poppy? ' [15] Buffon sees his animals in terms of feminine elegance to such a degree that the zoological description of the swan in the *Histoire naturelle* might be a description of a nude in one of Boucher's panels: ' Coupe de corps élégante, blancheur éclatante et pure, mouvements flexibles et ressentis . . . tout étalant ses beautés et développant ses grâces.' [16]

The obvious example of an erotic landscape is the *Embarkation for Cythera* (see Fig. 46) by Watteau. It is, as Jeanne Magnin puts it,

a fairy tale, a mirage, beautiful hopes of youth setting out for life under the guidance of love . . . an allegory penetrated by the emanations of spring . . . a song, a flame, a flight, a poem, a dream . . . atmosphere of a festivity, woods dominating the sea, the crowd of elegant pilgrims, the noise of the cupids climbing around in the tackles of the ship dressed with flags and describing a flowery parabola up to the highest sky. The rising sun irradiates the horizon . . . the light is sparkling . . . nature sings her epithalamium.[17]

46. Watteau, *Embarkation for Cythera*, Louvre. (Foto Marburg)

Rodin, in his *Propos sur l'art*, describes the different couples:

> The action starts from the foreground to the right and ends in the background to the left. The first group is composed of a pilgrim kneeling at the feet of a young woman who, insensible of his supplications, plays indifferently with her fan; a little Cupid pulls at her in vain by the hem of her gown in order to tell her to be less cruel. The second pilgrim is already more advanced; the one he is courting accepts, without waiting to be persuaded, the hand which he extends to her in order to help her stand. The third couple, almost in the center of the composition, represents love triumphant, because here, the young woman, standing erect, is prepared to follow her cavalier who clasps his arm around her waist, and she seems, before she leaves, to throw a glance of encouragement to her more timid companions. In front of her scores of couples, holding hands, move downwards to the shore where pilot Eros expects them. . . They advance carelessly towards the gilded ship, without hurrying, without hustling, as though they had an awareness of the fact that desire is the better part of love and that the moment of possession must not come too soon.[18]

Nature seems to follow this same pattern, for there are the realistic shadows in the foreground, the parklike scene with the statue, and the majestic tree. The undecided lady is sitting beside this majestic tree whose outspread branches point softly to the fairy landscape in the background, where the island for which the loving couples are longing may be found.

This picture has a close counterpart in literature, for Watteau has actually painted the finale of Florent Carton Dancourt's comedy *Les Trois Cousines*. The stage directions specify: 'The boys and girls clad as pil-

grims prepare to make a trip to the temple of Cupid,' and Mademoiselle
Hortense sings:

> Venez dans l'isle de Cythère
> En pèlerinage avec nous.
> Jeune fille n'en revient guère
> Ou sans amant ou sans époux;
> Et l'on y fait sa grande affaire
> Des amusements les plus doux.[19]

Paul Jamot has pointed out that everything in this picture is stage setting.
The personages are the actors of Dancourt's vaudeville, even to the point
that the beautiful pilgrim in the center, Hortense, with her face turned
toward the onlooker, is a portrait of Charlotte Desmare, who played this
part; Watteau was in love with her at the time he painted the scene. Watteau's dream of an escape to Cythera had been a part of the Frenchman's
illusion ever since Fénelon's Télémaque had been told by Venus (Book
IV): 'Tu arriveras bientôt dans cette île fortunée où les plaisirs, les ris et
les jeux folâtres naissent sous mes pas.' On the other hand, the rococo generations were influenced by Watteau's picture. For example, Gentil-Bernard
praises a wondrous nature arranged for love:

> Gazon, berceau, trône et lit de verdure
> Sont à l'Amour offerts par la nature
>
>                 . . .
>
> Asille heureux des tendres voluptés.
> Dans chaque objet, l'expressive nature
> De l'union rend la vive peinture.[20]

Watteau's nature, almost transfigured by powder and rouge, also influenced Rousseau, whose descriptions are erroneously supposed to be
direct from nature. Actually his nature bends to the yearnings of the
heart and to a picturesque fireworks, as seen from such expressions as:
sweet rays; sad shade; arrows of fire; brilliant points; a brilliant net of dew,
silvery trembling, verdant lawn; enameled meadows; tufted woods; sinu-
osity of mountains; large expanses of clear and crystal water; perspective of
mountains; blue water; the soft and sweet walk on the lawn.[21]

## III. Intimacy in Social Life and Institutions

The essential quality of the social life of eighteenth-century France is
its intimacy. Because of its delicacy, rococo eroticism supersedes the or-
chestral baroque with a finer chamber music. This quality is reflected also
in the *intérieurs*. The rococo shows its civilizing power when it challenges
the pompous *Galerie des glaces* of Versailles with such a *bijou* as the Salon

47. Salon of the Princess. Hotel Soubise, Paris. (Photo Giraudon)

of the princess in the Hôtel Soubise, by the architect Boffrand (see Fig. 47). The contemporary sensibility and reaction to such a room of light and illusion can be described in terms used by Voltaire in his *Le Mondain*. There are the mythological panel paintings surrounded by *chinoiseries* and ornamentalized garlands and cornucopias. Contemporary Hellenistic stories or the idyllic fairy tales of Hamilton, Moncrif, and Count Caylus are wreathed with symbols of love. These mythologies

> . . . sont vingt fois répétés
> Dans des trumeaux tout brillants de clartés.

There is also always a combination of a decorated wall panel and a mirror, just as the bouquet of the cavalier is accompanied by an epigram; so the room appears indeed as something 'half gilded and half transparent.' Color and stucco are indistinguishable at the border of walls and ceiling, as are truth and fiction in the innumerable *Mémoires* of the century and in the fanciful plays in the theaters. It is the same everywhere:

> L'art de tromper les yeux par les couleurs,
> L'art plus heureux de séduire les cœurs.

Such a room is, in its dainty oval form, the same kind of intimate art as a madrigal or a sonnet. Yet nature, despite all this artistry, is not entirely excluded. Through the windows the trees of the garden can be seen and the murmuring of the cascades and fountains can be heard:

De ce salon je vois par la fenêtre,
Dans des jardins, des myrthes en berceaux;
Je vois jaillir les bondissantes eaux.

The same intimacy is found in the rococo portrait of a young lady, *Love Letter* (see Fig. 48), by Fragonard. The eighteenth-century portrait is a surprised, intimate action — a snapshot of a lady sealing her letter, or reading one she has just received, or powdering her face, or interrupting her reading, as here in Fragonard's picture. She and her little watchful dog seem to look toward somebody entering the room. Her most hidden thought must be veiled now, as formulated by Diderot: 'One presses always against one's bosom the man one loves, and the art of writing is only the art of lengthening one's arms.' [22] In another Fragonard portrait, called *Study*,[23] the lady has that evasive look, typical of eighteenth-century women and men, the look of the bad conscience of a Christian society turning voluptuous, sophisticated, and pagan, so opposed to the clear and clean portraits of the seventeenth century. Furthermore, as far as the dress is concerned, its low-cut neck is in striking contrast to the narrow, long sleeves and the lace collar mounting high in the back. Such a style in dress betrays what Restif de la Bretonne calls the *Art de se dévêtir*, a sym-

48. Fragonard, *Love Letter*. (Foto Marburg)

bol of all the painful confidences or confessions of the century and of those unhampered *monologues intérieurs,* which are found for the first time in Marivaux. This exterior reflects such inner thoughts as those expressed by the girl in a Marivaux novel who watches the progress of her sentiments as if before the mirror: ' I enjoyed a secret pleasure which occupied me so completely that I halted my frivolity; and to indulge in my daydreams, I forgot everything else.' [24]

Diderot's *Neveu de Rameau,* too, likes the melancholy of a charming beauty: ' Oh, let her cry, suffer, simper, have excited nerves, provided that she be pretty, amusing and coquettish.' Jean Jacques Rousseau was objecting to this type of portrait when he criticized the work of a painter who had portrayed Julie, the *nouvelle* Héloïse: ' He put the hair line much too far from the temples. . . The color of the cheeks is too close to the eyes. . . One is inclined to think that it is artificial.' [25] Certainly Fragonard's young lady has not only her cheeks but also her lips painted with that same *rouge* which found a place and a biting definition in the *Grande Encyclopédie:*

> Rouge s.m. (cosmétique), espèce de fard fort en usage que les femmes mettent sur leurs joues, par mode ou par nécessité. En d'autres termes, c'est
>
> > Cette artificieuse rougeur
> > Qui supplée au défaut de celle
> > Que jadis causait la pudeur.

## IV. Mask and Disguise

The psychology of intimacy sometimes is obliged to use mask and disguise in order both to veil and to unveil. Jean Marc Nattier (1685–1766) became famous for having represented the princesses and ladies of the court as goddesses — Mme Henriette as Flora, Mme Adelaïde as Juno, Madame Victoire [26] as Diana with quiver, bow, and arrows. His portraits reflect intimacy in that they depict ' the princesses of blood as rustic divinities disrobed.' [27] Nonetheless he has nothing to do, to use the poet Gresset's words, with a painter like

> Vanloo le fils de la gaîté,
> Le peintre de la volupté.

He simply remains himself

> Nattier, l'élève des grâces
> Et le peintre de la beauté.[28]

Refined, like Largillière, he has recourse to the mask, almost as if to keep beauty within the bounds of genuine bashfulness. His choice of the integrity of the princesses, while others were indiscreetly painting the royal mistresses, is indicative of a certain *pudeur* — a quality rare at the time but still praised by the contemporary moralist Joubert: 'Decency is a certain fear attached to our sensibility which has the effect that the soul . . . folds and hides in itself (it is so delicate and tender) at the slightest appearances of whatsoever could hurt it by impressions too vivid or by unnecessary clarifications [*clartés*].' [29]

Dancourt also uses disguises as a mask of decency. Therefore in his *La Foire de Saint Germain* he garbs the young girls offering food and drinks in exotic costumes as a protection and a justification of their somewhat free behavior. There Manon appears *en Turque* and Lorange *en Arménienne*. Mme du Chatelet, too, appeared at a fancy-dress ball as a Turk, accompanied by Mme de Boufflers as *sultane* Roxane. Voltaire tells them the undisguised meaning of their disguise:

> Sous cette barbe qui vous cache,
> Beau Turc, vous me rendez jaloux!
> Si vous ôtiez votre moustache
> Roxane le serait de vous.[30]

The rococo mask, however, must deal with more serious problems. The deep melancholy behind a smile and a fancy dress, which characterizes the epoch, comes best to the fore in the downcast clown *Gilles* (see Fig. 49) by Watteau. His model was the famous Italian comedian Giuseppe Balletti, but in the face there is something of the painter's awareness of his own imminent death from an advanced stage of tuberculosis. There is something extremely sad in playing the fool before the madding crowd — a laughing prostitution, a disguise of despair. Jean Jacques Rousseau sees here the tragedy not only of the clown but of every actor: 'The art of falsifying oneself, of donning another character than one's own, of appearing different from what one really is . . . of saying other things than those one believes . . . a trade where one exhibits oneself for money. . . Would you not die of shame, if you had to play a part before the public's eyes . . . exposed to the hooting of the populace?' [31] The sadness of Rameau's nephew, which he tries to mask, does not escape the penetration of his interlocutor. Diderot reveals him as the most tragic Gilles of all:

> He: When you suffer you make others suffer too. This is not my affair . . .
> I have to be gay, subtle, pleasing, buffoon, funny . . . I have to be
> ridiculous and foolish; if nature had not made me such, the shortest
> way would be to look like that.
> I:    I am afraid, underneath it all, you have a delicate soul.

Rameau's nephew only *seems* more cynical, but he tragically feigns not to care for anything, as does Watteau's *L'Indifférent*,[32] who has been well described by C. Lewis Hind: 'Through Watteau's dream world trips "L'indifférent," rainbow-hued, mercurial, his indifference assumed, not

49. Watteau, *Gilles*, Louvre. (Foto Marburg)

troubling to conceal the sad thoughtfulness that lurks in his expression.' [33]
This *indifférent* looks indeed like another Arlequin, the one whom Lau-
rent Bordelon introduced in a fictitious letter from the other world written
by Cardan, who blames the treatment of Arlequin in our world where ' he
had been placed among the merrymakers [*farceurs*], buffoons and other
people despicable because of their social status . . . this was not at all in
harmony with his wit . . . when he appeared without a mask . . . [Here]
he was called to go to the place of the philosophers.' [34]

Whereas all these types of art are, to use Verlaine's words, *tristes sous
leurs déguisements fantasques*, literature uses still other masks. There are
all those exotic Persians, Hurons, Turks, Chinese, Polynesians, and so on,
who are disguised for political reasons and who sharply criticize Paris,
France, and Frenchmen. They need this mask to escape the censorship
about which Figaro makes the caustic remark: ' Provided that I do not
talk about authority, cult, policy, morals, opera and other performances, I
am free to print everything under the control of two or three censors.' (v, 3)

## V. ' Esprit '

The greatest asset of rococo civilization is perhaps its *esprit*. This is the
case with Watteau's picture *Gersaint's Signboard* (see Fig. 50). The art

dealer Gersaint proposed that Watteau, during a period of apparent creative stagnation, paint a signboard for his store. Watteau surprised his friend and protector with a picture that shows Gersaint as an efficient art dealer in splendid showrooms, which did not exist at that time, and with the most exquisite and elegant public as buyers and connoisseurs meeting there as at an official exhibition. Brinckmann has described the elegant refinements of this masterpiece in a convincing way:

> The well-known connoisseurs of bad repute are viewing pictures at Gersaint's. Gersaint himself explains with nimbleness a large oil painting done in Watteau's style to a lady standing erect and to a kneeling gentleman, both provided with lorgnettes, whereas young Mrs. Gersaint née Sirois [i.e. the daughter of Watteau's landlord] shows somewhat bashfully a miniature . . . to two cavaliers and a lady who is very consciously elegant and pretentious. On the left side there is a discussion in progress; he, persuading, perhaps analyzing; in addition, there are people wrapping pictures, among which is a portrait of Louis XIV, in whose honor and remembrance Gersaint had called his store ' Of the great monarch '; on the outer left there is a porter leisurely looking on, probably *le facteur de la maison*.[35]

This is indeed a lofty compliment to Gersaint, telling him pictorially, ' You have no art store, but you are the art center of Paris.'

Compliments of this kind are well known. When Voltaire wishes to compliment Madame Lullin on her one-hundredth birthday, in 1759, he tells her that her *esprit* is no less pleasing than was once her youthful beauty, admired by his grandfather's generation:

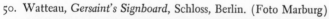

50. Watteau, *Gersaint's Signboard*, Schloss, Berlin. (Foto Marburg)

Nos grands-pères vous virent belle;
Par votre esprit vous plaisez à cent ans,
Vous méritiez d'épouser Fontenelle
Et d'être sa veuve longtemps.

The sister of Frederic the Great of Prussia is told by Voltaire in a madrigal that he dreamed he was king and had fallen in love with her. At his awakening he was, unfortunately, no longer king, but nevertheless his dreamed love for her remained:

Souvent un peu de vérité
Se mêle au plus grossier mensonge:
Cette nuit, dans l'erreur d'un songe
Au rang des rois j'étais monté,
Je vous aimais, princesse, et j'osais vous le dire!
Les dieux à mon réveil ne m'ont pas tout ôté;
Je n'ai perdu que mon empire.
                    (*Poésies mêlées*, no. 306)

At seventy-four, Voltaire writes some stanzas to his former pupil, Mme du Châtelet, expressing regret that he has reached an age when it is impossible to love her and to appear lovable to her, and saying that only regretfully does one change love into friendship — an operation more terrible than death itself:

Si vous voulez que j'aime encore,
Rendez-moi l'âge des amours;
Au crépuscule de mes jours
Rejoignez, s'il se peut, l'aurore . . .

On meurt deux fois, je le vois bien:
Cesser d'aimer et d'être aimable,
C'est une mort insupportable;
Cesser de vivre, ce n'est rien.

One can imagine Watteau's Flemish teacher, Weughels, a little old for participation in a *Fête d'amour* (*Les Fêtes Vénitiennes*),[36] paying similar compliments to the young lady in front of him. Weughels fits into this picture as little as the Persian Rica in the Tuileries Gardens, where, in a very similar manner, the curious Parisian ladies encircle him in their light, rainbow-colored dresses. Here Montesquieu's style, with its rare but effective metaphors, coincides absolutely with the style of Watteau:

Si j'étais aux Tuileries, je voyais aussitôt un cercle se former autour de moi; les femmes mêmes faisaient un arc-en-ciel nuancé de mille couleurs, qui m'entourait.
                    (*Lettres persanes*, no. 30)

In the works of Montesquieu and Voltaire one meets a form of French rococo *esprit* that cannot be painted: irony. This irony, however, is chiseled in marble by Jean-Antoine Houdon in his famous statue of Voltaire [37] (see Fig. 51), now in the Comédie Française. According to Alfred Noyes, this irony in Voltaire, like the man himself, is representative of the whole century. The following examples are typical of eighteenth-century sarcasm.

Montesquieu: 'A great lord is a man who is accustomed to see the king, to talk to the ministers, to have ancestors, debts, and pensions.' [38] 'The king of France is a sorcerer, because he extends his domination even over the thoughts of his subjects.' [39]

Voltaire: 'We [philosophers] agree on two or three points which we understand, and have arguments about two or three thousand which we do not understand.' [40] 'Louis XI had mistresses, he had three bastard sons, he made novenas and pilgrimages.' [41] 'The calendar reveals the age of the moon and that of all the princesses of Europe.' [42]

Chamfort: 'Most of the noblemen remind us of their ancestors almost as an Italian Cicerone reminds us of Cicero.' [43]

The *fait divers* invented by Voltaire to avenge himself on his bitter critic, the Abbé Fréron, is perhaps still more biting and undoubtedly more poisonous than were the Abbé's reviews:

> L'autre jour, au fond d'un vallon
> Un serpent piqua Jean Fréron.
> Que pensez-vous qu'il arriva?
> Ce fut le serpent qui creva.
> (*Poésies mêlées*, no. 345)

The impact of the rococo on the bourgeois, who was responsible for the *comédie larmoyante* and other monstrosities, results in a manifestation different from any of those previously discussed; for the bourgeois, while conniving with its obscene, lascivious, voluptuous, and vulgar implications, turns sensuality into a so-called natural virtue. The painter of such aberration is Jean Baptiste Greuze. In *The Broken Pitcher* [44] (see Fig. 52) he paints the fallen girl with a sorrowful face, tinged, however, with an indestructible, sensuous seduction and attraction — her fall symbolized by the broken pitcher and her attraction by the disarranged dress and scarf. This virtuous corruption depicts a 'womanhood bare of any ingenuousness and true candor.' [45] This is exactly the taste of Sébastien Mercier, author of sentimentally vulgar comedies whose subjects run to betrothals and weddings, with such accessories as 'the frisky groom impatient to see the light of the evening star, and the next day, the bride a little pale, confused and happy, astounded and triumphant.' [46] Unfortunately the Swiss bourgeois, Rousseau, in his passionate and pseudo-virtuous *Nouvelle Héloïse*, also destroys with a similar vulgarity the ethereal fancies of Watteau and Montesquieu, Lancret and Marivaux. The only author who keeps his mind

51. Houdon, Statue of Voltaire, Comédie Française, Paris. (Foto Marburg)

clear is Choderlos de Laclos, and that at a time when the pornographic Diderot, author of *Les Bijoux indiscrets*, can state: ' Greuze, c'est la peinture morale.'

These parallels between rococo art and literature make clear the inseparability of gracefulness and *esprit* in this civilization as long as it remains aristocratic. The efficiency of the one without the other would appear to be a miracle, as Voltaire tells the beautiful and intelligent princess Ulrica of Prussia in one of the finest of his fine compliments:

> Qui vous voit, croit que les appas,
> Sans esprit, suffiraient pour plaire;
> Qui vous entend, ne pense pas
> Que la beauté soit nécessaire.
> (*Poésies mêlées*, no. 234)

All this is a comparative, cultural psychology of literature and art during the rococo period. Further investigations may follow the line of interpretation of the rococo *forms* by such parallels as that between pastel and short sentences, and that between perspective in painting and narrative suspense. These problems are as far from being solved as they were two hundred years ago, when Diderot proposed the parallelism between the arts as a program:

Rassembler les beautés communes de la poésie, de la peinture et de la musique; en montrer les analogies; expliquer comment le poète, le peintre et le musicien rendent la même image; saisir les emblèmes fugitifs de leur expression; examiner s'il n'y aurait pas quelque similitude entre ces emblèmes, etc., c'est ce qui reste à faire.[47]

For the present, Voltaire's program at least is fulfilled:

> Tous les arts sont amis ainsi qu'ils sont divins;
> Qui veut les séparer est loin de les connaître.
> (*Poésies mêlées*, no. 496)

52. Greuze, *The Broken Pitcher*, Louvre. (Foto Marburg)

*Romanticism*

1789–1850

NINETEENTH–CENTURY romanticism stems first from Rousseau's emotionalism; secondly, it comes distinctly to the fore in a new, archaeological, Hellenistic concept of antiquity arising from the scholarly research of such men as Winckelmann and the Abbé Barthélemy. It has a third early incarnation in the imitation of 'Roman virtue' born of the French Revolution. Then comes the literary discovery of America, with its virgin woods and all the exotic implications seen by Chateaubriand. Senses reel from the lush, graphic impressions; the novelists begin to tell their stories in brilliant colors and the painters hasten to illustrate and to imitate them. With this interest in far-off countries, the distant epochs in history become important for the colorful life imagined there. Man and his soul lose importance. The great gift of the seventeenth century, consisting in a psychological anthropology, is temporarily lost. Soulless, beautiful women are described; their features and their dresses become more important than their feelings and ideas. Picturesqueness becomes the expression even of lyricism, and the borderline between the poet and the painter is less sharp than heretofore. The *Ut pictura poiesis* of Horace is misunderstood in a rather barbaric way.

As far as great themes are concerned, Napoleon, his cult, and his myth are of paramount importance. Passages of local color produce the greatest sensation when the stress is on the gruesome and the sensuous. Stifled by these tendencies, symbolism struggles through errors and difficulties. But French romanticism has no real center of gravitation. Love, in the most banal sense of the word, family life, and a poor religiosity supply the enthusiasm of which the romantics are so proud and which they believe they share with Germany and England, misinterpreting Germanic idealism and Anglo-Saxon pantheism.

Up to now, however, in no other epoch does painting follow literature so closely, because never before does literature itself depend so much on stimulation by visual forms, colors, and lines, as a result, unfortunately, of the abandonment of everything spiritual and truly intellectual. French romanticism turns out to be a civilization of sensations for eye and ear, of surface interests, and of a fancy running wild. What should be dramatic is melodramatic; what should be shaded is violent. The aristocratic trends are frustrated by the popular and even vulgar ones.

## I. The Neoclassic Concept of Antiquity

The romantic neoclassicism (fundamentally different from the baroque classicism of the seventeenth century) is strikingly visible in a picture such as *The Rape of Psyche* (see Fig. 53) by Pierre Paul Prud'hon (1758–1823). This picture shows, against a wild landscape steeped in moonlight, Zephyr and Cupids supporting and carrying through the air a naked, smiling Psyche, sleeping upon a yellow drapery. It is a lyrical picture. The painter is interested in the chaste beauty of a youthful body, in a rare and unusual landscape, in contrasts so mitigated that they produce a pale harmony, which was considered classical in an age when it was believed that Greek statues did not even have the eyes painted.

This is the ideal of beauty of the half-Greek André Chénier (1762–94), who depicts a *Jeune Tarentine* drowned during a sea trip that was destined to bring her to her wedding in Sicily. He uses Racinian Alexandrines in order to give her classical greatness and dignity, as Prud'hon sees flesh through Greek statues. But Chénier cannot prevent a lyrical, modern complaint over the premature death of the beautiful girl from creeping into the marblelike verse, as Prud'hon cannot entirely forget Rubens. Chénier describes how Myrto's beautiful dead body, after having been tossed by the waves, is brought by mournful Thetis and her Nereids into the protecting harbor of a hollow rock. The form and sentiment expressed are the same as those of Prud'hon:

> Elle est au sein des flots, la jeune Tarentine!
> Son beau corps a roulé sous la vague marine.
> Thétis, les yeux en pleurs, dans le creux d'un rocher,
> Aux monstres dévorants eut soin de le cacher,
> Par ses ordres bientôt les belles néréides
> L'élèvent au-dessus des demeures humides.

The Hellenism of Prud'hon and Chénier is romantic because the modern sentiment of the vibrating admiration of beauty, the fear of its destruction, and the care for its preservation is not expressed directly, as it once was done by François Villon, but in the conscious, although gratuitous, assumption that the ancients would have shared the same modern feelings. Their re-enacted, mythological forms and assumed aesthetic norms must therefore be derived from the ancients in spite of a new sen-

53. Prud'hon, *The Rape of Psyche*, Louvre. (Foto Marburg)

sibility and a new ideology unknown to the Greeks. According to the words of André Chénier himself:

> Pour peindre notre idée empruntons leurs couleurs;
> Allumons nos flambeaux à leurs feux poétiques,
> Sur des pensers nouveaux faisons des vers antiques.

The Roman pose, dear to the Revolution, Directory, and Empire, already appears strikingly in *The Oath of the Horatii* (see Fig. 54) by Jacques Louis David (1748–1825). David, who became the State's art supervisor during the Revolution, anticipates its spirit in this picture. Although it is the old Cornelian theme, the moment of the oath itself has something of the patriotic and military gesture that will become an element familiar to the Revolution. It is made particularly theatrical by the overtones, implying that these Romans defending their young republic are, of course, Frenchmen on the alert against any conspiracy from within or aggressive reaction from without. The romantic, emotional contrast is not lacking; whereas the three young men are eager to receive their swords from the hand of their father, their mother and their sisters are weeping in the background. More than in Corneille the emotional element is stressed in contradistinction to the real, proverbial, unshakable *virtus romana.*

The roman neoclassic Abbé Delille (1738–1813), translator of Vergil and Milton, in one of his epics, *L'Homme des champs,* also sketches the effect of mobilization on the country people. He couches the *appel aux armes* in classical allusions and Vergilian periphrases, but, like David, also adds emotional overtones, portraying the sadness of the mothers and sisters of the men to be drafted:

> Mais pourquoi ces concours, ces urnes, ces billets?
> Ah! Mars vient demander des soldats à Cérès. . .
> Dans le cirque fatal le village s'assemble:
> Les noms sont agités; tout attend et tout tremble:
> Chaque père en secret déjà se sent frémir.
> Quelles sœurs vont pleurer? Quelles mères gémir?
> Les noms sortent! Soudain sur les ponts se déploie
> D'un côté la douleur et de l'autre la joie.[1]

The full-fledged revolutionary spirit and military *élan* appear on one of the bas-reliefs of the Arc de Triomphe de l'Etoile in Paris — namely, in *Le Départ pour la guerre* (see Fig. 55) by François Rude (1784–1855). In this sculptured hymn of warriors' enthusiasm, the Frenchmen actually have become Romans, superhuman heroes in ancient garb, gathered around the banner and determined to vanquish or to die. This time the Roman garb gives the right dignity and spirit to this *Marseillaise de pierre,* as the bas-relief has been called; and no doubt the hymn these Romans entone is no other than Rouget de Lisle's *Marseillaise,* the first modern song of a mass upheaval in a pagan 'Roman' spirit:

> Allons enfants de la patrie,
> Le jour de gloire est arrivé. . .

54. David, *The Oath of the Horatii,* Louvre. (Foto Marburg)

55. Rude, *Le Départ pour la guerre*. (Archives Photographiques)

The same spirit, with much less *élan*, however, is expressed also by Marie-Joseph Chénier:

> La république nous appelle,
> Sachons vaincre ou sachons périr,
> Un Français doit vivre pour elle,
> Pour elle un Français doit mourir . . .
> Les Français donneront au monde
> Et la paix et la liberté.[2]

Romanticism in the making has a particular penchant for Homer. Not too abstract and not too realistic, he seems the ideal for an epoch that still considers itself classical — disgusted only with classical tragedy. Homer is now considered the father of poetry. This conviction, coming from Herder's Germany and early romantic England, finds a repercussion in France in new translations of the *Odyssey* and in *L'Apothéose d'Homère* [3] (see Fig. 56) by Jean Auguste Dominique Ingres (1780–1867). At first sight this classicism resembles a romantic carnival. As in the *Martyrs* of Chateaubriand, a kind of unconsciously sacrilegious Christian mythology is attempted. Here a Christian angel crowns the pagan poet. At Homer's feet are allegories of his own creations, the *Iliad* and the *Odyssey*. There are

also all the later poets inspired by that archpoet: not only Aeschylus with
the scroll of his tragedies and Pindar with his lyre, but also Dante, Tasso,
and Shakespeare, each in the garb of his own epoch, and Racine, Molière,
and Fénelon with their wigs *à la Louis XIV*. Their gestures indicate that
without Homer their own writings would not exist. The place seems to be
an Olympus or an Elysium, where all the ' Homerides ' are united and the
lines of Girodet-Trioson ask:

> Quel magique pouvoir assemble ici les dieux?
> Tout l'Olympe à la fois a-t-il quitté les cieux?
> Ou, l'artiste lui-même, admis dans l'empyrée
> En a-t-il pu franchir la barrière éthérée? [4]

This assembling of mythical and historical beings of different epochs,
however, is only half of the problem. The other is one of form, namely the
slight coloring of sharply delineated figures, which similarly occur in Lamartine's *Le Lac* or *L'Isolement*. In both cases a romantic device of expressing admiration or reflection according to the wishful yearning of the mind
is not granted all the coloring for which it clamors. The feelings are kept at
bay by the great classical lines with their reduced vocabulary and not too
picturesque metaphors. The famous *Apothéose* appears in exactly the same
taste as the fine brush strokes of Lamartine, which never disturb the primacy of the line. This is clearly seen from the description of the picture by
Louis Hourticq:

> Taking up once more the linear delicacy of the Florentine school, Ingres
> was bound to take over also its toned-downed coloring.
> If in the *Apotheosis of Homer* the figures gave us the illusion of reality,
> if the head of Boileau and that of Longinus were living portraits, if the
> Iliad and Odyssey were real women, this gathering of allegories and his-
> toric . . . personalities would at least arouse our incredulity. . . But by

56. Ingres, *L'Apothéose d'Homère*, Louvre. (Foto Marburg)

its unreal color, its design without relief, its abstract light, this Apotheosis carries us to a world which is not the one known to us through our eyes; in this world . . . men and things lose every material character to preserve only those qualities which depend on form; disburdened in that way reality can follow intelligence in the daring of its fictions; the very same immaterial forms may contain ideal persons or personified ideas.[5]

This is exactly the art of Lamartine. His *Lac* does not evoke the reality of a love experience or of the place where it happened. This 'realistic' way was left for Victor Hugo in his *Tristesse d'Olympio*. In Lamartine's *Lac* Madame Charles, the tubercular, adulterous young woman, has been transformed into a stylized, ethereal, angel-like Elvire. To repeat Hourticq's words, because of her unreal color, the drawing without embossing, the abstract landscape not recognizable as the Lac du Bourget, Elvire's apotheosis leads into a world of sheer poetry, where landscape and persons lose their material character and earthbound implications and become simply an outline of being. The whole of nature, therefore, may reasonably be conjured to testify to the importance and greatness of their love, or rather, of Love:

> O lac! . . .
> Que le vent qui gémit, le roseau qui soupire,
> Que les parfums légers de ton air embaumé,
> Que tout ce qu'on entend, l'on voit ou l'on respire,
>     Tout dise: ' Ils ont aimé.'

This is the last attempt at classicism, whose forms were not able ultimately to contain these romantic feelings in the making. This artificial classicism, which was not genuinely French, as was that of the seventeenth century, but merely German Hellenism of the Winckelmann brand propagated in France by Quatremère de Quincy, proved an inappropriate vehicle for the exotic and Anglo-Saxon concepts and motifs overflowing French literature at that time.

## II. Exoticism and Historicism

When Chateaubriand published *Atala* (1801) and *Les Natchez* (1827), he opened to an astonished Europe the virgin woods of North America by means of sheer imagination. This love story of Atala and Chactas, which is intended not as a 'meditation' on love but as a tragic idyl, is told in such striking forms and colors that Girodet-Trioson attempted to reproduce Chateaubriand's story. He did not need to create something new when he painted his well-known picture *The Burial of Atala* [6] (see Fig. 57). Anne-Louis Girodet-Trioson (1767–1824) thus contributes a classroom example of how a painter can, in his own medium, imitate a writer. Chateaubriand combines feeling for nature and lyrical tenderness with a power of descriptive representation. The atmosphere created by Chateaubriand depends on stylistic means at the disposal of the literary artist only, such as melancholy epithets, solemn metonymies, allusions to things past that give the present an air of particular sadness, comparisons that convey a special mood to the reader, symbolic language that gives depth to human sorrow, locutions that breathe sweetness and a preciosity not entirely out of accordance with the artistic tendencies of Chateaubriand. The painter has other advantages. Showing the dead Atala in a dignified pose, he need not call her stiffly *la statue de la virginité endormie*; the transitory moments of the burial are as impressive as the slowly developing story of Atala's death and *enterrement* in Chateaubriand. But the painter falls short of the text. He actually translates only the following from Chateaubriand's description: ' At one of the openings of the grotto . . . the hermit had wrapped Atala in a piece of linen . . . Her head, her shoulders, and a part of her breast were uncovered. Her lips seemed to smile. Her eyes were closed, her feet joined, and her hands pressed a crucifix upon her heart . . . a young savage and an old hermit were kneeling, one in front of the other . . . in the dry bed of a mountain torrent.'

The full text of Chateaubriand has not only the additional beauty of more details and a poetic language full of figures of speech, the description not of simultaneous but of successive details given as the action progresses, but also the element of a melancholy air and a sentimental rhythm. Consequently there are *demi-teintes* and minor tones that are lacking in the work of Girodet-Trioson. Chateaubriand's full text is as follows:

57. Girodet-Trioson, *The Burial of Atala*, Louvre. (Foto Marburg)

58. Delaroche, *The Young Martyr*, Louvre. (Archives Photographiques)

Vers le soir, nous transportâmes ses précieux restes à une ouverture de la grotte, qui donnait vers le nord. L'ermite les avait roulés dans une pièce de lin d'Europe, filé par sa mère; c'était le seul bien qui lui restât de sa patrie, et depuis longtemps il le destinait à son propre tombeau. Atala était couchée sur un gazon de sensitives; ses pieds, sa tête, ses épaules et une partie de son sein étaient découvertes. On voyait dans ses cheveux une fleur de magnolia fânée. . . Ses lèvres, comme un bouton de rose, cueilli depuis deux aurores, semblaient languir et sourire. Dans ses joues d'une blancheur éclatante, on distinguait quelques veines bleues. Ses beaux yeux étaient fermés, ses pieds modestes étaient joints, et ses mains d'albâtre pressaient sur son cœur un crucifix d'ébène; le scapulaire de ses vœux était passé à son cou. Elle paraissait enchantée par l'Ange de la Mélancolie et par le double sommeil de l'innocence et de la tombe. Je n'ai rien vu de plus céleste. Quiconque eût ignoré que cette jeune fille eût joui de la lumière aurait pu la prendre pour la statue de la virginité endormie. . . O mon fils! Il eût fallu voir un jeune sauvage et un vieil ermite . . . creusant un tombeau! [7]

Reciprocally, Chateaubriand imitates Girodet-Trioson's *Le Sommeil d'Endymion* in his description of the sleep of Eudore in *Les Martyrs*.

Geographical exoticism is counterbalanced by a historical sentimentalism.

The young Christian neophytes in the American woods find brothers and sisters in the Christian martyrs of the late Roman centuries. The spirit of Girodet-Trioson's *Atala* reappears in *The Young Martyr* (see Fig. 58) of Paul Delaroche (1797–1856). The dead body of a young woman with fettered hands drifts along a dark river. A halo encircles her head. The dark waves have silvery streaks and the white gown of the dead girl shines bleakly in the light of a half-hidden, yellowish moon. What the painter aims to express can be found again very explicitly described in the text of Chateaubriand. This time, however, not one but several passages can illustrate the sentimental implications of the picture. There is, first, a more sensational portrayal of Prud'hon-Chénier's tender, feminine body carried by water or air, but this time the water is brilliant with light; and there is also something more mysterious and at the same time more picturesque and less linear. So Chateaubriand in *Les Natchez* writes of the swimming Indian girl Mila as though he were describing Delaroche's picture in part:

> Mila s'ébattait au milieu de ces ondulations brillantes comme un cygne qui baigne son cou et ses ailes. . . Enveloppée d'un voile . . . elle ne montrait au-dessus de l'eau que ses épaules demi-nues et sa tête humide. Sa figure brillait à la clarté de la lune, au milieu de l'ébène de ses cheveux; des filets d'argent coulaient le long de ses joues.

(Op. cit. III, p. 356)

In the *Jeune Martyre* there is also an expression of sorrow for a girl prematurely doomed to death. This feeling is exemplified by Chateaubriand's Amélie, described as a narcissus broken by a storm or a bird fallen from its nest before its wings have developed:

> La blanche et souffreteuse Amélie . . . ressemblait à un narcisse abattu par l'orage, ou à un oiseau tombé de son nid avant d'avoir des ailes.

59. David, *Madame Récamier*, Louvre. (Foto Marburg)

The skyscape with the moon and its light effects comes beautifully to the fore in Chateaubriand's apostrophe to the moon, the music of the well-chosen words affording a kind of incantation:

> O Lune! tes regards veloûtent l'azur du ciel; ils rendent les nues dia-phanes; ils font briller les fleuves comme des serpents; ils argentent la cime des arbres, ils couvrent de blancheur le sommet des montagnes, ils changent en une mer de lait les vapeurs de la vallée.

If it is remembered that Chateaubriand himself dedicated a whole novel to the topic of *Les Martyrs*, then there is nothing implicit in Dela-roche that is not explicit in Chateaubriand. His text gains in importance if one considers how little modern art historians have to say about Dela-roche's picture, for example, ' Sainte Cécile morte passant au fil de l'eau sous la caresse de la lune.' [8]

### III. Soulless Physical Beauty: the Costume Portrait

Atala, Cecilia, Mila, and Amélie interested the artists from a sensa-tional rather than psychological point of view. What they seem concerned with is an exterior beauty in an arrangement that is striking, attractive, or fascinating for any reason whatsoever. This is a clue to the understanding of a more realistic picture, that of a beautiful and leading society lady of the Empire, *Madame Récamier* (see Fig. 59) by Jacques Louis David. Madame Récamier, dressed in a white gown, the long folds of which are arranged so as to reveal her bare feet, is reclining on a couch upon cushions of pale yellow bordered with delicate grayish blue. The pure outlines of her head and figure are clearly defined against the plain surface of the back-ground. At the head of the couch is a tall bronze lamp, the only ornament introduced into the apartment, which is severe in its simplicity.

Thus the leader of Empire society is represented in the ideal Empire style, the romantic color spots in the linear pseudo-classical style still being weak. The typical kind of beauty painted here by David is again explained in a passage by Chateaubriand from the *Martyrs*:

> Cette femme était extraordinaire. Elle avait, ainsi que toutes les Gauloises, quelque chose de capricieux et d'attirant. Son regard était prompt, sa bouche un peu dédaigneuse et son sourire singulièrement doux et spirituel.
>
> (Op. cit. p. 140)

Returning to the painting, we may note that, as a matter of fact, Mme Récamier did not like David's picture of herself. She probably looked too much like a vestal, and she preferred the type of beauty *qu'on arrache au sommeil*. To this ideal corresponds her second portrait, *Madame Réca-mier* (see Fig. 60) by François Pascal Simon Gérard (1770–1837). The best description of this painting is simply a continuation of Chateaubriand's text:

Les manières étaient tantôt hautaines tantôt voluptueuses; il y avait dans
toute sa personne de l'abandon et de la dignité, de l'innocence et de l'art
. . . Ses cheveux étaient relevés à la grecque sur le sommet de sa tête. . .
Elle portait pour tout vêtement une tunique blanche; fille de roi a moins
de beauté, de noblesse et de grandeur.

(p. 141)

Although Chateaubriand is describing here not Mme Récamier but the
daughter of a Druidic chieftain in fifth-century Gaul, he betrays exactly
the same taste as that of David and Gérard. His concept of a theatrical,
languishing, voluptuous feminine beauty is psychologically so inept that
he fails to depict in these exterior features an admixture of dignity and
nobility. It may be noteworthy that Lamartine, too, once caught a glimpse
of Mme Récamier as she was riding in a carriage with Mme de Staël. To
him also she appeared to have a supernatural beauty, so that he remarks in
his *Souvenirs et portraits:*

Mme Récamier m'éblouit comme le plus céleste visage qui ait jamais
éclairé les yeux d'un poète, trop beau, comme un éclair, pour être autre
chose qu'une apparition.

(I, p. 293)

60. Gérard, *Madame Récamier*, Petit Palais, Paris. (Archives Photographiques)

Sainte-Beuve has described Gérard's picture in an advanced romantic, sensuous, and psychological language that vies in Greco-Roman color with the painter himself who belonged to the first generation of the romantics. Sainte-Beuve interprets the setting and the transitory moment of the painting in which a lady rests after her bath:

> Dans ce frais pavillon de marbre et de verdure
>
> . . .
>
> Quand le rideau de pourpre assoupit la lumière,
> Quand un buisson de rose achève la cloison;
> Chaste au sortir du bain, ayant laissé derrière
> Humide vêtement, blanche écume et toison;
>
> De fine mousseline à peine revêtue,
> Assise, un bras fuyant, l'autre en avant penché;
> Son beau pied, non chaussé, d'albâtre et de statue
> S'éclairant au parvis, d'un reflet détaché;
>
> . . .
>
> Simple, et pour tout brillant, dans l'oubli d'elle-même,
> A part ce blanc de lys et ces contours neigeux,
> N'ayant de diamant, d'or et de diadème
> Que cette épingle en flèche attachant ses cheveux,
>
> . . .
>
> Mêlant un reste heureux d'insouciante enfance
> A l'éclair éveillé d'un intérêt naissant
>
> . . .
>
> Elle est trouvée enfin, la Psyché sans blessure,
> La nymphe sans danger dans les bains de Pallas;
> C'est Ariane heureuse, une Hélène encor pure,
> Hélène avant Paris, même avant Ménélas.[9]

As for masculine characters, romanticism makes the discovery, of doubtful value, that costume can be more important than personality. The hero seems to depend on a pseudo-historical makeup. The adage, ' L'habit ne fait pas le moine,' is reversed at this time. Historicism in style characterizes the 1830's. The costumes in Velasquez's paintings are the sources of the clothing of the heroes from D'Arlincourt to Dumas *père*. The historians of style report that Paris at that time was enthusiastic about *le pourpoint tailladé à l'espagnole, le chaperon à la Buridan, la dague de Tolède, les souliers à la poulaine, les éperons à la burgrave.* Jean Louis Ernest Meissonier (1815–91) has eternalized this superficial ideal in *The Cavalier* (see Fig. 61). It is unnecessary to describe this picture, since these painters are practically *enlumineurs* of the romantic historical novels. It would really seem that Meissonier had painted a cavalier according to the pattern given by Alfred de Vigny in *Cinq Mars:*

Et l'on voit entrer un jeune homme d'une assez belle taille; il était pâle, ses cheveux étaient bruns, ses yeux noirs, son air triste et insouciant: c'était Henri d'Effiat, marquis de Cinq Mars . . . son costume et son manteau court étaient noirs; un collet de dentelle tombait sur son cou jusqu'au milieu de la poitrine; des bottes fortes, très évasées et ses éperons faisaient assez de bruit sur les dalles . . . pour qu'on l'entendît de loin.

(Edition Larousse, I, p. 29)

The French were determined to cling to picturesqueness at a time when Hegel in Germany was philosophizing about the manifestation of ideas in forms.

## IV. Picturesqueness as an Expression of Lyricism

Eugène Delacroix (1798–1863), in his famous picture *La Barque de Dante* (see Fig. 62), is much more than an illustrator or an *enlumineur* of the *Divine Comedy*. With this picture the painter gives perhaps a greater shock of terror than does the poet whose vision he translates. The eighth canto of the ' Inferno ' relates how, while Dante is crossing the infernal River Styx in a rowboat, Philip Argenti tries to grasp the boat,

61. Meissonier, *The Cavalier*. (From the original in the Wallace Collection, by permission)

62. Delacroix, *La Barque de Dante*, Louvre. (Archives Photographiques)

but Dante cruelly pushes him back into the muddy, burning stream where those who sinned by pride are to suffer for eternity. According to Henri Marcel,[10] Delacroix has also given, by his own means as a painter, a vision of the horror of Hell: the water of the Styx shines in the darkness like a sweat of terror, despair, and rage; and the red, purple, and orange colors, together with the livid, naked bodies, evoke a mysterious horror.

Parallels of this form of expression can be found in the poetry of Victor Hugo. Hugo strives to express at all costs his philosophy about God and nature in a concrete-symbolic form. As a man of the senses so much opposed to the aerial, pantheistic attitude of a Shelley or a Keats, he attempts to formulate a pantheism that is almost animistic. If the involved jargon, always rampant in Victor Hugo, can be overcome, one sees the same mysterious horror emanating from the poetry as comes from the colors of uncanny bodies in Delacroix's painting; for Hugo's polytheistic evocations are couched in half-metaphors and half-personifications in an eery, synesthetic mixture that translates the poet's emotions of horror, rampant fear, anguish, doubt, and spiritual experiences: *l'océan ouvrant sa gueule . . . ; souffler une vapeur de bruit . . . ; l'ouragan qui vole . . . ; le tombeau d'herbe et de nuit vêtu . . . ; la rumeur des frissons de la foudre . . . ; tout parle, vent, ondes flammes . . . tout est plein d'âmes.* When seen in their full pattern, these mosaic elements by the Delacroix of French romantic poetry echo the climate of the canvas:

> Crois-tu que l'océan qui se gonfle et qui lutte
> Serait content d'ouvrir sa gueule jour et nuit
> Pour souffler dans le vide une vapeur de bruit
> Et qu'il voudrait rugir, sous l'ouragan qui vole,
> Si son rugissement n'était une parole?
> Crois-tu que le tombeau, d'herbe et de nuit vêtu,
> Que la création profonde qui compose

La rumeur des frissons du lys et de la rose,
De la foudre, des flots, des souffles du ciel bleu
Ne sait ce qu'elle dit quand elle parle à Dieu . . .
Tout parle. Et maintenant, homme, sais-tu pourquoi
Tout parle? Ecoute bien. C'est que vent, onde, flammes,
Arbres, roseaux, rochers, tout vit. Tout est plein d'âmes.
Mais comment? Oh! voilà le mystère inouï.

(Contemplations, VI, 26)

Picturesqueness in French romantic painting and literature has thus become a means of expressing sentiments and lyricism. Dante's themes combined with Germanic pantheism are reflected in the works of a generation standing on the shoulders of the writers of Gothic novels. This picturesqueness also serves to clothe a political myth, that of Napoleon.

## V. The Napoleonic Myth

Napoleon himself, as dictators usually do, started the Napoleonic myth. There is striking evidence of this in the fact that he ordered the Pope to Paris for his coronation as Emperor in Notre Dame on 2 December 1804. Publicly Napoleon wanted to assume the functions of a new *Imperator Romanus* and, with the blessing of the Church, overrun the Holy Empire; privately in Fontainebleau he used all kinds of intimidation to force Pius VII to change his residence from Rome to Paris in order to be subservient to him. When one recalls that the Pope excommunicated Napoleon in 1809, that Napoleon had actually made the Pope his prisoner for five years, and that in 1805, when Napoleon ordered the great coronation picture from David, the relations between State and Church in France were tense, in spite of the Concordat of 1801, it is clear that Napoleon wanted to have the moment painted when he himself was putting the crown on the head of the empress. The following is a description of David's *Coronation of Napoleon and Josephine* (see Fig. 63):

63. David, *Coronation of Napoleon and Josephine*, Louvre. (Archives Photographiques)

David has represented the moment when the emperor, already crowned by the Pope, Pius VII, who is seated behind him, is about to place the crown upon the head of Josephine. Clad in a white robe and long crimson mantle lined with ermine and bordered with gold, she kneels before him. He himself standing with upraised arms upon the steps of the high altar, is arranged in robes of state and wears a laurel wreath upon his brow.[11]

David was ordered to create in this picture the mythical *Empereur* who ostensibly triumphs over the Pope in the cathedral of Paris. Alfred de Vigny later (1835) gives the scene behind the curtain in the last *récit* of his *Servitude et grandeur militaires,* when the Emperor, in a closed room at Fontainebleau, tries to persuade the Pope to transfer the Holy See to Paris and is scored by the Pope as a political charlatan:

> L'Empereur était fort agité . . . s'avança vers la fenêtre et se mit à y tambouriner une marche avec les ongles. . . Le pape . . . avait un visage . . . plein d'une noblesse sainte et d'une bonté sans bornes. . . Bonaparte alors poussa du pied une chaise près du grand fauteuil du pape:
> Je n'ai jamais eu le temps d'étudier beaucoup la théologie, moi; mais j'ajoute encore une grande foi à la puissance de l'église . . . Saint Père . . . Moi, je ne sais pas . . . pourquoi vous auriez de la répugnance à siéger à Paris pour toujours . . . Pourvu que la guerre et la politique fatigante me fussent laissées, vous arrangeriez l'Eglise comme il vous plairait. Je serais votre soldat tout à fait. Voyez, ce serait vraiment beau; nous aurions nos conciles comme Constantin et Charlemagne, je les ouvrirais et les fermerais. . .
> Le pape qui jusque-là n'avait cessé de demeurer sans mouvement . . . sourit avec mélancolie, leva ses yeux en haut et dit, après un soupir paisible:
> Commediante!

Bonaparte himself, further, conveys the myth of the people's own Emperor to his soldiers, when, exactly one year after his coronation, on the eve of the Battle of Austerlitz, he addresses his soldiers in one of his famous *ordres du jour*, in which his telegraphic military style is patched up with *grands mots trompe-l'oeil*. Gustave Lanson can thus call this style *du dix-huitième durci de gréco-romain*. This *appel aux soldats* tries to make it clear that the soldiers are defending the legitimate crown against those (Austrians and Russians) who are trying to take it away from him in order to put it on the head of an enemy of France and of her liberty:

> Soldiers! When the French people put the imperial crown upon my head, I confided myself to you in order to keep it always in that high state of glory, which alone was able to make it valuable in my eyes; but in the very same moment our enemies thought to destroy and to debase it. And they wanted to force me to put this iron crown, conquered by the blood of so many Frenchmen, upon the head of our most cruel enemies.[12]

The spirit and the *grand geste* in the calculation of the repercussion on the soldiers are well illustrated by David's conception of the coronation. Vigny's text serves as an x-ray for both the painting and the *ordre du jour*.

Throughout the romantic period, however, the Napoleonic myth was always stronger than the truth in spite of the Emperor's defeat. This is almost unique in history and actually a result of the spirit of romanticism. Typical is the Emperor's appearance in simple array on the battlefield: it is the famous silhouette of the great general, on whom depends the destiny of the world, sitting on horseback, wearing his gray riding-coat and his three-cornered hat, the chart of the general staff in one hand, a telescope in the other. He was thus pictured on a strategic hill during battle by Horace Vernet (1789–1863) in *The Battle of Wagram*.[13] This silhouette appears greater in tragic situations, as is the case with the picture by Antoine Gros (1771–1835), *The Battle of Eylau* (see Fig. 64), described by Raymond Escholier as follows:

> In the foreground heaps of corpses already half covered by snow, wounded Russian soldiers busily tended by French military surgeons.
>
> In the distance, fire has just devoured Eylau, the church steeple of which served as observatory for Napoleon. . . Long rows of prisoners file off in front of our troops, which form anew in columns in order to be reviewed by the Emperor. Here and there dying horses, shaking off the hoarfrost of the night, rear on their weakened legs by a last effort and fall back to stretch out in death near to their masters.
>
> The central group gives this great poem of death all its meaning, all its tragic and simple accents. The marshalls and at their head King Murat, prancing like his bay horse, are only the frame from which comes the figure so human and so grave of the victor upon his dun-colored horse. . .
>
> Whilst a Lithuanian lancer presses against his lips the knee of the man who is touched by so much misfortune, the beautiful hand of the Emperor, an enchanting and magnificent hand, rises and hovers above the icy field like a dove . . . accusing the evils of war.[14]

Victor Hugo also supports this myth of Napoleon's simplicity and expresses very pertinently what is found in the pictures of Vernet, Gros, and others — that is, the inspiration coming from this simplicity:

> Puis, empereur puissant dont la tête s'incline,
> Gouvernant un combat du haut de la colline,
> Promettant une étoile à ses soldats joyeux,
> Faisant signe aux canons qui vomissent les flammes,
> De son âme à la guerre armant six cent mille âmes,
> Grave et serein, avec un éclair dans les yeux.
>                         ('Lui,' *Les Orientales*, 1829)

Furthermore, Napoleon is the greatest example of that spirit of gratuitous daring which the French romantics, according to the example of the Germans, were accustomed to call enthusiasm. It is the young Napoleon,

64. Gros, *The Battle of Eylau*, Louvre. (Archives Photographiques)

the general of the Republican armies, who is considered the enthusiastic hero. It is that Bonaparte who, on 17 November 1796, was the first to jump onto the bridge of Arcole, an Austrian stronghold that seemed unassailable, drawing all his soldiers after him to glory and to victory. This story is told in the painting *Napoleon at Arcole* (see Fig. 65) by Antoine Gros. The same enthusiasm permeates the short and breathtaking lines of Victor Hugo's *chanson* celebrating the same event:

> Napoléon dans la bataille,
> Grave et serein
> Guidait à travers la mitraille
> L'aigle d'airain.
> Il entra sur le pont d'Arcole,
> Il en sortit.
> (*Les Châtiments*)

The picture by Gros and the poem of Victor Hugo illustrate that quality praised in a general way by Madame de Staël, Napoleon's enemy, who certainly was not thinking of him when she wrote the following lines in *De l'Allemagne*:

> L'enthousiasme que le beau idéal nous fait éprouver, cette émotion pleine de trouble et de pureté tout ensemble, c'est le sentiment de l'infini. Nous nous sentons comme dégagés . . . des entraves de la destinée humaine. . . L'infini agit sur l'âme pour l'élever et la dégager du temps. L'œuvre de la vie, c'est de sacrifier les intérêts de notre existence passagère à cette immortalité qui commence pour nous dès à présent, si nous en sommes déjà dignes; et non seulement la plupart des religions ont ce même but, mais les beaux arts, la poésie, la gloire et l'amour sont des religions dans lesquelles il entre plus ou moins d'alliage.

And Madame de Staël underscores particularly:

> L'enivrement d'un jour de bataille, le plaisir singulier de s'exposer à la
> mort, quand toute notre nature nous commande d'aimer la vie, c'est en-
> core à l'enthousiasme qu'il faut l'attribuer.
>
> (Part IV, ch. 1)

When Napoleon is shown after his defeat in Russia, it is with another
romantic gesture, which, contradicting the facts 'enthusiastically,' hints
at something like invincibility, as in the *Episode de la retraite de Russie* [15]
by Boissard de Boisdenier.

The soldiers, clad in rags, dying and freezing to death, as shattered and
broken as their guns, lie near the wagons and the black corpses of the
horses, which contrast with the snowy landscape. But a glimpse of hope
on the faces of the suffering soldiers expresses one idea: Defeat is impossible.

This is the great military myth that Victor Hugo has expressed in a
superior way in his poem *L'Expiation:*

> Il neigeait. On était vaincu par sa conquête
> Pour la première fois l'aigle baissait la tête.
>
> . . .

65. Gros, *Napoleon at Arcole*, Louvre. (Archives Photographiques)

On ne distinguait plus les ailes ni le centre.
Il neigeait. Les blessés s'abritaient dans le ventre
Des chevaux morts; au seuil des bivouacs désolés
On voyait des clairons à leur poste gelés . . .
Stupéfait de désastre et ne sachant que croire
L'empereur se tourna vers Dieu; l'homme de gloire
Trembla; Napoléon comprit qu'il expiait
Quelque chose peut-être, et livide, inquiet,
Devant ses légions sur la neige semées:
— Est-ce le châtiment, dit-il, Dieu des armées? —
Alors il s'entendit appeler par son nom,
Et quelqu'un qui parlait dans l'ombre lui dit: ' Non.'

(*Les Châtiments*)

The romantic element of a popular, democratic devotion to great political and military personalities is highlighted in this aspect of the Napoleon cult. It comes to the fore particularly in the faithfulness of the
French people when Napoleon had to wage a defensive war in 1814.
Meissonier (1815–91) understood something of this when he painted
*The Campaign of France 1814.*[16] Napoleon is now dependent on the good
will of his people, who are surrounded and cornered with him in the open
country by the armies of the Holy Alliance. Nevertheless, the lion in his
den is isolated. Napoleon, riding his white horse, is pondering, lonely. The
officers of his staff follow him like a dark, dumb mass, foreboding disaster;
his army marches in silence, trodding heavily on the cold snow.

The poet Pierre-Jean de Béranger (1780–1857) dramatizes this feeling
in his poem 'Le Souvenir du peuple' (1821). As a poet, he chooses a
more lyrical angle of the situation. In this song *grand'mère* reports to her
astonished grandchildren the different instances in her life when she saw
Napoleon, triumphant until his year of disasters, when he knocked at her
very own door to ask for something to eat, being always *en campagne.*
Béranger uses the technique of details developing successively in time; the
little dialogue-refrain by which the children echo their grandmother's admiration is particularly powerful:

— Mais quand la pauvre Champagne
Fut en proie aux étrangers,
Lui, bravant tous les dangers,
Semblait seul tenir la campagne.
Un soir, tout comme aujourd'hui,
J'entends frapper à la porte;
J'ouvre. Bon Dieu! c'était lui,
Suivi d'une faible escorte.
Il s'assoit où me voilà,
S'écriant: Oh, quelle guerre!
Oh quelle guerre! —

— Il s'est assis là, grand'mère!
　　Il s'est assis là! —
— J'ai faim, dit-il; et bien vite
　　Je sers piquette et pain bis;
　　Puis il sèche ses habits;
　　Même à dormir le feu l'invite.
　　Au réveil, voyant mes pleurs,
　　Il me dit: Bonne espérance!
　　Je cours de tous ses malheurs
　　Sous Paris, venger la France.
　　Il part; et, comme un trésor,
　　J'ai depuis gardé son verre,
　　　　Gardé son verre. —
— Vous l'avez encor, grand'mère,
　　Vous l'avez encor! [17]

The full extent of the Napoleonic legend is reached when the Emperor is no longer represented as a person but as a symbol of military glory and of heroic France herself. This is the case in the painting *Officer of the Imperial Guard* (see Fig. 66) by Théodore Géricault (1791–1824). In-

66. Géricault, *Officer of the Imperial Guard*, Louvre. (Archives Photographiques)

stead of a description of this gigantic neighing and prancing horse and
the hussar in splendid battle array, the precise comment on the painting
is that made by Victor Hugo, who, son of a Napoleonic general, betrays
the same feelings as those expressed by Géricault:

> Mon envie admirait le hussard rapide,
> Parant de gerbes d'or sa poitrine intrépide,
> Et le panache blanc des aigles des lanciers,
> Et les dragons, mêlant sur leur casque gépide
> Le poil taché du tigre aux cris noirs de coursiers.
>
> . . .
>
> J'entendais le son clair des tremblantes cymbales,
> Le roulement des chars, le sifflement des balles;
> Et de morceaux de morts semant leurs pas sanglants
> Je voyais se heurter au loin, par intervalles,
> Les escadrons étincelants.
>
> (Odes et Ballades, ' Mon Enfance ')

Napoleon is even represented as military Glory riding a symbolic horse —
La France. This idea is treated by Auguste Barbier. He actually visualizes
Napoleon as the booted horseman who subdues, breaks in, and tames the
Horse in battles as though for training. Thus Barbier, though criticizing
Bonaparte, pays tribute to his military genius, as does the picture of
Géricault:

> O Corse! . . . que ta France était belle
>      Au grand soleil de messidor;
> C'était une cavale, indomptable et rebelle
>      Sans freins d'acier ni rênes d'or;
>
> . . .
>
> Tu parus, et sitôt que tu vis son allure,
>      Ses reins si souples et si dispos,
> Centaure impétueux, tu pris sa chevelure,
>      Tu montas botté sur son dos.
> Alors, comme elle aimait les rumeurs de la guerre,
>      La poudre, les tambours battants,
> Pour champ de course, alors, tu lui donnas la terre
>      Et des combats pour passe-temps. . .
>
> (L'Idole)

It is rather certain that Barbier's outspoken idea is hidden in the gesture
of Géricault's mounted officer.

From this point of view, the Homeric epithets and metonymies of Cha
teaubriand do not seem so ridiculous and the style troubadour, when applied to the military-glory complex of the Empire, makes sense. Géricault's,
Hugo's, and Barbier's cavalrymen are actually ' Centauri clad in green
whose helmets are crowned by a golden dragon '; their artillerymen are
' cyclopes,' handling ' the fire of death '; and their infantrymen, with their
rifles and bayonets, are carrying ' a flaming tube surmounted by a sword

of Bayonne.' [18] And so, as symbolic, mythical beings, these soldiers are going to die with the Emperor's last glory in the Battle of Waterloo, described in Hugo's *Les Misérables*, in Stendhal's *La Chartreuse de Parme*, in Thackeray's *Vanity Fair*, in the historical novel *Waterloo* by Erckmann-Chatrian (1865), and praised as 'La garde qui meurt, mais ne se rend pas' in 'Expiation' by Victor Hugo:

> Leur bouche, d'un seul cri, dit: Vive l'empereur!
> Puis, à pas lents, musique en tête, sans fureur,
> Tranquille, souriant à la mitraille anglaise,
> La garde impériale entra dans la fournaise.

There are other parallels that can be investigated — for example, in the lithographs of Raffet and in Balzac's *Le Médecin de campagne, La Femme de trente ans, Colonel Chabert*, and so on.

## VI. Local Color as the Expression of Sensation

From a poetic point of view the progress of the picturesque following the progress of romanticism in France is not a fortunate development; for, from being a new expression of lyricism it degenerates into a simple means of arousing sensations. Those who condemn realism and naturalism for their cruelty and sensuality should put the blame on the earlier evolution of local color and *fait divers*. The romantic painters leave no doubt in mind that they want their paintings to be a feast for the senses, a carnival of colors for the eyes, a vying between movement and grouping of figures in a historical setting.

If the movement toward the use of radical local color for sensational reasons has a concrete starting point in painting, it certainly is *The Raft of the Medusa* (1818) (see Fig. 67) by Théodore Géricault. Here are brutality, horror, sadism, couched in delightful colors and splendid effects of

67. Géricault, *The Raft of the Medusa*, Louvre. (Foto Marburg)

light. The *fait divers* told by Géricault is the following: The ship *La Méduse* had been shipwrecked in 1817 in the Mediterranean. Some of the passengers were fortunate enough to climb on a raft, which drifted for twelve days on the sea. The salvaged ones suffered terribly from exposure, cold, fear, weakness, thirst, and hunger. Murder and cannibalism were related later. Those who died, died painfully. Two eyewitnesses, the physician Savigny and the sailor Corréard, reported these facts. They reported further, and this is Géricault's subject, that on the twelfth day the people on the raft sighted a ship, *L'Argus*, which finally came to the rescue of the survivors of the *Méduse*. When the *Argus* is spotted, the weak, sick, dying, and dead are left alone, spread over the back of the raft, falling into the sea, and drifting on the water. The more vigorous ones, full of new hope, make a desperate attempt to signal the *Argus* of their dangerous situation. Some of the people seem in an ecstasy of hope. In picturesque rags they are grouped around the empty water barrel. They form an elegant pyramid, with the wounded officer sitting at the mast and with the highest-placed men waving pieces of white cloth.

The romantic writers of historical novels, viewing things in a manner similar to that of the painters, aimed at this type of captivating *tableau*. The gypsy dancer at the stake in Hugo's *Notre Dame de Paris* and the trial of the 'possessed' nuns of Loudun in de Vigny's *Cinq Mars* are of the same sensational cast. The language — technical and crude, insisting on colors, on details of body and costume, using the most irritating but motley similes to convey a mood — enhances the sensation intended. An example from *Notre Dame de Paris* is the terrible but picturesque scene of Quasimodo tortured and whipped at the pillory:

> They thrust him on to his knees on the wheel, they stripped him to the waist; he made no resistance. They bound him down with a fresh arrangement of cords and leathern thongs; he let them bind and strap him. Only from time to time he breathed heavily, like a calf whose head swings and bumps over the edge of a butcher's cart. . .
>
> There was a great burst of laughter from the crowd when, stripped naked to their view, they caught sight of Quasimodo's hump, his camel's breast, his brawny, hairy shoulders. During the merriment, a man in the livery of the Town, short of stature and of burly make, ascended to the platform and stationed himself beside the culprit. . .
>
> He . . . divested himself of his party-colored doublet, and dangling from his right hand there appeared a scourge with long, slender, white thongs — shining, knotted, interlaced — and armed with metal claws. With his left hand he carelessly drew the shirt-sleeve up his right arm as high as the shoulder. . .
>
> The torturer now stamped his foot; the wheel began to move. Quasimodo swayed under his bonds, and the amazement suddenly depicted on that misshapen countenance gave a fresh impulse to the peals of laughter round about.

Suddenly, at the moment when the wheel in its rotation presented to Master Pierrat Quasimodo's enormous back, the torturer raised his arm, the thongs hissed shrilly through the air, like a handful of vipers, and fell with fury on the shoulders of the hapless wretch.

Quasimodo recoiled as if suddenly startled out of sleep. Now he began to understand. He writhed in his bonds, the muscles of his face contracted violently in surprise and pain, but not a sound escaped him. He only rolled his head from side to side, like a bull stung in the flank by a gadfly.

A second stroke followed the first, then a third, and another, and another. . . Soon the blood began to flow; it trickled in a thousand streams over the dark shoulders of the hunchback, and the keen thongs, as they swung around in the air, scattered it in showers over the multitude.[19]

It is evident from *The Raft of the Medusa* and the description of the flogging of Quasimodo that sensational *faits divers* have become the working material of the romantic artists, painters as well as writers, not only for local color, evocational power, and visionary presentation, but also for their effects on the onlooker and reader but unfortunately do not produce a catharsis.

It remains to be seen how these artists must nevertheless follow the intrinsic laws of Lessing's *Laocoön*, each artist in his own field. For this purpose two from among the many common topics and mutual imitations may be chosen: *Mazeppa* and *The Massacres of Scio*.

Mazeppa (1644–1709) was a Polish gentleman who sided with Charles XII of Sweden against Peter the Great. The Russians punished him by binding him, naked, on a wild horse. The horse ran with its living charge to his native Ukraine, where the animal broke down and died. Peasants, however, detached the exhausted Mazeppa, still alive, and made him their hetman. In 1819 Lord Byron told the story poetically. The painters Horace Vernet and Louis Boulanger followed him. Finally, Géricault and Victor Hugo approached the subject. The *Mazeppa*[20] of Géricault depicts a picturesque moment from the mad gallopade of the horse. A better choice than Boulanger's initial fettering or Vernet's harassing by wolves, Géricault's selection is the instant that horse and unwilling rider have just crossed a river and the horse is climbing up the banks. The poet can include all these moments and more in some few lines and finish the story with the horse's death and its becoming a prey of the carrion vultures:

> Enfin, après trois jours d'une course insensée,
> Après avoir franchi fleuves à l'eau glacée,
> > Steppes, forêts, déserts,
> Le cheval tombe aux cris de mille oiseaux de proie.
> > (*Les Orientales*, ' Mazeppa ')

Nevertheless the comparison of Hugo's with the painter's presentation of Mazeppa as a full-fledged epic story is not ideal. Painter and poet are in their proper domains only if the painter conveys the mood of a scene by

68. Delacroix, *Les Massacres de Scio*, Louvre. (Foto Marburg)

stressing the lyrical details and the poet leaves the detailed description to
the imagination, but works out the mood by suggesting the lyricism
evolving from a situation. Ideal examples of this problem are *Les Massacres de Scio* (1824) (see Fig. 68) by Eugène Delacroix and ' L'Enfant
grec' (1829) by Victor Hugo. Delacroix paints with all his Oriental colors
the raging of some Turkish soldiers among the population of the island of
Chios. He stresses the cavalryman at the right who drags behind his horse
the fettered and vainly resisting women; he stresses an exhausted, crying
mother who is dying beside her babe; he underscores the terrified grandmother who is as motionless as a statue because her grief transcends the
faculty of weeping. To the left a married couple in affliction and despair
find a last consolation in their mutual love before the Turkish soldiers
come to separate them.

Victor Hugo does not show this scene; he supposes it known to the
civilized world. He intimates instead that after the Turks have extermi-
nated the Greeks of Chios, the island has become a desert. But a forgotten and abandoned boy wanders among the ruins, with one single thought
in his young head — revenge. And Hugo puts his lyrical re-evocation into
the following form:

Les Turcs ont passé là; tout est ruine et deuil.
Chio, l'île des vins n'est plus qu'un sombre écueil . . .
Tout est désert: mais non, seul près des murs noircis,
Un enfant aux yeux bleus, un enfant grec, assis
    Courbait sa tête humiliée . . .
Ah! pauvre enfant, pieds nus sur les rocs anguleux,
Hélas! pour essuyer les pleurs de tes yeux bleus . . .
' Que veux-tu? bel enfant, que te faut-il donner . . .
Veux-tu, pour me sourire, un bel oiseau des bois,
Qui chante avec un chant plus doux que les hautbois,
    Plus éclatant que les cymbales?
Que veux-tu? fleur, beau fruit, ou l'oiseau merveilleux? '
— ' Ami, dit l'enfant grec, dit l'enfant aux yeux bleus,
    Je veux de la poudre et des balles.'
                    (*Les Orientales*, ' L'enfant grec ')

Orientalism with all its local color reverts to the mysteries, sensuous rather than psychological, of the woman of the East and the South who is kept under a constant, vigilant watching, and who is thought to be interesting and full of unknown passions. The local color surrounding her brings the most passionate note into the painting and literature devoted to her. With their overtones of sun, lethargy, jealousy, and flesh, Ingres's *Odalisque* and *Bain turc*, Victor Hugo's ' Sara la Baigneuse' and Alfred de Vigny's ' Le Bain' exhale a perfume of curiosity and sin, *une pâture à l'imagination* (Courthion). Delacroix's ' hunt' for the Algerian woman may be compared to Mérimée's ' hunt' for the Spanish gypsy.

Delacroix, more seriously than Musset and almost anticipating Baudelaire and Flaubert, discovered the Oriental woman during his trip to North Africa and fixed the atmosphere surrounding her in *Femmes d'Alger dans leur appartement* (1834).[21] Three women sitting on Oriental rugs, served by a Negro girl and made dull by hashish and opium, are like quiet animals. Delacroix has done it so well that Baudelaire found in this quasiharem ' an I-do-not-know-what strong perfume of a place of bad reputation which leads rather abruptly to the inexplored limbo of sadness.' [22] These women are also capable of poison and destruction, as expressed by Alfred de Musset when he has Don Juan in ' Namouna ' (strophes 46–52) review his quest for the unknown woman:

Quelle est donc, disent-ils, cette femme inconnue
Qu'il appelait toujours et qui n'est pas venue?
Où l'avait-il trouvée? où l'avait-il perdue? . . .
Tu n'as jamais médit de ce monde stupide . . .
Et la vierge aux yeux bleus sur la souple ottomane
Dans ses bras parfumés te berçait mollement . . .
Tu retrouvais partout la vérité hideuse . . .
Partout l'hydre éternel qui te montrait les dents.
                    (*Premières Poésies*)

The ' Oriental' woman as presented by Mérimée is reflected in the description of Carmen by her lover-to-be, who finally kills her. She, too, has something poisonously fascinating about her, with a flower pinned on her blouse, another in her mouth, with holes in her stockings, a short red skirt, red strings to fasten her shoes, a provoking gait, a mantilla slipping from her shoulders, her hands on her hips and making the glad eye:

> Elle répondait à chacun, faisant les yeux en coulisse, le poing sur la hanche, effrontée comme une vraie bohémienne qu'elle était. D'abord elle ne me plut pas, et je repris mon ouvrage; mais elle, suivant l'usage des femmes et des chats qui ne viennent pas quand on les appelle et qui viennent quand on ne les appelle pas, s'arrêta devant moi et m'adressa la parole.[23]

It can be easily understood that romantic local color is the decisive element that is to drive romanticism into realism — the art of crude and sensual individual details without any attempt at abstraction or symbolization. Nevertheless, experiments in symbolism were made during the period of romanticism.

## VII. Errors and Assets of Symbolism [24]

In the competition between painter and poet during the romantic period, as far as symbolic presentation is concerned, the poet, being symbolic by definition, should in theory be superior to the painter, who is supposed to be a realistic imitator of nature. In practice, however, owing to the exceptional cases of genius, the roles may appear changed. The painter Pierre Prud'hon, whose *Psyché* has been discussed, cannot compete with the poet Victor Hugo, but Honoré Victorin Daumier (1808–79) can very well compete with Honoré de Balzac (1799–1850).

In 1804, at the request of the prefect of the department of Seine, Pierre Prud'hon painted for the Palais de Justice in Paris a symbolic picture: *La Justice et la vengeance divine poursuivant le crime* (1808) (see Fig. 69). Prud'hon made things very simple for himself. He presented Crime as a criminal who is just leaving his assassinated victim. But at once he is persecuted by Justice in the form of two avenging angels, one of whom is characterized by the torch, the other by the sword and the balance. It may be evident that these Angels of Justice fill the criminal with dismay and terror, but it is doubtful whether a symbolism simply personifying Crime as a criminal and Punishment as avenging angels is artistically a fit one, and whether the gigantic angels covering the picture like dark clouds are well-chosen details. Prud'hon mixes two different styles for painting Justice and Vengeance. He expresses this idea by two humanized angels with allegorical attributes, and by their dark garments, which fill the role of fear-inspiring clouds.

Victor Hugo, in his *Légende des siècles,* has symbolized Crime pursued by Divine Justice in a dramatized story of Cain, called ' La Conscience,' expanding the text of Genesis iv. 13–24, which begins:

> And Cain said unto the Lord, My punishment is greater than I can bear.
> Behold, thou hast driven me out this day from the face of the earth; and from thy face shall I be hid; and I shall be a fugitive and a vagabond in the earth . . .

Victor Hugo's symbolism has proved to be a great achievement. The Eye of God is the leitmotif, piercing all of Cain's hideouts and accusing him relentlessly for having killed his brother.

> Echevelé, livide, au milieu des tempêtes
> Caïn se fut enfui de devant Jéhovah.

This is the uncanny setting: a hunted man is shown against a landscape beaten by a hurricane; night is approaching; Cain tries to sleep but the Eye of God looks down upon him from the firmament and his remorse takes all sleep away:

> Ayant levé la tête, au fond des cieux funèbres
> Il vit un œil tout grand ouvert dans les ténèbres
> Et qui le regardait dans l'ombre fixement.

Cain flees again. Thirty days and thirty nights he wanders with his entire family. Now he is far away from God's accusing Eye and, exhausted, he sits down to rest, but

> . . . comme il s'asseyait, il vit dans les cieux mornes
> L'œil à la même place au fond de l'horizon.
> Alors il tressaillit en proie au noir frisson.

69. Prud'hon, *La Justice et la vengeance divine poursuivant le crime,* Louvre. (Archives Photographiques)

Desperate, Cain accepts the advice to retire to a fortress above whose entrance is written, as an expression of this despair, 'Défense à Dieu d'entrer.' But what happens?

> On mit l'aïeul au centre en une tour de pierre.
> Et lui restait lugubre et hagard. — O mon père!
> L'œil a-t-il disparu? dit en tremblant Tsilla.
> Et Caïn répondit: — Non, il est toujours là.
> Alors il dit: Je veux habiter sous la terre
> Comme dans son sépulcre un homme solitaire;
> Rien ne me verra plus, je ne verrai plus rien. —
> On fit donc une fosse, et Caïn dit: C'est bien!
> Puis il descendit seul sous cette voûte sombre.
> Quand il se fut assis sur sa chaise dans l'ombre
> Et qu'on eut sur son front fermé le souterrain,
> L'œil était dans la tombe et regardait Caïn.

Hugo's clever solution of a symbolic Crime pursued by Divine Justice is exclusively poetic, the effectiveness of which consists in the geometric gradation of the conscience motif from moderato to fortissimo, strongly dependent on successive scenes in progression. Therefore, it is out of the question that a painter like Fernand Cormont (1845–1924) or a designer like Chifflart could possibly translate Hugo's poem into the language of the arts of design. By painting an eye looking down from a dark sky upon a Cain hiding his face with his hand, they almost make Hugo's grandiose idea grotesque, if not ridiculous.[25]

In contrast to Prud'hon, Honoré Daumier solved the problems of symbolism by graphic means that are genuinely artistic. His La République (1848) [26] presents France as a gigantic, fertile mother with twins at her breast — her natural and spiritual forces. She is a superhuman mother defending her children, energetically grasping the flag, a symbol of protection, over the boy on the left, touching the one on the right with another protective gesture. This is, of course, for Daumier a free France, a republican France, La République, a generous Mother. Her contours are effaced, the style is simplified. It is the formal expression of a symbol in which the borderline between the thing itself and its deeper meaning is hazy.

This is exactly the wavering manner in which Hugo represents God's Eye as Conscience. But Hugo also represents, as far as the subject matter is concerned, the great forces helpful to mankind as superhuman suckling mothers:

> Ces mères aux triples mammelles
> La Nature et la Charité.[27]

He represents Old Egypt, invaded by Cambyses, as a mourning mother protecting the pyramids, her outraged children, under the folds of her robe of desert sands:

Comme une mère sombre, et qui, dans sa fierté
Cache sous son manteau son enfant souffleté,
L'Egypte, au bord du Nil assise
Dans sa robe de sable, enfouie, enveloppés
Les colosses camards, à la face frappés
Par le pied brutal de Cambyse . . .

Daumier's power of symbolic creation finds its best testing ground in his illustrations of Cervantes' *Don Quixote*, as, for example, *Don Quixote and Sancho Panza* (see Fig. 70). Here the *caballero de la triste figura* has become a symbol of the gallantry that attacks, with superhuman folly, not only windmills but whatever can be in the slightest way detrimental to weak orphans, innocent virgins, the rights of widows, the peace of the poor. Superhuman protection on the march; this is what Daumier realizes in his dynamic, symbolic caricature, brought to a climax by its contrast to the despair of the timid Sancho. Illimited and unconsidered courage is counterbalanced by cowardice, embodied in the short, heavy figure of Sancho, swooning from fear on his donkey. Jacques Lassaigne writes:

> Daumier has tackled without hesitation the greatest myth of all modern literature, Don Quijote . . . He found it up to his stature. Thus there was born that sublime reincarnation, the only one, I believe, which is not literary, that is, literature in art. ' Coming from the background of the horizon,' writes Elie Faure, ' [Don Quijote and Sancho] are so great when they come nearer, that we retire.' Daumier, who did not know Spain, has evoked her with a superhuman and super-real reality, a reality which makes his heroes live in the aridity and the mystical detachment which make this land itself seem to be a creation of the spirit.[28]

Daumier, although a painter, has even outdone Hugo in symbolism, anticipating Baudelaire by the simplicity of his means of expression. Hugo had also tried to render the symbolism of the radical and unswerving fight for right and justice in his older Don Quijote, called Eviradnus. As is evi-

70. Daumier, *Don Quixote and Sancho Panza*. (Foto Marburg)

71. Daumier, *The Uprising*. (Courtesy of the Phillips Gallery, Washington, D.C.)

dent from the decisive lines dedicated to him, his manner is quixotic, line four even hinting at Cervantes' text:

> Il est toujours en marche, attendu qu'on moleste
> Bien des infortunés sous la voûte céleste,
> Et qu'on voit la nuit bien des mains le supplier.
> Sa lance n'aime pas moisir au râtelier.
> Sa hache de bataille aisément se décroche:
> Malheur à l'action mauvaise qui s'approche.
>
> (*La Légende des siècles*)

Daumier's superiority in modern symbolism consists in avoiding the great, elaborate gesture and in pointing up the universal implications in observed occurrences in life. His representatives of everyday life cannot hide the deeper meaning of that for which they work. Daumier's washer-women mean hard labor; his revolutionaries mean *the* revolution; his leader of a group in upheaval means *The Uprising* (see Fig. 71). Henri Focillon describes the picture as follows:

> In a Parisian street, the high houses of which are sketched in the back-ground with their sad and lurid appearance, a man in shirtsleeves is rush-ing ahead followed by a group of insurgents. He utters a slogan or a song repeated by the crowd. His opened lips prolong its outcry. His lifted arm underscores its rhythm and its dash. . . His long head, his fine features imprinted with a nobility of the people, and his flowing hair designate the type of the aristocratic artisan. His eyes are open, but do not see. The glance is turned inward. The rioter is possessed by a dream to which he lures the crowd. A magnetic attraction draws the figures in the mob; to the right a man with a face as though it were cut out by a bill-hook, a long and sharp nose, the head bent down, a peasant face of Paris with thin lips and a stubborn eye; to the left a townsman with hollow cheeks, on his

head a silk hat rounded by long wear; and close to him, two profiles which seem to converge somehow towards the man in shirtsleeves, the chief, the magnetic center. All the generous passions of an epoch are there together with the eternal insurgent, the nomad of the spirit haunted by the future, the anonymous fighter of nameless battles.[29]

The literary parallel that Focillon chooses from Balzac as being symbolic, namely the description of the Pension Vauquer in *Le Père Goriot*, is not entirely convincing. It is true that Daumier and Balzac both try to apply romantic symbolism to situations occurring in their own time, causing them to be erroneously called ' realists.' Balzac by literary means can evoke with a particularly visionary force almost the same picture of an exalted young man as Daumier's *l'émeutier*. It is the portrait of the writer Daniel d'Arthez in *Les Illusions perdues*:

> Petit, maigre et pâle, ce travailleur cachait un beau front sous une épaisse chevelure noire assez mal tenue, il avait de belles mains, il attirait le regard des indifférents par une vague ressemblance avec le portrait de Bonaparte gravé d'après Robert Lefèvre . . . Les yeux ont de l'esprit, comme des yeux de femme. Le coup d'œil est de l'espace et désireux des difficultés à vaincre. . . Simple en ses gestes, il avait une contenance grave.[30]

To create a literary type that is really symbolic, Balzac makes such a tremendous effort that he jeopardizes the symbol to a greater extent than Daumier does by drawing it as a caricature. One of the best examples of this technique of the ' Daumier of literature ' is the exaggeration of the old miser Grandet in *Eugénie Grandet*. To make sure that he is the new Shylock and the new *Avare*, Grandet is presented as a man who, in spite of his immense wealth, is concerned with choosing cheap and durable clothing, which he uses as sparingly as possible.

> Ses forts souliers se nouaient avec des cordons de cuir; il portait en tout temps des bas de laine drapée . . . un gilet de velours à raies alternativement jaunes et puces . . . et un chapeau quaker. Ses gants, aussi solides que ceux des gendarmes, lui duraient vingt mois, et, pour les conserver propres, il les posait sur le bord de son chapeau à la même place, par un geste méthodique.[31]

But Balzac does more. He shows Grandet also as a miser in his household and describes this trait by means of a dialogue between the thrifty employer and his housekeeper Nanon. They fight over whether or not to grant a piece of sugar to Grandet's visiting nephew:

> With his keys in his hand, the old man had come to measure out the provisions necessary for the day's consumption.
> ' Is there any bread left from yesterday? ' he asked Nanon.
> ' Not a crumb, sir.'

Grandet took a large round loaf, well sprinkled with flour, moulded in one of those flat pans which are used in Anjou for baking bread, and was on the point of cutting it, when Nanon said to him, ' There are five of us today, sir.'

' Very true,' replied Grandet; ' but the loaf weighs six pounds, and there will be some left. Besides you'll find that these young Paris fellows don't eat bread.'

' They eat *frippe*, then,' said Nanon.

In Anjou, *frippe*, a word of the popular vocabulary, expresses any accompaniment of bread, from butter spread upon a slice, which is common *frippe*, to peach marmalade, which is the most celebrated of *frippes*. Every one who in the days of his childhood has licked off the *frippe* and left the bread will comprehend the meaning of this expression.

' No,' replied Grandet; ' they eat neither *frippe* nor bread. They are something like girls who want to get married.'

After having given out, with great parsimony, the supply of food for the day, Grandet was about to procede towards his fruit-room, not, however, until he had shut the doors of his larder, when Nanon stopped him with these words: ' If you will give me some flour and butter, I will make a cake for the young people.'

' Do you want to pillage my house because my nephew is here? '

' I thought no more of your nephew than I did of your dog — not more than you think of him yourself. You have only given me six pieces of sugar, and I want eight.'

' Come, Nanon, I have never seen you like this before. What idea have you got into your head now? Are you mistress here? You shall have no more than six pieces of sugar.'

' Very well; but what will your nephew sweeten his coffee with? '

' With two pieces; I will go without.'

' You go without, at your time of life! I would sooner buy you some out of my own pocket.'

' Mind your own business.' [32]

Finally Balzac presents the miser making his daughter, in the presence of a notary, renounce her maternal inheritance during her father's lifetime. Grandet, furthermore, from time to time assembles all his gold just to gaze at it and finally dies in a ' gold intoxication,' kissing blasphemously the golden crucifix offered to him by the priest who administers the last Sacraments. Greed for gold is also symbolized by the painter Thomas Couture in his *L'Amour de l'or*, shown in the salon of 1843.

The *rapprochement* between the symbolism of Daumier and that of Balzac, accordingly, seems more to the point in cases in which Daumier's symbolism takes the form of caricature. It is, indeed, this particular caricatural symbolism that made both of them collaborate on the comic paper *Charivari*. The objects of their common hatred are ' les gens de la robe,' the barristers and judges, attorneys and *procureurs*. Among Daumier's many caricatures of the advocate, there is a particularly impressive one: *L'Avocat triomphant*.[33] This lawyer, in an arrogant attitude of splendid isolation, is descending the steps of the Palais de Justice after having won a case — subjectively, a half-god; objectively, a scoundrel. The pride of this lawyer certainly is that of a scoundrel. It symbolizes all the bad tricks he has played hitherto. Daumier himself has described a whole series of these tricks in the captions to his caricatures of French justice in *Charivari*. For example,

> The jovial fellow decidedly seems to be a great criminal; all the better, if I am successful in getting him acquitted, what an honor for me! [34]

Balzac's greatest scoundrel, Vautrin, having become a *procureur*, is highly interested in appearing as a sacred and feared personality to the populace. In order to keep the mask of an ancient Roman pontifex, he would give up all the flattery of social life. His words make him the worthy competitor of Daumier's lawyer:

> Oh! the true magistrates . . . look! They ought to live separated from any society, as did the pontifs in earlier times. The world would see them only when they leave their cells at fixed hours in a grave and venerable attitude, passing judgment in the way the high priests in the ancient societies did who united in themselves the judiciary and the priestly power. People are accustomed to see us in the drawing rooms and thus we may appear grotesque instead of appearing dreadful.[35]

Even here the higher quality of art is certainly Daumier's. Balzac himself knows that, for he makes the famous statement about Daumier: ' This fellow here has something of Michelangelo under his skin.' Balzac does not know the particular technique of the art of the ellipsis, the art of not saying everything, which is Daumier's very secret, and as important for the writer as it is for the painter.

A final aspect of romantic symbolism is that of elucidation by the poets of hidden symbolism in painting. Doubtless *The Sower* (see Fig. 72) by Millet (1814–75) has a symbolic meaning. *Le semeur* is not an individual sower; he may be the sower in the famous parable of the Gospel. Nonetheless the interpretation of writers who were Millet's contemporaries is more reliable and more expressive than a subjective, modern interpretation. Théophile Gautier deepens the symbolism of the picture considerably by his description of it:

> La nuit va venir, déployant ses voiles gris sur la terre brune, le semeur marche d'un pas rhythmé jetant le grain au sillon . . . de sombres haillons le couvrent; sa tête est coiffée d'une sorte de bonnet bizarre. . . Il y a du grandiose et du style dans cette figure au geste violent, à la tournure fièrement délabrée et qui semble peinte avec la terre qu'il ensemence.[36]

In other words, Gautier, critic and poet, has seen many symbolic traits in the picture. The sower seems timeless because he ignores the approaching darkness; he himself belongs to the rhythm of time and space; he belongs to a world superior to everyday trifles, where there is no style, no mode, as seen from his bizarre cap; he is violent in his gestures, because

72. Millet, *The Sower*. (Courtesy of the Museum of Fine Arts, Boston)

violent must be the fight with the earth; he is rooted in the soil, and therefore is painted in brown. In spite of this excellent observation, Gautier does not exhaust the symbolism and the climate of Millet's picture. Victor Hugo's apocalyptic approach penetrates still more profoundly. The sower is an old man, so he belongs to the evening that surrounds him. The sowing symbolizes the provisions the passing generation is making for the coming one, on the immense plane of the clan and even of mankind. This peasant is a conscious link in the chain of being. He throws the seed far, and his gesture, too, appears immense in the twilight between day and night, life and death, seeming to reach up to the stars. This makes him appear really a sower *sub specie aeternitatis*. Hugo calls his poem, which is supposed to be a meditation on Millet's painting *Saison de semailles*, ' Le Soir.' Some believe it is older than Millet's picture.

> C'est le moment crépusculaire
> J'admire, assis sous un portail,
> Ce reste de jour dont s'éclaire
> La dernière heure du travail.

Dans les terres, de nuit baignées,
Je contemple, ému, les haillons
D'un vieillard qui jette à poignées
La moisson future aux sillons.

Sa haute silhouette noire
Domine les profonds labours.
On sent à quel point il doit croire
A la fuite utile des jours.

Il marche dans la plaine immense,
Va, vient, lance la graine au loin,
Rouvre sa main et recommence,
Et je médite, obscur témoin,

Pendant que, déployant ses voiles,
L'ombre où se mêle une rumeur,
Semble élargir jusqu'aux étoiles
Le geste auguste du semeur.

There are also striking parallels between Millet's *The Reapers* (see Fig. 73) and *L'Angélus* [37] and Hugo's ' Booz Endormi ' and Lamartine's ' L'Angélus.' Whoever has commented on Millet's gleaners has underscored their symbolic character. Paul de Saint Victor calls them ' les trois Parques du paupérisme,' and according to Julien Cain: ' Millet evokes Homer and Vergil with the grayish ground where the straw [*chaume*] is still lying, the straw which the family has cut, with the three women gleaners bent and tired, and in the background the farm people load the wagons.' [38] Victor Hugo has projected the eternal story of the poor gleaner who gleans after others have harvested into the Biblical atmosphere of Ruth and Boaz, as, incidentally, Millet too had originally planned. In ' Booz endormi ' Hugo praises the wealthy landowner who purposely leaves something for the poor:

73. Millet, *The Reapers*, Louvre. (Archives Photographiques)

[La gerbe de Booz] n'était point avare ni haineuse;
Quand il voyait passer quelque pauvre glaneuse:
'Laissez tomber exprès des épis!' disait-il.

*(La Légende des siècles)*

For Hugo it is imperative to maintain this Biblical atmosphere in order to preserve the symbolism; Millet can rely on the eternal gesture of the reapers for this function.

In regard to the *Angelus*, the naturalist Joris-Karl Huysmans dislikes the painting because it is symbolic: 'These peasants are as conventional, as fictitious as the "Petites Fadettes" and the "Champis" invented by that old spinner of the ideal called George Sand.' [39] The restrospective criticism of Huysmans is, however, as illuminating as Lamartine's parallel, in which the outspoken statement that symbolism is implied leaves no doubt of the interpretation. 'Les Laboureurs' of his *Jocelyn* breathes the same spirit, at once timeless and realistic, 'although it is more "idealized" than "real"': [40]

C'est l'Angélus qui tinte et rappelle *en tout lieu*
Que le matin des jours et le soir sont à Dieu.
A ce pieux appel le laboureur s'arrête,
Il se tourne au clocher, il découvre sa tête,
Joint ses robustes mains d'où tombe l'aiguillon,
Elève un peu son âme au-dessus du sillon.

(9e épisode)

## VIII. The Family Idyl

There is, however, a mirage in French romantic symbolism: birth, marriage, death, and the implications of family life, couple, parents, child, all possess a symbolism that is obvious. It is at hand for everybody and, when handled poetically, may provide under certain circumstances an idyl but not a new insight into life or nature, as comes from a true symbol. Realism begins at this point, as may be seen in two other works by Millet: *Feeding Her Birds* [41] and *The First Step* [42] (see Fig. 74). Concerning the first subject, the meaning for the romantics is explained by Julien Cain, who draws attention to the little girls' resemblance to birds protected by their mother. The father also, by intimation, belongs to the sympathetic grouping of mother and children. He is the man in the background who tills the soil for the mother and children.

All these elements are also in Lamartine's *Jocelyn*. Twenty years earlier Lamartine had chosen the scene of the lunch hour of a couple working in the fields, the baby in the cradle beside them:

> Le repos achevé, la mère, du berceau
> Qui repose couché dans un sillon nouveau,
> Tire un bel enfant nu qui tend ses mains vers elle,
> L'enlève et, suspendu, l'emporte à sa mamelle,
> L'endort en le berçant du sein sur ses genoux,
> Et s'endort elle-même, un bras sur son époux.

On the other hand, Millet's picture *Le Premier Pas* evokes the poem by Victor Hugo:

> L'enfant charmant . . .
> Riait, et par ses mains sous les bras soutenu
> Joyeux. . .
> Il grandit. Pour l'enfant, grandir, c'est chanceler.
> Il se mit à marcher, il se mit à parler.
> ('Le Revenant' in *Les Contemplations*)

Or, in a more sentimental way:

> Lorsque l'enfant paraît, le cercle de famille
> Applaudit à grands cris. Son doux regard qui brille
> Fait briller tous les yeux,
> Et les plus tristes fronts, les plus souillés peut-être
> Se dérident soudain à voir l'enfant paraître,
> Innocent et joyeux.
> ('L'Enfant' in *Feuilles d'automne*)

With these idyls romanticism becomes realism in literature too, the symbol being so weak that it disappears. A new genre in painting and literature begins, not without danger to the artistic principles themselves. As Charles Clément points out:

> Genre painting could be defined as painting in which, entirely or partly, the great qualities of art are lacking, namely importance and dignity of the subject, strength, nobility of the composition . . . But it compensates for its inferiority by the truth of the details, the cleverness of the workman-

74. Millet, *The First Step*. (Courtesy of the Museum of Fine Arts, Boston)

ship, the charm of color. A painter of this kind astonishes, interests, and seduces people. He sells his paintings at very high prices because they correspond to mediocre taste and to the average preoccupations of the crowd.[43]

## IX. Religiosity without Religion

As the great writers of the classical seventeenth century turned to the symbols of antiquity to fill them with a deep Christian sentiment, so the romantics of the nineteenth century turn to the great Christian symbols to fill them with modern doubt, sentimentalism, despair, political propaganda, and beauty for beauty's sake. This trend begins even with Prud'hon's *The Crucifixion* (1822) (see Fig. 75), which, when its details are explained with some pertinent texts, is bound to reveal its true meaning. There is, first, Christ himself, far from the romanesque Rex, far from the Gothic *Ecce Homo*, but close to the beardless youth with the beautifully modeled body of the Renaissance, without any wounds or lacerations. This Christ is indeed a romanticized 'young athlete,' conforming to Alfred de Vigny's anti-Christian, Dionysian concept of Him:

> Un soir, il arriva que l'antique planète
> Secoua sa poussière. — Il se fit un grand cri:
> 'Le Sauveur est venu, voici le jeune athlète . . .
> (*Les Destinées*)

The Blessed Virgin is not standing under the Cross but has collapsed, her suffering and her pain immense. She is suffused with the somber light from the darkened sky, which symbolizes the pain of nature. There is the modern sentiment of abysmal sadness, as in Lamartine's 'Mother in tears and Nature in mourning' expressed in one of the strophes of 'Le Crucifix':

> De la croix où ton œil sonda ce grand mystère,
> Tu vis ta mère en pleurs et la nature en deuil,
> Tu laissas comme nous tes amis sur la terre
> Et ton corps au cercueil!

A very young Madeleine (already Renan's Madeleine) embraces the Cross lovingly, but does she ardently believe in the Crucified One? Or do her stylish short sleeves *à la mode* betray rather that she is an *enfant du siècle*, perhaps the least believing one in a century without faith, who prays:

> O Christ! Je ne suis pas de ceux que la prière
> Dans tes temples muets amène à pas tremblants;
> Je ne suis pas de ceux qui vont à ton Calvaire
> En se frappant le cœur, baiser tes pieds sanglants! . . .
> Eh bien! qu'il soit permis d'en baiser la poussière
> Au moins crédule enfant de ce siècle sans foi,
> Et de pleurer, ô Christ! sur cette froide terre
> Qui vivait de ta mort, et qui mourra sans toi!
> (Musset, 'Rolla')

Prud'hon, like Vigny, Lamartine, and Musset, conceives of a Christ who is still Christian because he is ' of an extremely attractive sweetness, tenderness and molding.' [44] Therefore to make Prud'hon and Lamartine the heralds of Renan besides the internal analysis, still another proof is required. It may be found in the diary of Delacroix. After having painted in 1826 *La Mort de Sardanapale*, an orgy, he began a mural in the church of Saint Paul and Saint Louis called *Le Christ au jardin des oliviers*. The subject, writes Delacroix, did not appeal to him at all. But he became interested in it as soon as he conceived of Christ's agony simply as despair in spite of the consoling angels, who in his picture are two ' angels of death, sad, austere, who cast melancholically their eyes on Him.' [45] The unbeliever Delacroix practically discloses that he is painting the same Gethsemane that Alfred de Vigny sketched in his ' Le Mont des Oliviers '; ' Un Christ désespéré dans les ombres de la nuit,' in the midst of a black cloud, threatening monsters, and black angels of death:

> Le fils de l'Homme alors remonte lentement;
> Comme un pasteur d'Egypte, il cherche au firmament
> Si l'Ange ne luit pas au fond de quelque étoile.
> Mais un nuage en deuil s'étend comme le voile

75. Prud'hon, *The Crucifixion*, Louvre. (Archives Photographiques)

76. Bouguereau, *The Madonna of Consolation*, Ancien Musée de Luxembourg.
(Archives Photographiques)

> D'une veuve, et ses plis entourent le désert.
> Jésus, se rappelant ce qu'il avait souffert
> Depuis trente-trois ans, devint homme, et la crainte
> Serra son cœur mortel d'une invincible étreinte.
> Il eut froid. Vainement il appela trois fois:
> ' Mon Père! ' Le vent seul répondit à sa voix.
> Il tomba sur le sable assis, et, dans sa peine,
> Eut sur le monde et l'homme une pensée humaine.
> — Et la terre trembla, sentant la pesanteur
> Du Sauveur qui tombait aux pieds du Créateur.

The theatrical Madonnas of William Adolphe Bouguereau (1825–1905),
for example *The Madonna of Consolation* (see Fig. 76), are living statues
with the Guido Reni upward look and the traditional sacred gestures. A
mother, half-statue, whose child lies dead on the pedestal of the *Mater
afflictionis*, has thrown herself over the lap of the enthroned Madonna. It
brings to mind the story retold by the contemporary poet Théophile
Gautier, according to which the Blessed Virgin loved so very much one of
her medieval portraits painted at Toledo that she came down from Heaven
to embrace herself in the picture. Caustically Gautier asks if she would
do the same today:

Si la Vierge, à Paris, avec son auréole
Sur les autels païens de notre âge frivole
Descendait et venait visiter son portrait,
Croyez-vous, ô sculpteur, qu'elle s'embrasserait?
(' La Vierge de Tolède ')

Furthermore, in *Les Beaux-Arts en Europe* Gautier described Bouguereau's type of Madonna as ' a beautiful young woman who might be considered the Blessed Virgin.' René Ménard, in view of Bouguereau's imitation of the Italians and his modern lack of religious sentiment, commented:

> In his picture *The Virgin of Consolation* in the Luxembourg Museum, he addresses in particular afflicted mothers and makes the dead child the kernel of his composition. Bouguereau has given the Great Consolatrix a quite personal note of such a modern kind that the onlooker feels closer to the *Méditations* of Lamartine than to the Holy Families of the Renaissance.[46]

As far as religious feelings are concerned, incidentally, the *Méditations* are also rather cheap.

When Ary Scheffer (1795–1858) paints *The Temptation of Christ*,[47] he is simply practicing, as one of his critics remarks, a technique: ' He attaches a great importance to attitudes, gestures and effects of foreshortening. He is not able to touch the emotions because he is no longer sincere.' [48]

The Satan of the romantics, of course, is a gentle lie minimizing the sinful and the hideous. Therefore Satan does not appear disgusting but as a tolerable Mephistopheles, a ' fallen angel who remembers Heaven,' a kind of Eloa (Vigny), a Satan who, finally graced, will leave Hell, as did Victor Hugo's hero in *La Fin de Satan*, a poem whose lines are like an involuntary parody of Ary Scheffer's picture:

Ils ont mis l'astre avec la fange en équilibre,
Et du côté hideux leur balance a penché.
Quoi, d'une part le ciel, de l'autre le péché;
Ici l'amour, la paix, le pardon, la prière,
La foudre évanouie et dissoute en lumière,
Les malades guéris, les morts ressuscités;
Là, le tueur sous qui l'épouvante se creuse,
Tous les vices, le vol, l'ombre, une âme lépreuse.
(' Ténèbres ')

Finally, art and literature, using Christian topics, seem interested only in aesthetic problems. ' The important thing was,' says M. Gautier, ' to make manifestations in aesthetic intransigencies, not in a noble candor of piety.' [49] All these romanticists must confess, with Alfred de Vigny:

J'adorais sans amour, priais sans espérance;
J'entrais au tabernacle avec indifférence.[50]

In creating a historical relativism and turning religion into *l'art pour l'art,* the artists turn to imitating older masters and techniques in subjects of piety. Delacroix, in a baroque Tiepolo setting, copies old Venetian concepts in *Jesus and the Disciples of Emmaus,*[51] just as Eugène Dévéria (1805–65) and Jean Jacques Henner (1829–1905) paint groups of martyrs simply as light-and-shade studies in the Caravaggio style.

When literature, lacking proper religious feeling, undertakes such a historic revival, it can at least surround its aesthetic delight in earlier naïve piety with an empathic, ironic halo to make it tolerable, as did José Maria de Hérédia in describing his ' Gothic ' Holy Family:

> Le bon maître huchier, pour finir un dressoir,
> Courbé sur l'établi depuis l'aurore, ahane,
> Maniant tour à tour le rabot, le bédane
> Et la râpe grinçante ou le dur polissoir.
>
> Aussi, non sans plaisir, a-t-il vu, vers le soir
> S'allonger jusqu'au seuil l'ombre du grand platane
> Où madame la Vierge et sa mère Sainte Anne
> Et Monseigneur Jésus près lui vont s'asseoir.
>
> L'air est brûlant et pas une feuille ne bouge;
> Et saint Joseph, très las, a laissé choir la gouge
> En s'essuyant le front au coin du tablier;
>
> Mais l'Apprenti divin qu'une gloire enveloppe
> Fait toujours, dans le fond obscur de l'atelier,
> Voler les copeaux d'or au fil de sa varlope.[52]

## Impressionism and Surrealism

### 1860–1940

I N THE period following romanticism, art influences literature to such
an extent that the writers neglect psychological and philosophical implications; they forget the wisdom of the Laocoön, come to believe
again the Horatian mirage, *Ut pictura poesis*, and thus follow as closely as
possible the principles of the art of painting. With impressionism (1860–
1910) this situation becomes more acute, because the painters discover new
technical means of representing the visual. Then with a curious reverse
movement the painters make a desperate attempt to express *états d'âmes*,
an exclusively literary task. The results are such things as absurd renditions
of ugly dreams, or concepts and ideas in geometric forms.

With both painters and writers, the problems of form become so important that it would be preposterous to veil them by stressing only the
underlying sociological and revolutionary problems: the new sentiments
of pantheism, unanimism, the spirit of soil and *terroir*, the liberties and
perversions of love, the questions of capital and labor, war and peace,
fascism and communism. The varying aspects of these art forms have decisive values in themselves, apart from the fact that they give expression to
all these previously listed topics and their implications. These subjects,
interpreted through the new art forms, are of interest only from one
point of view, their validity for art. Aside from this initial decision, the
problem resolves itself into the following points of discussion: the triumph
of description over narration; the new spiritual climate of the great cities;
intoxication with life, water, sun, rhythm; enthusiasm for movement, dancing, horse races; the problem of line in contrast to color, ornament rather
than topic; abstract art and pure poetry; the obsession with the psychological and its expression.

## I. Triumph of Description over Narration

After 1850 art turns to a new concept of life, which, even before the
technical consequences are fully realized, can be called impressionism.

77. Courbet, *Funeral at Ornans*, Louvre. (Archives Photographiques)

Clearly, poetry and art are not to be lavished on historic or exotic subjects or on philosophical problems. The interest is in contemporary, everyday life, presented not in a plot or a story but in a fleeting moment, whatever it may be — an event, an impression. Therefore from a philosophical point of view any form of modern realism may be called impressionism. If poetry and art are to consist of snapshots of life, then a philosophy that concentrates on the sensibility of the moment without any symbolic or metaphysical implication is involved. Ashamed of this surface sensibility, the ideological impressionist feigns to be impassive, simply to be true, sincere, to give *tranches de vie*.

All this is implied in the revolutionary effect produced by *Funeral at Ornans* (see Fig. 77) by Gustave Courbet (1819–77). This is the burial of a peasant of Ornans, no more. The 'transitory moment,' postulated by Lessing in his *Laocoön* as the hallmark of a painter's choice, is paramount here. It is the burial at its close. The women in their white coifs are already leaving; only a few of the closer relatives stand at the open grave, weeping and meditating. The priest in his black cope is surrounded by the altar boys in their white and red vestments. One of the pallbearers holds the cloth that had covered the coffin. It is white with black crosses, bones, and tears. One peasant in shirtsleeves kneels down after having lowered the coffin. The *marguilliers* in old-fashioned, picturesque garb, some male mourners, the sexton in a white surplice holding the cross, and an onlooker with a white dog surround the grave in an excellent composition of colors and forms. This grouping comes not only from a casual snapshot of a burial but also from Courbet's study of the technique of the old masters. The realist and the worshipper of *l'art pour l'art* coincide from the very beginning. François Fosca can therefore write about this picture:

> This burial of an obscure peasant has an incomparable majesty and grandeur. Although the picture has the enigmatic beauty of a coat-of-arms and the vague and defaced naïveté of a chromo, it calls to mind the high-

est and most abstract works of art, the frescoes of Giotto and Piero della Francesca. There is nothing that tries to arouse our emotion or to touch our heart. The artist had only one thing in mind: to be true.[1]

The Courbet of literature is Gustave Flaubert. He describes in the same uncompromising way the burial of Madame Bovary (1857). He has the writer's advantage of being able to show the funeral in movement, its arrival at the cemetery and occurrences during the burial. But he stresses to such an extent the same details that it is difficult to believe that Flaubert worked without having Courbet's picture in mind. Flaubert thus describes the priests, singers, altar boys, the women in black mourning veils, the black coffin cloth sewn with white tears (conversely to the one in the picture), the turf and the prepared grave, and a man, Charles Bovary, kneeling at the grave. He describes additional details to those shown in the painting: the recitation of the Psalm *De profundis*, the smell of the candles, the pallbearers' weariness, the soft shoulder of the sand dripping slowly into the grave while the priest is talking, the three shovelfuls of sand thrown by the mourners upon the coffin and the uncanny sound arising from it, as though it came from eternity.

> People were at their windows watching the *cortège* pass. . . The priest, the choirmen, and the two acolytes recited the *De Profundis*. . . The women followed, draped in black mantles with the hoods lowered. They carried large lit candles. The endless prayers, the lights, the stale smell of wax and soutanes made Charles [the widower] feel faint. . .
>
> The black pall, sewn with white tears, occasionally billowed up and revealed the bier. The tired bearers slackened their pace. . .
>
> They arrived.
>
> The men went on to the far end, to a spot on the turf where the grave had been dug.
>
> They took up their positions round it. While the priest droned on, the red earth, piled along the edge, kept trickling from the corners in a noiseless cascade.
>
> The four ropes were adjusted, the coffin placed in position. He [Charles] watched them lower it. Down it went, down.
>
> At last there was the sound of a thud. The ropes grated as they were pulled up again. Bournisien [the priest] took the spade which Lestiboudois [the gravedigger] passed to him with his left hand. Still sprinkling holy water with his right, he gave a vigorous push to a large shovelful of earth. The wood of the coffin gave out, beneath the shower of stones, that terrible noise which strikes on the listening ear like the hollow echo of eternity.
>
> The priest handed the sprinkler to the man beside him, who happened to be Monsieur Homais [the pharmacist]. The latter gave it a solemn shake and passed it on to Charles, who sank to his knees in the loose earth and threw great handfuls into the grave, crying — ' Farewell! ' [2]

Flaubert's *tableau* has something else different from Courbet's picture. It is the harmonious insertion of the description into the whole of the

78. Corot, *Woman Gathering Fagots*. (Courtesy of the Metropolitan Museum of Art)

novel. Everything is therefore concentrated around Charles Bovary, the betrayed husband, whose awkwardness reveals his stupid innocence even after the death of his adulterous wife.

The link between the concept and the later technique of impressionism is a new sentiment of nature, which discovers the atmospheric haziness in landscapes, the particular climate of morning and evening, spring and autumn. In painting, this movement was started by such pictures as *Woman Gathering Fagots* (see Fig. 78) by Jean Baptiste Camille Corot (1796–1875). Here an effort is made to characterize the mistiness of a spring landscape in the morning with a particular light on foliage and trees. It is difficult to account for the captivating effect of such a landscape, called photographic by those critics who believe only in a creative art with everything transformed. A sensitive critic like the late Charles Du Bos apparently understood the essence of Corot's new type of landscape:

> Corot is so much inside whatever he reproduces that . . . nowhere else is there more emotion and tenderness than in the correct, pure, and flexible line of his trees, rendered so exactly and so precisely that it appears impersonal; but it is precisely in this kind of impersonality that emotion and tenderness stream like a natural sap. . . The lines of Corot make you see the undulation and movement of the earth.[3]

Attempts in literature to capture the atmospheric aspects of landscapes had appeared already in single instances in the works of Honoré de Balzac. In *Les Chouans* he speaks of the pearly color of water on which the moon is shining and of the impressive silence of a landscape covered with snow. In *Le Curé de campagne* he observes the thrilling impression that comes from the echo of a distant noise carried over the surface of a quiet lake. Flaubert, however, is capable of giving a consistent picture, and not merely fragments, of an early impressionistic landscape. Like Corot, he tries to catch, but by literary means, the atmospheric colors of a spring evening.

> It was at the beginning of April, when the primroses are in bloom. . . Through the lattice of the arbour, and all around beyond it, she could see the river meandering slow and carefree through the meadow grasses. The mist of evening was drifting between the leafless poplars, blurring their outline with a violent haze, paler and more transparent than a fine gauze hung upon their branches. Cattle were moving in the distance, but the ear could catch neither the noise of their hooves nor the sound of their lowing. The bell, continuously ringing, struck upon the air with its note of peaceful lamentation.
>
> (*Madame Bovary*, part ii, ch. vi)

Although the works of Flaubert reveal something of impressionism, the general principles of its technique for the arts of design can be best derived from programmatic manifestations, such as the *Lever du soleil, une impression* (1874) by Claude Monet and *Art poétique* (1885) by Paul Verlaine. Impressionism in painting means, in general: primacy of landscape, not story; subjective, unconscious transformation, but by no means conscious changes, of a subject *vu à travers un tempérament*; *plein air*; concentration on the nuances of light, not on form; large brush strokes and new colors for shading; suppression of single features; color perspective in horizontal parallels, indicating the shades of air changing with distance; and no perspective of design.

Impressionism in literature, coinciding to a certain extent with symbolism, means: primacy of atmosphere, *musique* rather than topic; unconscious transfiguration, not studies of eloquence ('Take rhetoric and break its neck'); impressions of *plein air* ('The great trembling light of noon'), that is, refined response to nature; concentration on the nuance ('The nuance only links dream to dream'), that is, suggestive art; effacing of contours ('The gray song in which the vague is joined to the precise'), that is, no logically constructed sentences; shading ('No color, nothing but shade'), that is, metaphors rather than similes; suppression of single, discursive elements ('Cruel wit and impure laughter'); perspective by vague expressions ('The odd, more vague and dissolvable in the air without anything ponderable'), generally effected by the nominal style without clarifying verbs.

Verlaine's own lines are the best interpretation of literature through art:

> Rien de plus cher que la chanson grise
> Où l'Indécis au Précis se joint.
>
> C'est des beaux yeux derrière des voiles,
> C'est le grand jour tremblant de midi,
> C'est par un ciel d'automne attiédi
> Le bleu fouillis des claires étoiles!
>
> . . .
>
> Que ton vers soit la bonne aventure
> Éparse au vent crispé du matin
> Qui va fleurant la menthe et le thym . . .
> Et tout le reste est littérature.[4]

The enthusiasm for the *indécis* is one of the elements that called forth the modern seascapes, generally combined with skyscapes. A pioneer in this line, without even using the strictly impressionistic technique, is again Courbet with his painting *The Wave* (see Fig. 79). The two little boats are the only objects that are *précis* in the picture. Take them away, as actually suggested by some critics, and there remain water and clouds. Bluish tones make the air seem somewhat heavy; the foam on the crests of the wave and at the bottom of the breakers conveys the notion of agitated waters. To describe such a seascape in a condensed form, for instance in a single sentence, has been attempted several times by nineteenth-century authors. Guy de Maupassant offers the following sketch:

> L'onde soulevée, souple et blanche d'écume, s'arrondissait et retombait, comme retombe, brune et lourde, la terre labourée des champs.

The writer who labored at length on such problems is Pierre Loti. He can do more than describe the waves. He evokes with striking details the pale, monotonous North sea in the dim daylight around the ship of the *Pêcheurs d'Islande* (1886). He even gives tactile and olfactory details — moist freshness, penetrating air, taste of salt — which a painter could never render:

> Autour d'eux, tout de suite, commençait un vide immense qui n'était d'aucune couleur, et, en dehors des planches de leur navire, tout semblait diaphane, impalpable, chimérique.
>
> L'œil saisissait à peine ce qui devait être la mer: d'abord cela prenait l'aspect d'une sorte de miroir tremblant qui n'aurait aucune image à refléter; en se prolongeant, cela paraissait devenir une plaine de vapeur et puis plus rien; cela n'avait ni horizons ni contours.
>
> La fraîcheur humide de l'air était plus intense, plus pénétrante que du vrai froid, et, en respirant, on sentait très fort le goût de sel. Tout était calme et il ne pleuvait plus; en haut, des nuages informes et incolores semblaient contenir cette lumière latente qui ne s'expliquait pas; on voyait clair, en ayant cependant conscience de la nuit, et toutes ces pâleurs des choses n'étaient d'aucune nuance pouvant être nommée.[5]

As the impressionists develop their general technique, they are able to enhance the mood of even a snapshot of modern life. In the contourless mass of hulks and sails in Edouard Manet's *Port of Bordeaux* [6] there is no rest, although a restful harbor with idle boats is represented. No technique can express better than the impressionistic one the latent restlessness of the hustling, bustling modern world, even though it appear serene. There is a whole forest of masts, which the onlooker's eye is not able to affix to their individual ships. The towers of the cathedral of Bordeaux in the background might be trees or clouds of smoke. The horizontal strokes that distinguish the small waves from the embankment give the water an oily aspect, whose smoothness makes the turmoil of the many sails to the left seem the more agitated.

Precisely the same mood is found in descriptions of harbors by contemporary authors. Daudet has a whole book on *Port Tarascon*, and in *Tartarin de Tarascon* he sketches the port of Marseilles in the following manner: ' C'était à perte de vue un fouillis de mâts, de vergues se croisant dans tous les sens.'

Maupassant in *Pierre et Jean* describes, with the ' wood of masts' and with the sea like an immense blue cloth, exactly the same contrasts of turmoil and rest, or entanglement and smoothness, as does Manet: ' Tous les mâts des navires donnaient l'aspect d'un grand bois mort. . . La mer plate [était] tendue comme une étoffe bleue immense luisante.'

Baudelaire has best grasped the ultimate meaning of the restlessness of idle ships in a harbor — it is the desire to travel to unknown shores (' Invitation au voyage') :

> Vois sur ces canaux
> Dormir ces vaisseaux
> Dont l'humeur est vagabonde.
> *(Fleurs du Mal)*

79. Courbet, *The Wave*, Louvre. (Foto Marburg)

80. Signac, *Entrée du port de Marseilles*, Musée d'Art Moderne, Paris.
(Archives Photographiques)

But when he continues:

> Les soleils couchants
> Revêtent les champs,
> Les canaux, la ville entière
> D'hyacinthe et d'or;
> Le monde s'endort
> Dans une chaude lumière,

the splendor of *hyacinthe et d'or* cannot be found in Manet's harbor. This splendor, however, emanates from the shimmering *Entrée du port de Marseilles* (see Fig. 80) by Paul Signac (1863–1935). It is a dream in colors of sun-saturated water and land, warm and heavy, but the pointillist technique excludes any repose, although the square sail in the center, white and sunny, enforces a sham rest on the onlooker.

The particular sensitivity of Signac's marine can be understood from Proust's interpretation of Elstir's marines. Proust sees them with the same hypersensitive approach as does the painter, and so he can write that they are metaphors in so far as the water and the ships in the foreground were expressed in more solid, ' urban ' terms, while the solid town in the background was expressed in evanescent, maritime terms, the whole being ' poudroiement de soleil et de vagues,' and even ' les églises . . . semblaient sortir des eaux, soufflées en albâtre ou en écume et, enfermées dans la ceinture d'un arc-en-ciel versi-colore, former un tableau irréel et mystique.' [7]

## II. The Climate of the City Captured by Impressionism

Refinement of details in the technique of impressionism proves to be an excellent means of grasping the atmosphere of cities as something new and typical of modern life. Since technique is primarily responsible for this artistic rendition, style will be considered first and subject matter second.

Though the so-called impressionism in literature is older than that in painting, its forms can be better explained by the forms of the later art. As previously discussed, these painters aim to give a fresh, total impression of a fragment of the outside world as seen at a certain moment, in a certain light, through a certain temperament. Their purpose is served by broad brush strokes or smaller dots of color, pointillism, and by a simplification of the details. A parallel impressionism is rendered in literature by means of the qualifying adjective, designating, for instance, a color: in *l'arbre vert* the adjective may be taken from its logical place in the phrase, *le vert arbre*; or it may be neutralized and substantivized, *le vert de l'arbre*, or even replaced by a substantive, *la verdure de l'arbre*. The word artist blurs the picture by giving the color green such a preponderance that the quality and not the form of the thing at issue is stressed. Abstract substantives of quality replacing adjectives, and anticipated or substantivized adjectives are the principal means of description in Emile Zola's *Le Ventre de Paris*:

> On ne voyait encore, dans la *clarté brusque et tournante* des lanternes, que l'*épanouissement charnu* d'un paquet d'artichauts, les *verts délicats* des salades, le *corail rose des* carottes, l'*ivoire mat* des navets; et ces *éclairs* de couleur intense filaient le long des tas avec les lanternes.

Furthermore, if the verb is omitted, or is relegated to a clause, or is reduced to an auxiliary, with the nouns dominating the sentence, there is another close analogy: color spots without verbal harmonization. Zola's description in *L'Assommoir* of the formation of a funeral has been called by Eugen Lerch typical of impressionistic style:

> De courts silences [nominal spot] se faisaient [pale verb], coupés de chuchotements [noun] rapides, une attente [noun] agacée et fiévreuse avec des courses [noun] brusques de robes, Mme Lorilleux qui avait oublié [verb in relative clause] son mouchoir ou bien Mme Lerat qui cherchait un paroisien à emprunter. . . Il y avait [auxiliary] un bruit prolongé de sanglots.

An effacing of contours is effected in literature by the hazy *style indirect libre*, a tricky presentation of half-direct, half-indirect speech, in which the author uses the vocabulary and locutions of his characters. As a result, the reader sometimes is at a loss to decide who is talking, the author or the character, so strong is the author's empathy, though in this empathy there is a sovereign, ironic criticism of habits in life and speech.

This method can be used moderately, as when Flaubert writes:

> Madame Bovary . . . déclarait adorer les enfants; c'était sa consolation, sa joie, sa folie, et elle accompagnait ses caresses d'expansions lyriques.

81. Renoir, *Les Grands Boulevards au printemps*, Munich. (Die Piperdrucke)

Or it may be used in an exaggerated way (pointillism), as when Zola himself uses the language of the lowest people to describe Coupeau's reaction
to the First Communion of Nana. It is as though Coupeau were reporting:

> At church, Coupeau wept all the time. It was stupid, but he could not
> help it. It affected him to see the priest holding out his arms, and all the
> little girls, looking like angels, pass before him clasping their hands; and
> the music of the organ stirred up his stomach, and the pleasant smell of
> the incense forced him to sniff, the same as though someone had thrust a
> bouquet of flowers into his face. . . There was a canticle especially, some-
> thing extra sweet, sung whilst the children were taking the communion,
> which seemed to run with a shiver down his neck and backbone.[8]

An impressionistic painting like *Les Grands Boulevards au printemps*
(1875) (see Fig. 81) by Auguste Renoir (1844–1919) shows how such a
style is extremely well-fitted to depict that atmosphere which created the
great French realistic novels. There is no previously arranged mixture of
colors on the palette, as there is no previously arranged, logical construc-
tion of the sentence; the colors on the canvas are to be mixed by the eye
of the spectator, as in analogous literary works the overstressed nouns and
strong epithets preceding the verb must be toned down and the pale verbs
intensified by the reader's judgment. As in the painting there is a color
perspective rather than a linear one, so in the nominal sentence depth
comes from the blocks of nouns and not from verbal subordination. As
the tones of light reappear in the shades and no particular color clings to
any particular object, so in the *style indirect libre* the action expressed
hovers always between the narrator and the person whom the narrator
causes to speak. The airy, half-indirect report cannot be localized; the language of the character appears as ' color shade ' in the language of the author. The exquisite finish in the technique of the impressionist painters

thus points to an explanation of all the refined implications in French realistic style, which, as reflected light, even have symbolic meaning, although not seen at first glance and only recently discovered in a style that was considered to be coarse and naturalistic.[9]

The subject matter of Renoir's picture conveys all the thrill of a Parisian boulevard on a spring day at a time when carriages were the normal means of transportation and people walked along the sidewalks *pour la promenade*. The spring atmosphere is wonderfully realized through the simple colors *rose-citron* for the light and purple-blue for the shade. And the light itself invades the shade. The objects are chosen according to their natural capacity for reflecting light: the lush green of the trees, the white horse, the bright suits and dresses of the people, the yellow soil, the clear color of the blinds and façades of the apartment houses. Added to this are the reddish-brown touches as shown on the waistcoat of the coachman and the rose-trimmed gown of the lady in the foreground.

What Renoir has painted is indeed the atmosphere that envelops a carriage driving down a boulevard, and he has done it in the only possible style for creating ' climate,' by the technique of impressionism. Twenty years earlier exactly the same topic with a similar climate expressed by literary impressionism was described by Gustave Flaubert in his revolutionary and allegedly objectionable scene of Emma and Léon driving in adulterous love in a carriage through the boulevards, quais, and streets of Rouen. Flaubert's impressionist innovations consist in showing only the driver and the carriage, the streets and the people, and then the white hand of Madame Bovary reaching out the window to scatter the pieces of the letter of refusal she had written Léon — a symbol of her succumbing to the adulterous love.

> The cab passed through the city gates, and once on the public promenade, trotted gently between the rows of great elms. The driver mopped his forehead, put his leather hat between his legs, and, cutting across the sidewalk, took a course along the river, skirting the turf.
>
> The cab . . . rumbled past the gardens of the Alms-Houses, where old men in black coats were sunning themselves, and along a terrace green with ivy. . .
>
> From time to time the driver cast despairing glances from his box at the taverns he was passing. It was beyond his comprehension what frenzy of locomotion forbade his fares to stop. . .
>
> Down at the harbour, in a hurly-burly of wagons and casks, along the streets, at various milestones, the citizens stared wide-eyed at that most extraordinary of all sights in a provincial town — a carriage with drawn blinds . . .
>
> Once, about mid-day, out in the open country, with the sun striking full on the plated lamps, a bare hand emerged from behind the little curtains of yellow canvas, and scattered some scraps of paper which eddied in the wind and settled afar off, like so many white butterflies, on a field of red flowering clover.

82. Monet, *Cathedral of Rouen*. National Gallery of Art, Washington, D.C.
(Chester Dale Collection — Loan)

The examples of Renoir and Flaubert coincide in their tendency to suggest the *indécis*; in this lies the realization of their principles of art. In Flaubert it is even the principle of decency, although his first critics interpreted it conversely.

Another method of seizing the climate of a modern city is to view its silhouette or some of its representative buildings in rain or mist, sunshine or darkness, and thus to evoke, so to speak, its ghost and soul instead of its body, since there are no details, but only vague *états d'âme*. The whole spirit of London, the town of fog and mist, is in *Houses of Parliament*,[10] a vague silhouette coalescing with the air and water of the Thames, by Claude Monet (1840–1926). In his novel *Bruges la morte*, Georges Rodenbach has done practically the same thing, couching the love story between a widower and an actress in the particular atmosphere of a town of continual drizzles and fogs, and consequently preparing, from the beginning, the tragic ending of a pseudo-idyl.

Another parallel can be found in Monet's attempt to catch the atmosphere of the *Cathedral of Rouen* (see Fig. 82) at different times of the day and in Zola's experiment in his novel *Une Page d'amour* of using Paris as a leitmotif, seen from the same window at different moments of the day. Monet's cathedral is so different in the morning and in the afternoon light that one picture has been called a blue-sugar icing and the other a rose-sugar icing.

Consideration of Zola's 'icing' procedure in literature calls for a slight introduction into the story itself. A young widow, Hélène, indirectly kills her own little daughter Jeanne, who becomes jealous when her mother falls in love with the physician Dr. Déberle. At the end of the first part of the story, mother and child are still in full harmony. It is in the morning that both, from their window, gaze on an awakening Paris, which seems to reflect their happiness. At the end of the second part, clouds are hovering; jealousy is rising. The light of the happiness of the mother and child, now looking at Paris in the evening, is becoming more dim. By the end of the third part, Dr. Déberle has blacked out the happiness of the child, who, sitting at her window, glares at Paris at night. At the end of the fourth part, it is even raining and Jeanne, sitting alone at the open window, can scarcely discern Paris behind the mist; she falls asleep and catches a cold from which she eventually dies. The fifth part closes with Hélène and Dr. Déberle two years later looking at Paris as they stand beside Jeanne's grave. 'Le cimetière était vide, il n'y avait que leurs pas sur la neige. Jeanne restait seule en face de Paris, à jamais.'

## III. Intoxication with Life

Impressionism means preoccupation with life, water, sun, rhythm, sometimes underscored by the subject, sometimes by the technique. The life depicted in the works of these impressionist painters and writers is that of artists, littérateurs, critics, actors, actresses, painters, models, cabaret singers — the whole Parisian Bohème. The preferred settings are outdoor scenes, with interest also in the theaters and concerts, music halls and circuses. Renoir and Manet, Flaubert and Maupassant delight in portraying excursions to the Bois de Boulogne or to the *banlieue* alongside the Seine for a picnic *au bord de la route*, or *pour manger de la friture*. A good example of this subject is *Luncheon of the Boating Party* (1881) (see Fig. 83) by Auguste Renoir. The boating party has reached Bougival on the Seine. They have just had luncheon with plenty of French claret. Now they are talking on the terrace of the Restaurant Fournaise. At the left sits Mlle Charigat, later Mme Renoir; at the right is the critic Charles Caillebotte. The man with the top hat in the background is Renoir himself. The picture has been called a poem of the simple pleasures of life. The portraits of his friends and these sculptured groups in splendid colors seemed more important to the artist here than the new manner of painting. Nevertheless, there is a beautiful central tone in the yellowish red of the sunlight coming through the arbor.

83. Renoir, *Luncheon of the Boating Party.* (Courtesy of the Phillips Gallery, Washington, D.C.)

Flaubert, too, is more interested in the spirit of such a *canotage sur la Seine* than in the impressionistic technique; as a writer he can fill in the details around Renoir's ' transitory moment,' the actual picnic, by including the departure and the return. Furthermore, Flaubert hints at other elements beyond the transitory moment, such as details of nature newly discovered by these couples in a glow of love:

> When evening came they took a boat with an awning and went out to one of the islands for dinner.
> It was the hour of the day when from every shipyard came the sound of caulking hammers working on the hulls. The smoke of burning pitch drifted up between the trees, and the surface of the river showed patches of oil heaving unevenly in the red light of the setting sun, like floating plates of Florentine bronze.
> They went downstream through a medley of moored vessels, whose long, slanting cables grazed the top of their little craft.
> Gradually the sounds of the town grew fainter, the rumbling of carts, the hubbub of voices, the barking of dogs on the decks of ships. . . They landed on their island, and sat in the low-ceiled public room of a tavern, which had black nets hanging round its door. . . It was not the first time that they had seen trees, blue sky, and green turf, or heard the lapping of water and the moaning of the breeze through the leaves, but it is doubtful whether they had ever before known the wonder of these things. It was as though nature had never before existed, or had taken on its full beauty only now that their desires were gratified.
> At night they went back.
>
> *Madame Bovary* (Part III, ch. III)

The technique is overdone in the elaboration of similar themes of life, water, and sun by Georges Seurat (1860–91), who painted in 1883 *La Baignade*,[11] showing some boys and men bathing in the Seine, the water almost vibrating with the sunbeams. Again he tries to get as much sun as possible into his neo-impressionist and pointillistic picture of a Sunday afternoon on *La Grande Jatte* (1886) (see Fig. 84), a small island near Neuilly. Seurat does consciously what the classical impressionists did unconsciously.[12] He reconstructs their impressions, after interminable preparations, by the logical use of a technique of producing light effects. He, too, follows the law of complementary colors and of dividing the compound colors into their elements on the canvas. But he uses small square dots or points instead of broad strokes and puts them carefully on the picture. He thus renders even the vibration of the air that can readily be seen on hot summer afternoons. His dots produce, above everything else, this vibration. The whole landscape and scene appear in an overwhelming clarity because of the extremely clean and bright touches. This was readily seen earlier in the painting *Port de Marseilles,* by a pupil of Seurat, Signac. Seurat inserts little red and yellow squares even in the shades, which contain nothing darker than blue and green. The whole picture has something of a careful architectural design.

This exaggerated and contrived pointillism in art corresponds to the *écriture artiste* of the Goncourt Brothers in literature. The *Grande Jatte* may therefore be compared to the description of the excursion of the painters to Trouville in *Manette Salomon* (1867); there is the same feigned impressionism. The Goncourts even use techniques of modern art to interpret the refinements of nature and to evoke a painted spring:

> A large perspective of shade like an India-ink drawing upon an underpart of blood color, a zone of fiery reds and tarry blacks, burned by those russet tones of frost and those warm winter colors found on the watercolor palette of the British. . .
>
> The air streaked with water had a washing of that purple blue by which painting imitates the transparence of solid glass. The first lively smile of green was beginning to show on the black branches of the trees, where

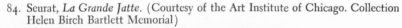

84. Seurat, *La Grande Jatte.* (Courtesy of the Art Institute of Chicago. Collection Helen Birch Bartlett Memorial)

one could almost see, like brush strokes, the touches of spring sowing a light haze of green ashes.[13]

The capturing of sunlight upon an object is of paramount importance in expressing the modern sentiment of life with its interest in open-air sports and the exposure of the body to water and sun. Whatever may be the objections to Seurat and Signac from the point of view of the impressionists themselves, they are the first painters who have the power of transfiguring, transforming, and changing life into something that is later called magic realism.

Paul Signac's *Le Pin de Bertrand*[14] is a kind of a mosaic made out of pigments that contain almost no green at all, as one should expect for a tree, but an intoxication of yellow, blue, and purple. This fairytale of light colors is a symphony and a harmony reflected against the sky from which the colors are supposed to come. The virtuosity in arranging colors evoked by a vague impression and then remembered in tranquillity reminds one spontaneously of the technique of Marcel Proust in literature. So far as delicacy of colors is concerned, other authors also tried to convey to their readers such shades as *bleu canard, bleu Nil, bleu cendre, jaune citron, jaune soufre, jaune de jonquille, rouge groseille, rose des Indes, couleur de verveine, brique, cerise, tabac d'Espagne*. But Proust has specific literary means for transforming his natural trees into something fanciful. His secret consists of dipping a scene visualized in nature into all the sentimental and historical reminiscences of life, art, experience, and civilization, thus in a magic manner transforming the first impression into something new and strange. He transfigures *temps perdu* into *temps retrouvé*. His procedure becomes evident in his famous description of the pink hawthorn among the white ones. The rosy blossoms remind him first of the ' tufts forming a wreath around the crook of a rococo shepherdess,' such as he had seen in pictures; then of the biscuits in a store in Combray, where the rosy biscuits were more expensive than the white ones; then of a particular cream cheese with which he was allowed as a child to mix his strawberries. He goes on to a higher series of impressions — the exquisite pink dresses of young girls, the altar laces on high feast days, the color of precious marble cups, and finally the flowers and girls around the statue of the Virgin during May. The transformation is now complete:

> Taking its place in the hedge, but as different from the rest as a young girl in holiday attire among a crowd of dowdy women in everyday clothes, who are staying at home, equipped and ready for the ' Month of Mary,' of which it seemed already to form a part, it shone and smiled in its cool, rosy garments, a Catholic bush indeed, and altogether delightful.[15]

Proust not only accounts for his personal reminiscences, which transform the shrub and the flower into a mythical, ' catholic' hawthorn in a land of memory and dream. He also appeals to the psychology of the reader and asks him by innuendo whether, after pale sketches of trees and bushes, this image is not the ideal of his dreams; whether he does not feel at its discovery as though his preferred painter has produced something surprising, unusual, unheard of; whether, finally, this is not like a painting of something that previously was only a drawing, or a piano piece suddenly performed by an orchestra.[16] So Proust's hawthorn study expresses the same jubilation felt on confronting for the first time Signac's sun-bathed, sun-scintillating tree.

There are other passages in *Du Côté de chez Swann* where, on such a tree as Signac's, the reflections of the light from the evening sun are grasped in the painter's way:

> La lumière du soleil, presque horizontale . . . dans le crépuscule com-
> mençant . . . s'allume comme une lampe, projette à distance sur le feuil-
> lage un reflet artificiel et chaud et fait flamber les suprêmes feuilles d'un
> arbre qui reste le candélabre incombustible et terne de son faîte incendié
> . . . elle greffait et faisait épanouir, impossible à discerner nettement dans
> l'éblouissement, un immense bouquet comme de fleurs . . .
>
> (Bk. ii)

Proust, like Signac, does not hide his surprise at the artificial element that enters into exact observation. At the same time he becomes enrap-tured, like the painter, by a beauty revealed only to a loving, sensitive eye, by a fairylike transformation of a tree into a nosegay.

This modern feeling of excitement comes also from the artificial light shining on groups of persons gathered at dances, theaters, and circuses, where costumes and movement make the *tranche de vie* particularly thrill-ing. Painters and writers often hesitate between a proletarian milieu or one of high society to bring out the details in which they are interested. The bourgeois meet the lower-class girls at the Parisian public dances, as pic-tured in *Le Moulin de la Galette* (1875) (see Fig. 85) by Auguste Renoir, and it is the realistic and naturalistic authors who describe the elements of this lively scene that captivated Renoir. Throughout the picture are young ladies about whom Maupassant could have been writing in *Pierre et Jean:*

> All these many-colored toilets that covered the sands like a bed of
> flowers . . . all the ingenious inventions of fashion, from the tiny shoe to
> the extravagant hat, the seduction of gesture, voice, and smile . . .[17]

The description conveys another kind of atmosphere than that of the pic-ture, because there can be some retrospective remarks that embellish the picture's frozen moment.

There are, furthermore, passages in Flaubert that describe the dancing couples in their attitudes and gestures. The lady of the second couple to the left abandons herself to the waltz as does Madame Bovary at Vaubyes-sard:

85. Renoir, *Le Moulin de la Galette*, Musée de l'Impressionisme, Paris.
(Foto Marburg)

> Moving to the rhythm of the orchestra, she swam forward with a gentle undulation of the neck. A smile showed upon her lips at certain tender passages on the violin. . . Then, with a crash of brass, the music would once more strike up loudly. Feet took up the measure, skirts swelled, swishing as they touched one another. . .
>
> (Part i, ch. viii)

Renoir's gentlemen in the picture, either talking or dancing, may be seen through Flaubert's eyes:

> Several men — fifteen or so — of all ages ranging from twenty-five to forty, scattered among the dancers, or standing in the doorways, talking, were distinguished from the general crowd by a sort of family likeness which linked them in spite of differences in age, face, or dress. . . Their necks moved freely above low cravats, their long whiskers fell over turned-down collars. . . Those on the threshold of middle age looked young, while the more youthful of their company had an air of maturity. . .
>
> The air of the ballroom grew heavy. . .
>
> Everyone in the room was waltzing . . .
>
> They began slowly, then started to move more swiftly. They turned and twisted, and everything about them turned and twisted, too. . .
>
> (Part i, ch. viii)

An impression of a popular ball is given by Edmond and Jules de Goncourt in their *Journal* — namely, the ball of the 'Elysée des Arts, boulevard Bourdon,' which, with some modifications, was put into their novel *Germinie Lacerteux*, chapter sixteen, as 'Les bals Musette.' The picture from the diary (9 February 1863) is more lively and more impressionistic so far as the technique is concerned:

> Today we attend a public dance in the Elysium of the Arts, Bourdon Boulevard. . .

A large room in which could be felt a vague restlessness, a somewhat spiritless movement. Gray, lack-lustre faces, complexions reflecting misery and the hospital. Young women dressed in brown woolen clothes, all dark shades without the gay strip of white linen around the neck, and nothing but dark bonnets with only an occasional burst of a red ribbon upon them. . . Most of the faces emerge from a neckpiece of cat fur. The men are all in caps, coats, colored shirts. The more elegant ones have a loose muffler whose two ends hang down the back in raffish negligence. . .

Here the men invite the girls to dance by catching the ribbons of their bonnets, which float behind them.

The orchestra struck up a quadrille and everybody joined in the singing. They were attracted at the same time by the sight of the only beautiful woman at the ball, a Jewess, a young Herodias, a flower of the perversion of Paris, a perfect example of those shameless girls who sell stationery in the streets at dusk.

As important as the technique are the details seen in this ' taking everyday life seriously' (Auerbach). In *Le Cirque* (see Fig. 86) by Seurat, the female equestrian performer on her white horse is obviously the center of interest. The clown behind her turns a somersault; the public, composed of different types, occupies the benches; and a group of club men stand at the entrance to the stables. If one were to call the horsewoman La Tompkins and the flying clown Nello, the description of the whole picture would be found in *Les Frères Zemgano* by Edmond de Goncourt:

At night Miss Tompkins is the attraction, with her body trained during the whole day, with its force, elasticity, feverish quaking, that type of dumb enthusiasm animating it, and still the dauntless fury with which the untiring woman throws herself into the danger of the most difficult exercises, uttering some low guttural sounds . . . a horsewoman putting her foot upon the thigh of the horse and bending back in a sylphlike movement. The frill of the short skirt over the colorless tights was tossing up and down, making her flesh appear to be the pale pink of a little old Saxon China statue.

The white horse whose name was Snow seemed a floating of silk in the midst of which were noticeable two humid eyes.

The eye of Tompkins looked steadily on Nello, the whole time this young man was in the circus, but he, for his part, was seized with an instinctive antipathy toward this American woman without being able to account for it. He avoided her glances by marching upon his hands and by teasing his sweetheart with an acrobatic thumb to the nose by joining his legs above his head.

The public of the circus, a motley assemblage under that light which makes the faces appear blurred and which is absorbed by the cloth of the dresses, did it not call to mind those admirable lithographs of Goya showing the scaffolds of the bullfight? . . .

As for the passage to the stables, despite the poster announcing seats in the tent, it was crowded to the point of obstructing the exit of the horses

86. Seurat, *Le Cirque*, Musée de l'Impressionisme, Paris. (Photo Giraudon)

and the riding-masters, for it was full of a crowd of sportsmen and notables from the club. . .[18]

The elegance of single persons is seen in the snapshot of a theater box with a distinguished couple in evening dress looking at other boxes during intermission, admiring and enjoying their partners in elegance, looking for flirtation and for *la chronique scandaleuse*. In *La Loge* (see Fig. 87) by Renoir, black and white dress, pink flowers, gold and pearl jewelry, purple velvet of curtains and balustrade make a colorful ensemble. Balzac and Flaubert fix the impressions of this type of scene. Balzac shows Rastignac accompanying the vicomtesse de Beauséant to her theater box, where she becomes jealous when Rastignac constantly directs his glasses to the box of Mme de Nucingen, née Goriot:

> A few moments later he was sitting beside Mme de Beauséant in a brougham, that whirled them through the streets of Paris to a fashionable theatre. It seemed to him that some fairy magic had suddenly transported him into a box facing the stage. All the lorgnettes of the house were pointed at him as he entered, and at the Vicomtesse in her charming toilette. . .
>
> 'You must talk to me, you know,' said Mme de Beauséant. 'Ah! look! There is Mme de Nucingen in the third box from ours. Her sister and M. de Trailles are on the other side.'

The Vicomtesse glanced as she spoke at the box where Mlle de Roche-fide should have been; M. d'Ajuda was not there, and Mme de Beauséant's face lighted up in a marvelous way.

'She is charming,' said Eugène, after looking at Mme de Nucingen. . .

'Her face is long.'

'Yes, but length gives distinction.'

'It is lucky for her she has some distinction. . . Just see how she fidgets with her opera-glass! The Goriot blood shows itself in every movement,' said the Vicomtesse. . .

Indeed, Mme de Beauséant seemed to be engaged in making a survey of the house, and to be unconscious of Mme de Nucingen's existence; but no movement made by the latter was lost upon the Vicomtesse. . .

'If you look at her so persistently, you will make people talk, M. de Rastignac.' [19]

Flaubert describes Monsieur and Madame Bovary attending a perform-ance of *Lucia of Lammermoor*. They are in a box at the Rouen theater and Flaubert gives Madame Bovary's bird's-eye view before the opera starts:

She went up the stairs leading to the First Circle. She took a childish pleasure in pushing the large curtained doors open with her fingers. She breathed in the dusty smell of the passages with delight, and, as soon as

87. Renoir, *La Loge*, London. (Archives Photographiques)

she was seated in their box, began to preen herself with the easy unconcern of a duchess.

The house began to fill. There was much extracting of opera-glasses from cases. The regular subscribers recognized one another from afar and exchanged greetings. . . Some of the older men, resigned and inexpressive, with whitish hair and whitish faces, looked like silver medals which had been tarnished by exposure to lead fumes. The young bucks-about-town strutted in the stalls, displaying a great expanse of pink or apple-green cravat in the openings of their waistcoats. Looking down on them from above, Madame Bovary admired the way in which they rested the palms of their hands in their tight yellow gloves on the gold knobs of elegant dress canes. . .

The curtain rose, revealing a country scene. . . Charles . . . confessed . . . that he was losing track of the story, because the music made it very difficult to hear the words.

' What does that matter? ' said Emma. ' Do be quiet.'

' But I like to understand what is going on, as you very well know,' he replied, leaning over her shoulder.

' Oh, please stop talking! ' she said, having by this time come to the end of her patience.

(Part ii, ch. xv)

## IV. Enthusiasm for Movement

Impressionism is driven to two extremes inherent in its tendencies: a radical *l'art pour l'art*, which is no longer interested in life but in the rhythm of life expressed by art; and a preoccupation with striking, beautiful, or surprising movements, as in dancers, running horses, or people at work. But interest in these movements leads the observer to people of the meanest and lowest classes and characters. This causes the *l'art pour l'art* and interest in formal movement to make a detour over the most pronounced naturalism. It is known that Degas' enthusiasm for movement and the beauty of artistic dance was inseparable from his attraction to and interest in the Montmartre girls, and so it was the dreams of beauty of Manet, Baudelaire, and the Goncourts, all of whom could say with Flaubert, 'L'ignoble me plaît.' In his painting *The Dancer* Edgar Degas enters the purest realm of movement. Degas himself felt this, as his few sonnets on the dancer reveal:

> Elle danse en mourant, comme autour d'un roseau,
> D'une flûte où le vent triste de Weber joue;
> Le ruban de ses pas s'entortille et se noue,
> Son corps s'affaise et tombe en un geste d'oiseau.
>
> Sifflent les violons. Fraîche, du bleu de l'eau,
> Silvana vient, et là, curieuse s'ébroue.
> Le bonheur de revivre et l'amour pur se joue
> Sur ses yeux, sur ses seins, sur tout l'être nouveau,

Et ses pieds de satin brodent, comme l'aiguille,
Des desseins de plaisir. La capricante fille
Use mes pauvres yeux, à la suivre peinant.

Mais d'un signe toujours cesse le beau mystère;
Elle retire trop les jambes en sautant:
C'est un saut de grenouille aux mares de Cythère.[20]

There is no doubt that the sensuous Degas envisions the idea of the pure movement of dance as expressed by his younger friend Paul Valéry:

. . . cette exaltation et cette vibration de la vie . . . cette suprématie de la tension, et ce ravissement dans le plus agile que l'on puisse obtenir de soi-même, ont les vertus et les puissances de la flamme . . . faisant briller à nos yeux ce qu'il y a de divin dans une mortelle. . .

Quelle vive et gracieuse introduction des plus parfaites pensées . . . l'art pur des métamorphoses.
(Eupalinos . . . pp. 19 and 41)

Delight in abstract movement is revealed in the notes of Charles Du Bos on the dancing of Isadora Duncan:

Paris 49, Rue de la Tour, Wednesday, 17 February 1909. One of the secrets of Isadora. . . When she is throwing her hands forward with out-stretched fingers, she seems at the same time to cleave space and to bewitch it. Is this not the very attitude which a philosopher ought to have when facing his problems? The idea of effort ought to be, I do not say banished, but at least transformed in an agreeable way.[21]

But the interest of Degas, like that of Manet in *Lola de Valence*, goes from the movement of the dancer to the dancer herself, as is the case in *The Dancer with the Bouquet* (see Fig. 88). Although surrounded, as Valéry phrases it, by 'les claires danseuses . . . un bosquet aux belles branches tout agitées par les brises de la musique,' the Prima Ballerina is here far from being pure movement. She is, as Degas says in another of his sonnets, a 'Mignonne avec ce populacier museau.' She is too near the desires of Baudelaire:

Que j'aime voir, chère indolente
De ton corps si beau
Comme une étoffe vacillante
Miroiter la peau!

. . .

A te voir marcher en cadence
Belle d'abandon,
On dirait un serpent qui danse
Au bout d'un baton.
(*Fleurs du mal*, xxix)

88. Degas, *The Dancer with the Bouquet*, Louvre. (Foto Marburg)

This dancer in repose is hardly ' pistil of flesh issuing from flower-cups of colored muslin, living bouquet in movement, snowflake flitting on the stage,' for she is too much woman and ' salaried figurant.' [22]

Still more naturalistic is *The Foyer*.[23] The Goncourts, commenting on Degas in their diary (13 February 1874), clarify the meaning of this and similar pictures:

> There is the foyer where, illuminated from a window, legs of dancing girls appear as fancy silhouettes, legs descending a small staircase, with the shining red patch of a tartan in all these fluttering white clouds, from which arises the comic figure of a *maître de ballet*, dark and heavy. And before your eyes there is, snatched from nature, the graceful turmoil of movements and gestures of these young girls, alert like little monkeys.
>
> And actually, the rosy shade of the skin, the white of the lingerie, the milky clouds of the gauze are the most charming pretext for light and delicate color nuances.

Before continuing the naturalistic line, in order to make a *rapprochement* between Degas and Zola, it must be stressed again that the problem of movement did mean something to Degas, as seen in his pictures of horse races, for example, *Aux courses* (see Fig. 89). The meaning of this picture of beautiful horses, which are being shown immediately before the races, is best expressed by Degas himself in the sonnet ' Pur Sang ':

On l'entend approcher par saccade brisée,
Le souffle fort et sain. Dès l'aurore venu,
Dans le sévère train par son lad maintenu,
Le bon poulain galope et coupe la rosée . . .

Et pour les coups divers où la cote l'emploie,
On le fait sur ce pré débuter en voleur,
Tout nerveusement nu dans sa robe de soie.

Horse races are also a subject of description by writers. There is a passage in Flaubert's *Education sentimentale*, ' Les jockeys en casaques de soie . . .' and one in Zola's *Nana*, ' Les chevaux arrivaient . . .' The interest of these authors is, however, different. There is no such thing in literature as *la peinture qui tourne*, as inaugurated by Constantin Guys, brought to a peak by Degas, and exaggerated by Toulouse-Lautrec. Flaubert and Zola are interested in the turf only as another snapshot from life.

The naturalism of Degas comes best to the fore in *Les Repasseuses* [24] (see Fig. 90). It is true that E. de Goncourt pays lip service to this picture as an attempt to catch heavier movements like ironing: ' Ironing and dancing women . . . I cannot blame his choice, because I, too, have praised in *Manette Salomon* these two professions as the ones which give the modern artist the most appropriate feminine models.' Hautecœur stresses, however, the naturalistic implications of the painting: ' Degas shows the ironing women in a state of untidiness, in the atmosphere of a humid steam-room, with laundry hung all around, the earthen water pot close to the starched shirt and the bottle which has been put down by the yawning laundress.' [25]

Actually, no painter comes closer to the naturalism of Zola, who, in *L'Assommoir*, shows Gervaise and Clémence, tired and exhausted, doing the ironing in their laundry shop:

89. Degas, *Aux Courses*, Louvre. (Photo Giraudon)

90. Degas, *Les Repasseuses*, Louvre. (Photo Giraudon)

> It was now the warm time of the year. One June afternoon, a Saturday
> when the work was pressing, Gervaise herself had piled the coke into the
> stove, around which ten irons were heating, whilst a rumbling sound is-
> sued from the chimney. . . The atmosphere was stifling. . . For some
> little while past, an oppressive silence had reigned in that furnace-like
> heat, interrupted only by the smothered sound of the banging down of
> the irons on the thick blanket covered with calico.
> ' Ah, well! ' said Gervaise, ' it's enough to melt one! It's almost impos-
> sible to keep a thing on.'
> She was sitting on the floor, in front of a basin, starching some things. . .
> Tall Clémence . . . was suffocating. . . No other workwoman could
> iron a shirt with her style. Shirts were her specialty.
> Back and forth moved the Polish iron, a small iron rounded at each end.
> Clémence . . . had reached her thirty-fifth shirt since the morning.[26]

Zola has depicted the same scene as Degas. He has shown a laundry shop
with tired women yawning after strenuous and enervating work on a hot
summer day. Zola surpasses Degas in vulgarity, as seen from the continuation of the text. The naturalistic parallels between Zola's writings and the
work of Manet,[27] between Bastien Lepage (1848–84) and Guy de Maupassant are so evident that further illustration is unnecessary.

## V. Line as Opposed to Color. Ornament rather than Topic

Impressionism and naturalism in literature and art overlooked two problems: the element of strict form and true psychology as the heart and
*raison d'être* of representation.

In regard to the return of strict delineation, the reintegration of the ornamental functions of art and the consequent return to symbolism brought about a devaluation of the *tranche de vie*, as the *tranche de vie* impression once devaluated the artistic narration and the invented story. The *indécis* of Verlaine has not influenced everybody. Baudelaire himself said: ' I hate the movement which disturbs the line.'

René Bray[28] is therefore correct in stating that it is more exact to consider Baudelaire rather than Verlaine as the source of modern poetry. The *Art poétique* of Gautier, which stresses the *contour pur* against wishy-washy romanticism, comes into its own with the contemporary painters: ' Sculpte, lime, cisèle,' as Gautier says.

The revolutionary painter whose ideals correspond to the Gautier-Baudelaire concept of art is Paul Cézanne (1839–1906). In his famous picture *La Montagne Sainte Victoire* (1887) (see Fig. 91) his analogous program can be readily seen: clear forms even at a distance, essential forms only, eschewing romantic detail as well as impressionistic blurring, but in any case sharply contoured forms to which the clear and sharply separated colors make the essential contribution. These colors underline the masses and volumes as structural forms and the interdependence of these forms. Greater details are taken into consideration only from the point of view of their submission and contribution to the ensemble. The colors themselves are few but well harmonized. Too loud or self-centered colors that would be detrimental to the idea of relegating details to the unity of the whole are carefully avoided. The result is majestic simplicity, leading to the great murals of Puvis de Chavannes (1824–98).

This particular feeling for landscape expressed by Cézanne was vital in

91. Cézanne, *La Montagne Sainte Victoire*. (Courtesy of the Phillips Gallery, Washington, D.C.)

his older contemporary, Théophile Gautier (1811–72), more than in any-one else. His enthusiasm for the Spanish Sierra, sublime without details of shrub and flowers, as opposed to dainty garden landscapes, impels him, too, to adopt this same majestic approach to nature. He underlines his love for 'proud and sublime mountains,' where little plants do not dare put their feet — no vines, no corn, no barley. The landscape is populated only with wild and great things, eagles and the echos of outlaws. These land-scapes, Gautier adds, certainly have nothing except their majestic beauty, but they are closer to God than the rich and fertile lands:

> J'aime d'un fol amour les monts fiers et sublimes!
> Les plantes n'aiment pas poser leurs pieds frileux
> Sur le linceul d'argent qui recouvre leurs cimes;
> Le soc s'émousserait à leurs pics anguleux;
>
> ·Ni vigne aux bras lascifs, ni blés dorés, ni seigles;
> Rien qui rapelle l'homme et le travail maudit.
> Dans leur air libre et pur nagent des essaims d'aigles,
> Et l'écho du rocher siffle l'air du bandit.
>
> Ils ne rapportent rien et ne sont pas utiles;
> Ils n'ont que leur beauté, je le sais, c'est bien peu;
> Mais, moi, je les préfère aux champs gras et fertiles,
> Qui sont si loin du ciel qu'on n'y voit jamais Dieu!
> (Dans la Sierra, España)

The shadeless landscape under the sun, clear, sharply cut, immense, without movement of men or animals, is also the ideal of Leconte de Lisle:

> Midi, roi des étés, répandu sur la plaine,
> Tombe en nappes d'argent des hauteurs du ciel bleu.
> Tout se tait. L'air flamboie et brûle sans haleine;
> La terre est assoupie en sa robe de feu.
>
> L'étendue est immense, et les champs n'ont pas d'ombre
> Et la source est tarie où buvaient les troupeaux;
> La lointaine forêt dont la lisière est sombre,
> Dort là-bas, immobile en un pesant repos.[29]

Adoration of the pure form leads very rapidly to a pure-form cult of tech-nical achievements. Cézanne himself included this in his theoretical for-mula after 1907: 'Peindre ce n'est pas copier seulement l'objectif: c'est saisir une harmonie entre des rapports nombreux.' This formula becomes very important for pure art, pure poetry, as represented by Valéry and Abbé Bremond, and pure architecture, as practiced by D'Ozenfant and Le Corbusier. It is an ideal of harmony and rhythm, more a virtual desire than an actual achievement, as desperately expressed by Baudelaire:

Je voudrais . . .
Que ton sang chrétien coulât à flots rythmiques,
Comme les sons nombreux des syllabes antiques,
Où règnent tour à tour le père des chansons,
Phœbus, et le grand Pan, le seigneur des moissons.
(Fleurs du Mal, ' La Muse Malade ')

The quest for absolute beauty of form has always incited the painter to attempt a well-arranged still life. In Cézanne's The Basket of Apples (see Fig. 92), his objects may still be distinguished: a basket with apples, a bottle, a platter with biscuits, a white tablecloth, napkins, and apples scattered around. But the desire to suppress the obvious colors is already visible. The drapery of the tablecloth and the steeply placed apple basket are drawn almost on the surface, and their gliding appearance hinders the onlooker from getting any feeling of depth. Where can one get a foothold in this beautiful world of forms and form-creating colors?

The very same question will come to the mind of a reader studying one of the most perfect sonnets of Mallarmé:

Victorieusement fui . . .

Victorieusement fui le suicide beau
Tison de gloire, sang par écume, or, tempête!
O rire si là-bas une pourpre s'apprête
A ne tendre royal que mon absent tombeau.

Quoi! de tout cet éclat pas même le lambeau
S'attarde, il est minuit, à l'ombre qui nous fête
Excepté qu'un trésor présomptueux de tête
Verse son caressé nonchaloir sans flambeau,

92. Cézanne, The Basket of Apples. (Courtesy of the Art Institute of Chicago. Collection Helen Birch Bartlett Memorial)

La tienne si toujours le délice! la tienne
Qui seule qui du ciel évanoui retienne
Un peu de puéril triomphe en t'en coiffant

Avec clarté quand sur les coussins tu la poses
Comme un casque guerrier d'impératice enfant
Dont pour te figurer il tomberait des roses.

In this verbally beautiful still life the striking feature is that the wishfully distorted word order and the purposely obscure metaphors hinder the perspective that logical syntax would convey in a clear manner. Forced to guess the meaning of elements purposely put at random solely for euphonic reasons (surface euphony being the new principle of composition and the *raison d'être* of this particular composition), different interpreters have given different meanings to the sonnet. Poizat interpreted it as ' the battle of Actium,' Thibaudet as ' the poet's triumph over the sun at his desk at night,' Spoerri as the ' flight from the temptation of suicide by an interior overcoming of the illusions of life.' In any case, if Mallarmé's still life in words is susceptible of any half-rational symbolic interpretation, the particular form of Cézanne may be eligible, too, for such an interpretation, and Paul Claudel would not hesitate to give it:

> All kinds of objects in a state of disequilibrium. You would think they are about to fall. There is a napkin at the moment of being unfolded, all kinds of vases or fruits shaken and dishes out of balance. A Mallarmé would be tempted to see here, as I do myself, a kind of dedication to something beyond. This impression comes from the almost moral immobility of the background and the lining up of half-airy witnesses in the foreground, which give meaning to all these material attitudes of falling down. This still life is an arrangement on the brink of disintegration; it is something like a prey of duration. The wine at the side establishes something of a feeling of eternity.[30]

## VI. Abstract Art and Pure Poetry

If Cézanne himself has not yet reached the logical meaninglessness of Mallarmé, who sacrifices everything to the power of form, the disciples of cubism and abstract art have done so. This is the case, for example, with *The Chessboard* [31] (1917) (see Fig. 93) by Juan Gris (1887–1927). This *Echiquier* is an introduction into a still more pure abstract art, which takes a more radical form in the paintings of Picasso and Matisse. The new ideal of still life is a compound of geometrical figures, regularly shaped *propriétés*: papers, cartons, parchments, cylinders, boards with squares, circles, ellipses — in other words, rhythmical ornaments. Because there are no practical objects but only fundamental forms, such arrangements have been called paintings in verbs as opposed to paintings in nouns.[32] Here is a new perspective of superimposed planes, where things are shown at random, *en profil, en face,* in totality, in sections, in full shape, and in projection.

If Mallarmé's hermetic poetry comes close to this concept of art, Paul Valéry embodies the idea of abstract art still more in his practice and theory of *poésie pure.* Just as abstract painting cannot contain practical objects, pure poetry cannot contain discursive thoughts and words, causal links between the phrases and sentences, or elaborate comparisons. Pure poetry will use instead difficult associations, enigmatic metaphors, and intuitive epithets, which make a formally arranged maze whose beauty is disclosed only on very careful analysis. The first four lines of Valéry's *Le Cimetière marin,* a poetical chessboard, lend themselves to an analytical chess play:

> Ce toit tranquille, où marchent des colombes,
> Entre les pins palpite, entre les tombes;
> Midi le juste y compose de feux
> La mer, la mer, toujours recommencée!

This is enigmatic so long as one does not see the calm sea behind the sign and form of ' the quiet roof.' Only then is it clear that the ' walking doves ' are the moving sails. Further, the ' roof that palpitates ' is the shimmering sea beating between pine trees and tombs. Consequently, the whole can only be the vision of an onlooker on the sea from a *cimetière marin.* Noon is ' the just one ' because of the equal and just division of the day into two halves. The noonday sun creates a sea of fire, because the sun's reflection in the calm waves gives the impression of a fiery surface. The repetition of ' sea,' reminiscent of Xenophon's *thalatta, thalatta,* gives the impression of immensity. The expression ' the sea always begun anew '

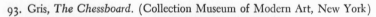

93. Gris, *The Chessboard.* (Collection Museum of Modern Art, New York)

is but another form of the same idea. Consequently, Valéry's pure poetry channeled into simple prose would mean:

> The quiet sea, where some sails are moving,
> Surrounds a promontory with a graveyard:
> The heat of the sun at noon provides firelike reflections
> To the endless, immense sea.

St. John Perse learned his lesson well, as Wallace Fowlie [33] has made clear, for he expresses in this manner the idea that even the merchant-traveler is stirred by the call of eternity:

> You traffic not in salt more strong than this, when at morning with omen of kingdoms and omen of dead waters swung high over the smokes of the world, the drums of exile waken on the marches.
> Eternity yawning on the sands.
>
> (*Anabase*, translated by T. S. Eliot)

Modern tendencies of abstract art become quickly deadlocked in the unsuccessful attempts at cubistic and futuristic *poésie pure*, an inevitable result of the fact that an abstract idea cannot enter the realm of art except by a metaphorical process. This metaphorical process may be a rhythm. Thus Georges Braque [34] tries to express the dynamism of *La Valse* and its successive three-tack movements by the static, simultaneous still life of tripartite groups of objects: on one hand, a glass, a fruit bowl, and a page of music; on the other hand, a fork, a pear, and the shadow of the pear. Take away the inscription *The Waltz* and a meaningless still life remains. Braque daringly crosses the Laocoön frontier, unaware that he cannot paint action by objects. There can be no *peinture en verbes*. What Braque wanted to do, Paul Valéry is able to do by more convincing metaphors, linking thought to dance and its movement to the branches shaken by the wind, or to flames. Using the medium of abstract terms balanced by the concrete dancer (*mortelle*), he fixes the symbol convincingly:

> Quelle vive et gracieuse introduction des plus parfaites idées . . . un bosquet aux belles branches tout agitées par les brises de la musique . . . cette exaltation et cette vibration de la vie . . . cette suprématie de la tension, et ce ravissement dans le plus agile que l'on puisse obtenir de soi-même . . . les vertus et les puissances de la flamme faisant briller . . . ce qu'il y a de divin dans une mortelle.

The metaphors of Valéry's highly artistic prose would fail to grasp the phenomenon of refined thought expressed through the symbol of the dance if the truly abstract material of language (*exaltation, suprématie, tension, ravissement*) did not give them that final *élan* into the ideological realm, which cannot be attained by a metaphorically expressed still life.

This does not mean that literature cannot fall into the same aberrations

LA CRAVATE
DOU
LOU
REUSE
QUE TU
PORTES
ET QUI T'
ORNE O CI
VILISÉ
OTE- TU VEUX
LA    BIEN
SI        RESPI
      RER[35]

in regard to its own boundaries as painting does when rendering a dance by rhythmical, abstract proportions. Guillaume Apollinaire's *Calligrammes* take the same step into a foreign domain, though a certain humor mitigates the issue. For instance, a protest against wearing neckties is expressed by arranging the words of this protest into the form of a necktie.

In connection with abstract art, there certainly must be a consideration of the boundaries of beauty. It is not in the spirit of scholarship to condone the attitude of the snobs who declare all forms of contemporary art acceptable, even though these forms are often a shock to any kind of human or, to put it more carefully, Western or Greek taste. Unfortunately, what P. Marie-Alain Couturier states about the latest development of Picasso can be applied to most of these works: 'The latest works are terrible: The ugliness assumes there such a character as seeming to *identify* itself with evil. All this appears to us shocking.' [36]

Beautiful, elegant forms, however, must be acknowledged, even if the aim of the artist is not fully recognizable. Such is the case with Constantin Brancusi's *Bird in Space* [37] (1919) (see Fig. 94). This bronze evidently tries

94. Brancusi, *Bird in Space*. (Collection Museum of Modern Art, New York)

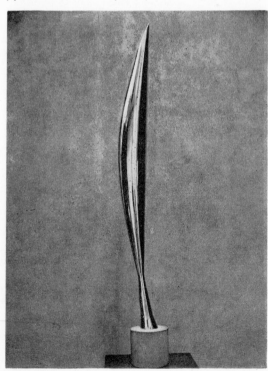

to give an idea of flight, *le vol d'oiseau*; it is something of an *élan vital*, of the bird itself taking the shape of the elegant form his flight has designed in the air. Such a form is not found in nature. It is a functional form, as Le Corbusier would say, a form like that of an ideal egg or an ideal shell, or any ideal form. It is movement in its pure essence or, as Paul Valéry would state, it is 'the design in which reality, the unreal, and the intelligible merge and are combined.'

Brancusi no more violates the limits of the possible in art than does Mallarmé with his dream of the flights that have not been flown by his swan, caught in the ice. These are impossible, beautiful flights, like those of a poet who lacks the technique to express his intuitions, like those of all the 'Raphaels without hands.' In this obscure sonnet the movement itself forms the design of the idea:

> Le vierge, le vivace et le bel aujourd'hui
> Va-t-il nous déchirer avec un cou d'aile ivre
> Ce lac dur oublié que hante sous le givre
> Le transparent glacier des vols qui n'ont pas fui!
>
> Un cygne d'autrefois se souvient que c'est lui,
> Magnifique mais qui sans espoir se délivre
> Pour n'avoir pas chanté la région où vivre
> Quand du stérile hiver a resplendi l'ennui.
>
> Tout son col secouera cette blanche agonie
> Par l'espace infligé à l'oiseau qui le nie,
> Mais non l'horreur du sol où le plumage est pris.
>
> Fantôme qu'à ce lieu son pur éclat assigne
> Il s'immobilise au songe froid de mépris
> Que vêt parmi l'exil inutile le Cygne.

### VII. Psychic Obsession

A second path, leading away from impressionism, has the serious goal of recapturing the soul, forgotten during the second part of the nineteenth century. In this endeavor the psychological, including the truly metaphysical, is so strong that one may speak of a psychic obsession, and, curiously enough, the pictures are often more clear than the dreamlike texts that represent the same trend.

'Mystique,' from *Les Illuminations* by Arthur Rimbaud (1854–91), seems absolutely dark, cryptic, and un-understandable:

> Sur la pente du talus, les anges tournent leurs robes de laine dans les herbages d'acier et d'émeraude.

Des prés de flammes bondissent jusqu'au sommet du mamelon. A gauche, le terreau de l'arête est piétiné par tous les homicides et toutes les batailles; et tous les bruits désastreux, filent leur courbe. Derrière l'arête de droite, la ligne des orients, des progrès . . .

La douceur fleurie des étoiles, et du ciel et du reste descend en face du talus . . . contre notre face, et fait l'abîme fleurant et bleu là-dessous.

The key to the meaning of these words can be found in a picture by Paul Gauguin (1848–1903) in the National Gallery of Scotland, Edinburgh, called *Vision after sermon* or *Jacob Wrestling with the Angel* (1889) (see Fig. 95). Whether this picture was remotely inspired by Rimbaud's text is not known with certainty. Gauguin's motif surely comes from his experience of finding in Le Pouldu (Brittany) very pious girls with second sight. The picture was actually painted there in 1889. Gauguin paints these Breton girls as they envision Jacob wrestling with the angel, the mystical story par excellence from the Old Testament, which they have learned during a sermon. It seems, however, as though Rimbaud's ' Mystique' (1873) was at the back of Gauguin's mind and, willy-nilly, he explained it by this painting. By painting the meadow in a provoking red he clarifies *des prés de flammes,* and this meadow on a ' fabulous hill . . . of rutilant vermillion ' [38] explains why the flames jump to the top of the hill (*bondissent jusqu'au sommet du mamelon*). It is true that Gauguin replaces *les anges* by the angel and Jacob, but by painting the angel blue (*robe de laine d'acier*) and Jacob green (*robe de laine d'émeraude*), he clarifies the purposely obscured sentence of Rimbaud, which should have a comma after *herbages,* because if the meadows were blue and green they could not at the same time be red. Thus the picture helps to unmask the syntactical trick well known in the technique of *poésie hermétique.* The division

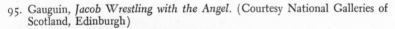

95. Gauguin, *Jacob Wrestling with the Angel.* (Courtesy National Galleries of Scotland, Edinburgh)

of the picture into two parts by the tree makes clear the division made by Rimbaud: sin and evil are on the left side, where the painter, following a Biblical procedure, condenses the *homicides, batailles,* and *bruits désastreux* into a symbolic animal that tramples down (*piétine*) everything good; whereas on the right, the side of virtue, Jacob extorts the angel's divine blessing before he is left alone. From this side comes grace, *la douceur fleurie des étoiles et du ciel et du reste,* to the enraptured Breton girls with their white coifs (*fleurant*) and blue dresses (*bleu là-dessous*).

The parallels between Gauguin and Rimbaud go far. Even Hautecœur, who generally gives no detailed parallels at all, cannot but see such a striking coincidence in the unusual intoxication with color of both artists that he quotes the text of Rimbaud's ' Enfance ' to describe *Chevaliers sur la plage:*

> Cette idole, aux yeux noirs et crin jaune . . . son domaine azur et verdure insolents court sur des plages nommées par des vagues sans vaisseaux. . . A la lisière de la forêt . . . la fille à lèvre d'orange, les genoux croisés dans le clair déluge qui sourd des prés, nudité qu'ombrent, traversent et habillent les arcs-en-ciel, la flore, la mer.

The fundamental parallelism, however, consists of the Baudelairian obsession of both Gauguin and Rimbaud to find at any cost the *inconnu,* an indefinable exoticism. This *inédit* must have haunted the dreams of both artists. The *Illuminations* of both, in addition to their splendor and psychological discoveries, belong to an existence different from the familiar Occidental one, because the persons and stories seem fanciful and strange, somewhat unearthly. Gauguin's landscapes have a real echo in the *Bateau ivre* of Rimbaud. *From Tahiti,*[39] by Gauguin, shows fascinating, rare colors in meadow, brook, trees, the clothes of the Polynesians, and the fur of the unreal animals. The contrasts worked out are agreeable contrasts. There is indeed something of *la musique du tableau.* There are no effects of atmosphere and therefore the figures appear as if glued to the background, foreshadowing the collage of the Dadaïstes.

Rimbaud's drunken boat (' Le Bâteau ivre ') dreams [40] of similar landscapes and men in maddening colors:

> Comme je descendais des Fleuves impassibles,
> Je ne me sentis plus guidé par les haleurs;
> Des Peaux-rouges les avaient pris pour cibles,
> Les ayant cloués nus aux poteaux de couleurs . . .
>
> J'ai rêvé la nuit verte aux neiges éblouies
> Baisers montant aux yeux des mers avec lenteur;
> La circulation des sèves inouies,
> Et l'éveil jaune et bleu des phosphores chanteurs . . .

J'ai heurté, savez-vous, d'incroyables Florides
Mêlant aux fleurs des yeux de panthères, aux peaux
D'hommes des arcs-en-ciel tendus comme des brides,
Sous l'horizon des mers, à de glauques troupeaux.

Like Gauguin, Rimbaud makes highly artistic *images d'Epinal*. He places
against a beautiful background sharply chiseled scenes and figures: red-
skins shooting at prisoners bound to colored poles; green skies over white,
sanded banks. The water of the streams appears phosphorescent because of
a strange fluid. In Florida-like countries flowers, wild animals, and men in
deerskins make a world shining in the colors of the rainbow, from yellow to
orange and red, purple and blue; an unreal world like an underwater woods
or a meadow with peculiar fauna.

*Ia Orana Maria* [41] (see Fig. 96), by Gauguin, is a brown Madonna of
Tahiti, standing in the woods with a brown Divine Child to whom an
angel in beautiful colors conveys two native women. The climate of this
devotional picture is that of 'a country perfumed and sun-kissed . . . under a canopy of purple woods and palm trees,' as Baudelaire describes it
('A une dame Creole'). This picture, in color and meaning, is in a minor
tone if compared to the one just described. And these tones of awe and

96. Gauguin, *Ia Orana Maria*. (Collection of Mr. and Mrs. Sam A. Lewisohn)

97. Rousseau, *The Sleeping Gypsy*. (Collection Museum of Modern Art, New York. Gift of Mrs. Simon Guggenheim)

calm can be found in Rimbaud's great pupil, Paul Claudel. In his *Connaissance de l'Est*, Claudel describes the approach to a grove dedicated to worship, and it is like an echo of Gauguin's picture in so far as the atmosphere is concerned:

> The cloud overshadows the whole west. Made of great masses of cumuli it presents that voluminous and plastic aspect that occurs sometimes by chance in the evening when a low illumination like a veiled footlight underlines the relievi in reversed fashion. Deep in the background dark woods and the fold of heavy mountains, in the front the soil is first of thin, dark charcoal humus, then of yellow sand, finally of red sulfurous or cinnabar clay. This burned soil, this low sky, this bitter enclosure, do they not respond to the dark and empty depth from which rise the visions of dreams?
>
> The forest of the *cryptomères* actually is a temple.

If the exotic-dream propensity loosens its grip on reality, it runs into a kind of provoking infantilism. This is the case with painters like the *douanier* Rousseau (1844–1910) and poets like Cocteau, Desnos, Soupault, Vitrac, André Breton, and the entire so-called surrealist school.

The literary critic is helpless before the waking-dream infantilism of a dadaïst like Robert Desnos, when he says, 'Dans le sommeil de Rose Sélavy il y a un nain sorti d'un puits qui vient manger son pain la nuit,' or before the stammering of an *avant-garde* like Roger Vitrac:

> Dans la forêt incendiée
> Les lions étaient frais.

This whole makeup of infantilism becomes very clear from the art of the *douanier*. He paints, with the technique of a child, the dreamer together with his dream, particularly in such pictures as *The Dream* [42] and *The Sleep-*

*ing Gypsy* [43] (see Fig. 97). In the first picture a naked girl is lying on an
elegant couch placed in a primeval forest. She could be called ' Rose
Sélavy,' particularly as she is a *rosa silvatica* among the other virgin plants
there, and she sees in her dream a savage playing a flute, while lions, their
faces illuminated by moonlight, look on amazed. Henri Rousseau, who
admired a Polish girl, Yadwigha, explained his picture in a way worthy of
a painter playing the naïve: ' You must not be surprised to find a couch
in a virgin wood. That is only for the wealth of the red color. You understand that the couch, of course, is in a room; mark my words, the rest is
Yadwigha's dream.' [44] In the other picture there are simply a sleeping gypsy
and a lion, with a river and mountains in the background. But Jean Cocteau comments: ' The lion and the river are perhaps the dream of the
sleeping girl. What peace! It is perhaps not without reason that the painter,
who never forgot any detail, does not mark the sand by any footprints
around the slumbering feet? The gypsy did not go there. She is not there.
She is in no human place at all.'

In such a spiritual no-man's land, the forest is burning but nonetheless
the lions therein remain untouched; dwarfs emerge from a well to eat their
bread and cause no surprise. It is in such a land of similar infantilism that
Francis Jammes talks to the donkeys:

> J'irai et je dirai aux ânes, mes amis:
> Je suis Francis Jammes et je vais au Paradis
> Car il n'y a pas d'enfer au pays du Bon Dieu.

Jammes has something in common also with Vincent van Gogh (1853–
90). They both present young girls in their mysterious, immature, excited
condition — their frightened, unconscious conflict between the first urges
toward motherhood and the defense of their virginity. Vincent van Gogh
in *The Blue Girl* (see Fig. 98) shows this apparent calmness by the apa-
thetic expression of the face, but the simple silhouette has restless, sharp
contours. The badly proportioned arms stress the immature girl between
childhood and womanhood. A similar language is spoken in the innuen-
does of Francis Jammes:

> La jeune fille est blanche,
> elle a des veines vertes,
> aux poignets, dans ses manches
>             ouvertes.     .
>
> On ne sait pas pourquoi
> elle rit. Par moments
> elle crie et cela
>             est perçant.
>         . . .

98. Van Gogh, *The Blue Girl*. (Collection of the Reverend Theodore Pitcairn)

> On dirait quelquefois
> qu'elle comprend des choses.
> Pas toujours. Elle cause
> tout bas.
>
> . . .
>
> Quand un jeune homme souffre,
> d'abord elle se tait,
> elle ne rit plus, tout
> étonnée.
>
> Dans les petits chemins,
> elle remplit ses mains
> de piquants de bruyères,
> de fougères . . .

Jammes describes three other 'blue girls' at the threshold of adolescence: Clara d'Ellébeuse, Almaide d'Etremont, and Pomme d'Anis, although he etherealizes them more than Vincent van Gogh does.

The real literary parallel to van Gogh, however, is Emile Verhaeren. Literature sometimes has the privilege of being able to give a specimen of art its place in history and in the circle of civilization to which it belongs.

Such a great connoisseur of Vincent van Gogh as Julius Meier-Graefe found no one comparable to him. Even the Japanese painter, Sharaku, whose work van Gogh's resembles, 'does not explain the demon in the European painter . . . whose flames resemble radiant gardens, flaming trees, chasing clouds, glowing suns.' [45] Yet there is a convincing parallel between the demoniac, ecstatic naturism of Vincent van Gogh and that of his Flemish countryman and contemporary, Emile Verhaeren. The same view of nature, the same enthusiasm, the same century-old romantic naturism is at issue in both cases, a supreme example of the unifying power of blood and soil. If one really wants to understand a picture like A Road in Provence [46] by van Gogh, with the whole landscape flaming, the road, the cornfield, the clouds, the sun, the moon, but particularly the beautiful tree in the middle of the picture, what help is it to speak about 'Rembrandt, Rubens, Greco, Delacroix, raised to a demoniacal pitch?' This characterization is doubtful, vague, and does not explain the sentiment that created the picture but merely the technique. To express the inner feeling of this picture, nothing is more eloquent than the poem by Verhaeren, 'L'Arbre,' burgeoned from the same vitalistic Flemish feeling for life and nature:

> Il impose sa vie énorme et souveraine
> Aux plaines.
> Les yeux aujourd'hui morts, les yeux
> Des plus lointains aïeux
> Ont regardé, maille après maille,
> Se nouer son écorce et ses rudes rameaux.
> Il est dans le secret des *violents* nuages
> Et du *soleil qui boude, aux horizons latents.*
> Avec tous ses bourgeons, avec toutes ses branches
> — *Lèvres folles et bras tordus* —
> Il *jette un cri immensément tendu*
> Vers l'avenir . . .
> Cet arbre d'automne et de vent traversé.
> Comme un *géant brasier de feuilles et de flammes*
> Il se dressait, tranquillement, sous le ciel bleu,
> Il semblait *habité par un million d'âmes* . . .
> Que son rythme profond et sa force totale
> *Passaient en moi* et pénétraient jusqu'à mon cœur.

Furthermore, Vincent van Gogh's work has metaphysical overtones. His painting Night Café [47] (see Fig. 99) focuses on modern persons and things in their intrinsic ugliness but still 'in forms of beauty.' It is the last minute in the café before the tired waiter ejects the last five doubtful guests — two sleepy drunkards, a newspaper-reading intellectual without a decent home, and an amorous couple. The colors are purposely dirty and ugly to symbolize this dirty-ugly spiritual climate of a night café and the vulgar guests.

99. Van Gogh, *Night Café*. Museum of Modern Art, New York. (Collection of Stephen C. Clark, New York)

Rainer Maria Rilke was fascinated by the form and spirit of this picture and wrote his wife about it:

> . . . in the late hours of the day, forsaken, and looked at, as it were, with eyes which have watched all night . . . The way in which the painter has rendered the oldish atmosphere of the lamps by concentric circles traced around the lamps and effaced gradually in space, is not painting, but a result obtained by force with the aid of colors, which is overwhelming; before such a thing you feel that you are getting old, you wither, fall asleep, and despair . . . a night picture of a café full of art with the wine-red tones, the yellow of the lamps, deep and dried-up green tones, together with the three mirrors, each of which encloses a different emptiness.[48]

This is a tableau of modern decay and disintegration, which van Gogh's friend Rimbaud has grasped in his *Une Saison en enfer* and *Illuminations*:

> J'aimai . . . les boutiques fânées, les boissons tiédis. Je me traînais dans les ruelles puantes. . .
> Une misérable femme . . . soupire après des abandons improbables. Les desperados languissent après l'orage, . . . l'ivresse et les blessures.

Van Gogh himself has pointed out that the café is a place where people are tempted to ruin, become mad, commit crimes. Apparently harmless things are full of diabolic temptations. Literature has invented an excellent expression for this situation: *l'acte gratuit*. A place, a situation, induces you to do something foolish. In a whim, Salavin, hero of Duhamel's meaningful *Confessions de minuit*, gives his employer a box on the ear and loses his position. Julian Green in his diary writes about an urge to stretch out his hand and pull the opera conductor by the sleeves. The stern Julian Green seeks an explanation of things strange and comes back to the baroque idea that life must be in some way a dream.

Among the authors who try to explain the metaphysical background of the *acte gratuit*, the most serious one is André Gide. Gide, weary of his own trifling, turns back to the sterner language of his Calvinistic youth. Then the *acte gratuit* appears to him as a fiend that possesses him: ' I feel in myself on certain days such an invasion of evil that the prince of evil already seems to take steps for establishing Hell there.' Or, ' Vincent lets himself be slowly permeated by the diabolic spirit. He believes he becomes the devil. He actually feels in a conspiracy with Satan.' [49] Gide's Christian language makes it perfectly clear that his discovery of the anarchic-amoral superreality is nothing more than a detour to reach a part at least of the forgotten Christian reality, ' the contemporary substitute for original sin and damnation.' [50] Gide, whether he likes it or not, does see the hellish forces in life, and so doubtless does van Gogh in his *Café de nuit*.

There are also truly Christian discoverers of the despair of the modern world, the solution of which is the cry for help with uplifted arms to God. The painter Georges Rouault (born 1871) and the novelist Georges Bernanos represent this situation in an impressive metaphorical style. The *Clown's Head* [51] (1917) by Georges Rouault embodies sadness, ugliness, and helplessness, but also weakness and resignation, emphasized by the technique of the *cerne* — that is, the imitation of the sharp black contours of the stained-glass windows of the Middle Ages. This clown's head speaks of the apparently lost battle against human injustice and cruelty. One critic even found that these black, infinitely sad eyes are the only jewels in the darkness of this picture. This clown is somber, heavy, ugly, horrible, but essentially good and sincere, and therefore an understandable outcry against sin. Because of his *cerne* technique, Rouault heads the *Fauves*, the group of painters whose passionate extravagances in technique were considered by their adversaries as the leaps of wild animals (*fauves*) in the jungle. The *fauve* Rouault enhances the horror of the picture even more for those who know that, in Rouault's philosophy, modern desperate types are interchangeable with Christ on the Cross crying aloud: ' My God, my God, why hast thou forsaken me? ' (Mark xv. 34).

Rouault's clown is on the verge of despair; there seems no vestige of hope in his face; he is the *Désespéré* of Rouault's friend, Léon Bloy; he is wounded to death; he is surrounded and pressed by evil in the maze of the godless world of the *Enfants terribles* of Cocteau, the *Faux-monnayeurs* of Gide, and the characters of Georges Bernanos: Abbé Cénabre (*L'Imposture*), Fjodor (*La Joie*), and Mouchette (*Sous le soleil de Satan*). In his disfigured face there is something of the struggle of Mouchette before her suicide, when the vision of all the sins of her family and her surroundings in which she participated drives her to final despair:

100. Denis, *The Annunciation*, Musée d'Art Moderne, Paris.
(Archives Photographiques)

Lies full of calumny, hatreds long fostered, shameful love affairs, calculated crimes of avarice and hate, all this was reshaped in her as a cruel image of a dream is reshaped in the state of waking.

The crowd, swarming before her mind's eye, a moment earlier when she had recognized all those of her family, shrank accordingly. Faces were superimposed one upon the other; they now formed only one single face, which was the face of vice. Confused gestures became fixed in one single attitude, which was the gesture of crime. The avaricious ones made a mass of living gold, the voluptuous ones a heap of bowels. Everywhere sin burst its wrappings and disclosed the mystery of its generation: Scores of men and women bound by the fibres of the same cancer, and the hideous fetters retracted like the cut-off arms of an octopus to the very heart of the monster, the initial sin. . .

And she understood that the hour had come to kill herself.[52]

These provocations for despair, visible in Mouchette, seem to transpire behind the forehead of the desperately sad clown, only the clown will not succumb; his eyes keep a spark of love. But Mouchette and the clown are creations of the religious spirit of the century, which despises sugar-coating. The *Clown* is a religious picture in so far as it challenges love, pity, charity, and brotherhood as expressed in the painter's strong and virile manner.

The interest of the *Renouveau Catholique* in the positive aspect of mysticism is illustrated by *The Annunciation* (see Fig. 100) by Maurice Denis, now in the Musée de l'Art Moderne. The purity of the young girl in the picture is signified by her white dress and also by the lily on the windowsill; her piety by the gesture of the raised and folded hands. Denis suggests the virtual possibility that any pure and pious young girl living at any time, even today, even though she be the daughter of a Parisian gardener, may hear and accept in a mystical way the message of the Annunciation so long as she is ready, through suffering (thorns in the framed picture), to be invaded by the flames of Divine Love. Christ will truly be born and live in her heart instead of her ego. She will be another Mary and she will truly be a spouse of the Holy Spirit on condition that she leave the door wide open to the flowering garden of God (Paradise), from which the breath of celestial air (the Holy Spirit symbolized by his messenger the Angel) conveys mystical and spiritual motherhood to her.

There is no doubt that the method of Maurice Denis is to embody the mystical element in an almost realistic picture, with only moderately symbolic elements. This corresponds to the poetic method of Paul Claudel in his parallel topic, L'Annonce faite à Marie. Likewise Violaine, a triumphantly pure girl living in the Middle Ages in the liturgical atmosphere of the farm of Combernon, suffering from unrequited love, mistrust, hate, and leprosy, becomes so saintly as a result of accepting these sufferings that on Christmas night a miraculous power is given to her to bring back to life her sister's dead baby, Aubaine. As a token of Violaine's spiritual motherhood, the child is given her own pure, spiritual, blue eyes instead of the dark, carnal ones of the mother Mara. Denis and Claudel thus attempt in art to fuse the mystical followers of Mary as closely as possible with their ideal and pattern.

Poetization of life in art has been roughly called magic realism. There are very few artists who can offer this evasion in a naïve and convincing way, but there is at least one artistic and one literary figure to represent it. Magic realism can be understood from a painting like La Chambre de musique [53] by Pierre Roy (born 1880). A woman clad in blue is playing a cello during the night in a top-floor room entirely empty of furniture. Through Gothic windows an unseen moon in a blue sky projects the yellow shades of the window upon the brown floor and gray wall and makes the door at the right appear green. Everything has a dreamlike, mysterious, clear, delightful, imaginative, and enchanting quality. In literature, examples of this magic realism, more transparent but pervaded with irony and preciosity, are found in the work of Jean Giraudoux. Only the novel Le Grand Meaulnes, by Alain Fournier, which appeared before World War I and again after World War II in a new edition, has the genuine qualities of magic realism. Fernand Desonay has fully understood the poetically transfigurative character of this novel.[54] The youthful dreamer, Augustin Meaulnes, escaping from his classroom to seek adventure, arrives at a château in Sologne at a moment when they are preparing for a festivity in fancy costumes. Meaulnes, intruding during the night, climbs from a barn full of carriages into an empty top-floor room, as real as that in Roy's picture, falls asleep, and is awakened in the morning by players in fancy-dress costumes, one of whom treats him as though he were a fairy prince. He is so surprised that reality seems to him to be transfigured.

He jumped over the wall and, stepping from one carriage to another, he arrived at the level of the window silently, and pushed it like a door.

He found himself not in an attic but in a large room with a low ceiling . . .

Soon it seemed to him that the wind brought to his ear the sound of faint music. It was like a remembrance full of charm and nostalgia. He recalled the time when his mother, still young, on certain afternoons sat down at the piano in the drawing room and he listened to her until nightfall. . .

Awfully tired, he fell asleep at once. . .

Meaulnes heard a match cracking. . .

The actor, passing by the alcove, said with a bow: ' Sir, fallen asleep here, you only need to awake, to get dressed as marquis, and to get down to the dress festival.' [55]

This enchanting beginning of the novel ends in tragedy when Meaulnes, having married the daughter of the owner of the magic castle, deserts her after their wedding day. Immense sorrow follows; there is no longer a spell over the reality of life. Much has been written on this imaginative story, and Henri Peyre comments on it decisively in words that may cover the picture by Roy also: ' This is real life, but with that slight intrusion of fancy. . . It is the real existence of a corner of a province seen through the enchanted eyes of childhood.' [56]

Artists like Roy and Fournier may be credited with reintroducing a dignified beauty at a time when art in general seems bound to indulge in discouraging problems and ruthlessly ugly forms. Thus even contemporary art and literature in France reveal that there is still a reservoir of poetry, which André Maurois has connected with the wonderland *Méipe*, which is ' in France, in our garden, two steps from here,' nowhere, everywhere, ' a nonexistent and real point at which heaven and earth meet.' [57]

# Consequences for Literary Criticism

I T WILL have been noted that these comparisons of art and literature have been restricted to examples within the same epoch in history. The observance of this principle is a guarantee that the comparisons selected are a meaningful expression of the common spiritual root
behind the related examples in literature and art. As knowledge of the cultural spirit at a given epoch becomes broader and deeper through the study
of these interrelations, the interpretation of history becomes more precise,
which is to say that this study thus far has served history. These same
parallels, however, can also serve literary criticism, for they illustrate topics
concerned with criticism *per se*.

If in the historical part the parallelism between the arts of the word and
the color consisted in psychological analogies with no possible proof of pri-
ority, sometimes art threw more light on literature or conversely literature
on art, depending on internal affinities which were more striking in the
language than in the painting or vice versa. If a formal parallelism was at
issue, an attempt was made to clarify the origin in the one or the other of
the two arts. Sometimes both arts seemed to depend simply on the spirit
of the time without a specific, direct interrelation. Finally, some of the examples discussed revealed clearly the technical limits for the mutual imitation of the arts. These considerations offer to criticism seven constant cases,
applicable to any historical epoch, as will become clear from this chapter.
In other words, there can be derived from our historical material seven
categories of literary criticism as well as of art criticism. They will corroborate the indissoluble unit of the historical and the aesthetic method.

## I. Details of a Literary Text Elucidated by a Picture

The approach to literature through art proved to be imperative in all
those cases where literary texts contained factual, psychological, or structural elements that would have remained obscure without the elucidation
of the arts of design.

This is true in such cases as the following: The hieratic epic king of the
*Chansons de geste* could hardly have come from the type of stereotyped

heroes in Greco-Roman literature, for this literary tradition had been interrupted. The form of the young, popular, epic king can be fully explained only by the art tradition of the Byzantine-Romanesque *Pantocrator* as depicted on the medieval tympana. The lively dialogues of cavalier love casuistry in the *romans courtois* are decisively linked to Scholastic disputations as their source, as proved by the presence on the cathedral portals of the apostles arranged in discussion groups. The striking mystical anachronisms in the poetry of Villon, for which no literary source can be found, are pictured by Enguerrand Charonton, Justus of Ghent, and Nicolas Froment.

The sudden appearance of realistic details and cozy *intérieurs* in fifteenth-century Burgundian flamboyant literature would seem to be without source in the literary tradition. In art, however, such things as the miniatures and pictures like *Birth of Saint John* and *Childbed of Saint Ann* had prepared the way by setting Biblical subjects in Flemish-French interiors, with the consequent development of the bourgeois *intérieur* for its own sake. The movement then simply goes from the tradition of secular painting into the early prose novels (*Petit Jehan de Saintré* and *Jean de Paris*).

Racine's use of a few epithets to evoke tragic and disastrous, lovely and promising climates and landscapes, giving the whole the lucent beauty of a slightly changing though constant scene, could easily escape the reader if there were not at the same time the stereotyped landscapes of Claude Lorrain, where the light suggestions of morning, noon, and evening apparently have the same meaning as Racine's epithets.

Discussions over the meaning of La Fontaine's ' human ' animals are resolved by a comparison with the sketches by Charles Le Brun depicting human heads shaped according to animal patterns, confirming the idea of a new anthropology that uses *ressemblances* as a basis for psychology. This parallel gives the problem of nature in La Fontaine a new orientation.

Mallarmé's beautiful, dreamed flights of an ideal symbolic bird in an ideal boundless space, not self-evident from the context, are crystallized in abstract form in *Bird in Space* by Brancusi; and lastly, the darkly cryptic *Illumination* by Rimbaud called ' Mystique ' is translated and commented on by Gauguin's picture *Jacob Wrestling with the Angel*.

## II. Details of a Picture Clarified by a Literary Text

Conversely, literature can be an aid to painting. Often a picture reaches its full meaning as an interpreter of cultural phenomena only by the literary parallel. It is in this function that literature reveals itself as the philosophically deeper and psychologically richer interpretation.

Specifically, details in the following works of art are explained by contemporaneous literary texts. The winged, apocalyptic animals and other enigmatic, symbolic beasts that appear on the Romanesque tympana reveal their zoological secrets only to the readers of the bestiaries, in particular that of Philippe de Thaün, while the monsters and dwarfs of the tympanum of Vézelay find their full explanation in the *Roman d'Alexandre*.

The ' Poem of the Assumption,' in which the concept is of the *dormitio* as opposed to the more frequent *resurrectio*, resolves the question of the famous *Assumption of the Virgin* on the west front of Notre Dame cathedral in Paris, much debated by the historians of art. The *Roman de Renart* is certainly the key to the nature of the very human animal gargoyles of Notre Dame in Paris, the literary and sculptural manifestation of a sympathetic preoccupation with the animal itself as opposed to its intended allegorical meaning: sin and Hell.

' Nature ' poems in the fifteenth century, such as those of Froissart and Charles d'Orléans, reveal that nature, whether in these poems or in the early miniatures (*April* by Pol de Limbourg), actually plays a secondary role to culture, the silent miniatures obviously needing the contemporaneous literary parallels to decide the issue about which art historians could not until recently agree. Similarly, the poems of Remy Belleau and Jean Antoine de Baïf corroborate the idea that the Renaissance writers were decidedly more disposed toward a witty interpretation of mythological subjects, while such paintings as *Amor Disarmed* by the Fontainebleau School sacrificed this element to a glorification of beautiful forms.

Knowing that the *Embarkation for Cythera* is actually a translation of the finale of *Les Trois Cousines*, the comedy by Dancourt, and that the actress who played the heroine also played an important role in Watteau's life, adds zest to the tableau and explains in particular why she turns her beautiful face to the public. Voltaire's rococo poem ' Le Mondain ' is the ideal guide through a rococo room like Boffrand's Salon of the Princess in the Hôtel de Soubise. The well-known phrase, ' La Marseillaise de Pierre,' fixes the spirit of the *Hymn of Departure for War* by Rude on the Arc de Triomphe de l'Etoile.

Again it is a poem that reveals the mythical, symbolic, and apocalyptic implications of the painting *The Sower*; this time ' Le Soir ' by Victor Hugo fulfils this function for Millet's well-known painting. Proust's study of the *aubépine* in *Du Côté de chez Swann* makes the light-shimmering *Pin de Bertrand* of Paul Signac consciously meaningful.

Verhaeren's ecstatic feeling for nature, expressed in his poem ' L'Arbre,' explains the unique ' burning trees ' of van Gogh as being an outgrowth of the intense Flemish spirit. Finally the Claudelian parallel to the *Annunciation* by Maurice Denis substantiates an interpretation of the picture as having mystical implications.

### III. Concepts and Motifs of Literature Clarified by the Arts of Design

Certain general concepts conditioned by propensities of a certain epoch appear as motifs in literature. Their exact meaning can be corroborated by parallel cases in the arts of design. The interpretations by art give to a mere descriptive, possibly subjective, interpretation a type of objectively verifiable proof.

Such concepts in literature are: the medieval element of the *tremendum* in the religious sphere, where the meaning of ambivalent epithets emanates clearly from the sculptural vizualization; the constant following of a *topos* receives its meaning from iconographic clichés; and the lively rhythm of movement in the *romans courtois* is highlighted by the turmoil scenes in sculpture. The Gothic ideals of feminine elegance are more vividly seen from the statues than in the elements of beauty scattered throughout the literature.

Renaissance hedonism and Reformation pietism form a more striking unity in the *Eva Pandora* picture than in the works of Marot, where love poetry and Psalms are relegated to different volumes.

Psychological shades of the theme of acceptance of death, which are found throughout a gamut of passages in literature, from Malherbe to Bossuet, are condensed in one single picture by Poussin, *Et in Arcadia Ego*. The feeling of uncanny uneasiness behind so many nocturnal scenes of Racine is focused more drastically in the St. Sebastian picture by Georges de la Tour. The typically baroque feeling of infinite space comes less vividly to the reader of Pascal than to one who views the gardens of Versailles. *Polyeucte* as a drama of religious heroism according to Jesuit piety is fully explained in Poussin's less mitigated picture of *St. Francis Xavier Awakening a Dead Girl*. The meaning of Jansenistic renunciation, abstention, and simplicity is brought home much more quickly in the *Ex Voto* painting by Champaigne than from a volume like Arnauld's *Fréquente Communion* or even from a drama like *Bérénice* by Racine.

The combination of learning and flirtation that permeates the elegant scientific treatises for ladies in the eighteenth century is contained in one glance at the *Music Lesson* by Lancret. The spirit of the lascivious rococo novel is caught in a moment from the *Escarpolette* by Fragonard. The same spirit in the *forme embourgeoisée* is hidden in Rousseau's *Nouvelle Héloïse* but distinctly unveiled in the pictures of Greuze.

The neo-classic ideal of beauty — that is, a slightly sentimentalized concept of the Hellenistic spirit — permeates, as is well known, the poetry of André Chénier. Its very details, however, are more exactly caught in certain of Prud'hon's pictures. Similarly it is possible to understand the mixture of devotion and sensuality that characterizes the romantic Catholicism of Chateaubriand (generally praised and misunderstood by the *bien pensants*) by confronting it with such a picture as *The Young Martyr* by Delaroche. There is no better illustration of the shallowness of Victor Hugo's type of metaphysics and mystery than the fact that it could be painted as a myth in Delacroix's settings of eerie dusks and darks, truly corresponding to Hugo's *ombre-sombre* type of rhyme. The enthusiasm of Madame de Staël and her followers, reflected in many a romantic face, finds its prototype in young Napoleon storming the bridge at Arcole, as painted by Baron Gros. The coarse sensuality behind the romantic search for the unknown woman, from Musset and Mérimée to Flaubert and Baudelaire, is laid bare in a picture like *Algerian Women* by Delacroix.

The paintings Paul Gauguin made in Tahiti can prove that the cryptic prose of Rimbaud, full of colorful, unheard-of evocations, represents the escapism of his epoch into exotic dreamlands rather than metaphysical yearnings, as Claudel would like to have it. The infantilism and dadaism of the surrealists cease to ' dumbfound the bourgeois ' if, while reading their poems, one keeps in mind the earlier pictorial attempts by the *douanier* Rousseau to combine heterogeneous elements by means of a child's drawing technique.

## IV. Motifs of Pictures Elucidated through Literature

In other cases, the clarification of certain general concepts and motifs in art comes from an outspoken parallel in literature. Mediaeval literature and literary theory make clear that the general preoccupation with light, brilliancy, and splendor, regarded as necessary constituents of heavenly beauty and grace, is the real *raison d'être* of the over-abundance of light on the tympanum of Vézelay: *Christ Sending Forth the Apostles.*

The tympanum of the *Last Judgment* on the cathedral of Bourges is an example of two contradictory trends in expression: the realistic and the symbolic. On this particular tympanum these trends are manifested in the realistic presentation of Hell and the symbolic presentation of Heaven, shown as Abraham sitting in a framed cubicle holding the souls of the just in his lap (bosom). Literature proves that one is confronted here with two different strata of different epochs, because in literature these two trends appear at different moments: the attitude of awe is found in the early half-liturgical plays, avoiding the realistic presentation of God (*Figura*) and Paradise; the new realistic, popular stage method appears during later centuries of the Middle Ages, using all imaginable horrors to produce the harrowing of Hell without developing any corresponding presentation of the joys of Paradise.

The beauty and wealth reflected in the harmonious features and opulent dress and jewelry of the young woman depicted in the portrait of *Elizabeth of Austria* by François Clouet do not reveal the sentiment of a self-conscious enjoyment of personal attractiveness behind it. A clear commentary can, however, be taken from a much earlier and more precise, almost jubilant, literary *Portrait d'une pucelle par elle-même*, by Eustache Deschamps.

The dignified sorrow and wordless pain expressed by Pierre Villatte in his *Pietà* receives the most illuminating commentary from Antoine de la Sale's *Réconfort de Madame du Fresne*. The new, naïve shamelessness of the

Renaissance, daring to appear harmlessly and gracefully in the picture of *Gabrielle d'Estrée dans son bain,* can be understood in all its implications as the normal spirit of the time if looked at through the sensuous love poems of Ronsard, where Gabrielle changes into Marie, *la belle paresseuse.* The attempt by Goujon to express the element of water, symbolic of nymphs, by giving the four feminine figures on his *Fountain of the Innocents* shimmering and flowing garments is outdone by Ronsard's ' nymphes quand l'eau les cache,' an expression of a considerable assimilation of Greek mythology into a more modern feeling for nature.

The picture by Poussin, *Orpheus Asking the Way to Hades,* gains in meaning if it is remembered that at the same historical moment Pascal was writing his *Pensée:* 'L'immortalité de l'âme est une chose qui nous importe si fort. . . .' Poussin's attraction to the topic of *Diogenes Throwing away His Bowl* causes no surprise in a century of renunciation, which produces *Le Cid* and *La Princesse de Clèves.* A bare landscape is intolerable to Poussin, who admits only a *Landscape with Fauns and Nymphs,* but this can only be intimated by the general interest of the century in man and psychological anthropology. The declaration by Corneille sharpens the point: ' Otez Pan et sa flûte; adieu les pâturages! ' Claude Lorrain's still more whimsical filling of landscapes with Biblical subjects arbitrarily arranged (*Marriage of Isaac, Flight into Egypt, Baptizing the Eunuch*) finds its explanation in Fénelon's concept of such scenes as *un caprice.* The overstressing and isolation of the protagonist in a victory parade, as is the case in Charles Le Brun's *Alexander Entering Babylon,* receives its elucidation from the classical tragedy, where all action is centered in the soul of the hero and not in the activities of supernumeraries.

The beautiful busts and portraits of the century receive their full meaning from the corresponding literary portraits, typical or individual, where the expressions are truly interpreted as different psychological attitudes. The ascetic restraint of Philippe de Champaigne's *Magdalen,* in contrast to all the contemporary baroque Magdalens of Europe, is best explained by the austere, Jansenistic Puritanism apparent in the whole literary production of Port Royal. The religious pictures of the classical age, such as *Christ on the Cross* by Charles Le Brun and *Christ and the Woman of Samaria* by Mignard, reveal all their seriousness if considered together with corresponding texts from Pascal. The paintings of the Le Nain brothers lose their stiffness if understood not as representations of *faits divers* in the Dutch manner, but as studies of man as given by Descartes, Pascal, La Rochefoucauld, and La Bruyère, which is to say that the Le Nain brothers are *moralistes.* The fact that in Poussin's famous picture, *Elieser and Rebecca,* the essential actors, the camels, do not appear is understood from the application of the requisite quality of *bienséance,* so important in classical literature, which also excludes lower animals from the language of tragedy and poetry.

The strange boldness of the petting scenes of the eighteenth century, as depicted in the paintings of Watteau (*La Danse dans un pavillon*) or in those of Pater (*Reunion of Comedians in a Park*), is explained not only by the obscene rococo novels but even by the correspondence between Diderot and Sophie Volland. The marble statues of Watteau, which seem living flesh, find their explanation in Diderot's theory of flesh and marble, as well as in the tendency of Buffon to see beautiful animals as women. The sad clowns and actors that are the subjects of Watteau's *Gilles* and *Indifférent* are lengthily interpreted by the sad-amusing discussions of the role of the actor by Rousseau and Diderot. *Signboard for Gersaint* by Watteau awakens to its full life as a *compliment* when surrounded by all the well-cut epigrams, poems, and remarks from the pen of Voltaire, which unite in the same unique form *esprit* and gracefulness.

The sensation of the gruesome, the cruel, and the crude, as evident in the *Raft of the Medusa* by Géricault, proves to be symptomatic of romanticism, for similar repercussions of sensation and unrefined passion are analyzed in the historical novels — for example, in the flogging of Quasimodo and the burning of Esmeralda in *Notre Dame de Paris*. That the realism of the romantics nevertheless still clings strongly to a super-individual, symbolic interpretation of life can be seen from the literary parallels to the apparently realistic paintings of Millet.

The sentimental and critical de-Christianization of the nineteenth century is still camouflaged in the traditional religious themes of Prud'hon's *Crucifixion*, Bouguereau's *Madonna of Consolation*, and Ary Scheffer's *Temptation of Christ*. But these pictures reveal their faithless atmosphere not simply because of their merely technical tradition, but because they reflect the new ' religious ' poetry, such as Lamartine's *Le Crucifix*, Vigny's *Le Mont des oliviers*, and Hugo's *La Fin de Satan*.

Pictures like *Les Grands Boulevards au printemps* by Renoir, stressing the sensations of life, great cities, and atmosphere, would not by themselves reveal the implications of a metaphysically meaningless world, but the description of the drive in Flaubert's *Madame Bovary* is an analyzed *Boulevard au printemps* and reveals these implications to the fullest extent. The same is true for Renoir's and Flaubert's *Luncheon of the Boating Party*, Renoir's *Le Moulin de la Galette* and Flaubert's description of *Le bal de Vaubyessard*, Seurat's and Edmond de Goncourt's *Cirque*, Renoir's and Flaubert's *Theatre Box*. If there were need to prove that the realistic-impressionist pictures without the analytical aid of literature could not express sufficiently the curious new merger of the beautiful with the ignoble in this grasping of life by a religion of *l'art pour l'art*, one could quote the fact that Degas himself commented on his ballet studies in meaningful sonnets that underscore either problem.

The yearning for a new landscape with simple and mighty forms is not necessarily explained as an individual innovation by Cézanne, because it is found also in the epochal trend of the poetry of Théophile Gautier and Leconte de Lisle, wherein are given explicit reasons for it.

The *Blue Girl* of Vincent van Gogh is made meaningful by the explicit poem of Jammes, 'La Jeune Fille,' just as van Gogh's *Café de Nuit* is elucidated by the detailed texts of despair of Rimbaud, Gide, Duhamel, and Green. The metaphysical despair of the modern world, as suggested in *Clown's Head* by Rouault, is described in such detail by Bloy and Bernanos as to become a literal comment on Rouault. The magic power of childlikeness and fancy to transform a sad world into beauty may be the message of a picture like *La Chambre de Musique* of Pierre Roy; the novel *Le Grand Meaulnes* by Alain Fournier makes this possibility a certitude.

### V. Literary-Linguistic Forms Made Comprehensible by Art Forms

Art has proved particularly helpful to literature in so far as formal problems in painting can account for formal problems of composition, style, and technique in literature.

The life of a saint, *La Chanson de Saint Alexis*, has an interior and exterior division based on the number five. This principle would remain an enigma (it is not a symbolic 'holy' number) if the groups of the oldest Romanesque tympana were not also based on this number five. Since psychologists have discovered that five units are the maximum the eye can embrace, a *transposition d'art* accounts much better for the five units appearing in composition, strophes, and verse of the *Alexius* than any other symbolic or dramatic explanation. The apparent chaos of endless monotonous fighting scenes in the *Chanson de Roland*, the more clumsy as they describe in detail the Christian side as well as the pagan and are interrupted, apparently quite arbitrarily, by digressions, turns into a well-understood order when checked against the marching nations on the tympanum of Vézelay, where a conscious additive technique has made monotony bearable by contrasting two groups striving to meet and by interrupting each one by opposite movements. The tripartite, gradational character of a biographical tympanum lends certainty to the theory that the hitherto much debated structural principle of the biographical and adventurous courtly novels of Chrétien de Troyes is also tripartition and gradation.

Pictures such as *Canon van der Paele* by Jan van Eyck, showing all the wrinkles, warts, folds, veins, and scars on the face, reveal the formal principle of minute realism, according to which the realistic details in the prose novels of the fifteenth century are enumerated with the naïve aim of attaining completeness and microscopic exactness. The illogical use of the tenses, the endless co-ordination, and the word order based on psychological criteria, which are found in the works of Villehardouin, Joinville, and other early prose writers, are less disturbing if it is understood that these elements correspond exactly to the wrong perspective, the simultaneous co-ordination of successively occurring scenes, and the size of the figures according to their psychological importance in the miniatures and first French *tableaux*, such as the *History of Saint Denis* by Malouel and Bellechose. On the other hand, one can understand the awkward attempt of Antoine de la Sale in the first genuine French prose novel, *Jehan de Saintré*, to give a slight, erotic plot an immense depth by moral-educational discussions and by the insertion of military problems and actions when one sees the same artistic principle used by Jan van Eyck. In his picture, *Virgin and Donor*, the action takes place in the foreground — the Chancellor Rollin adores the Divine Child held by the Virgin — whereas in the background one sees through a window in an immense perspective the town, river, and country with all their life and movement.

The classical-baroque structure of the seventeenth-century dramas, with the *longue carrière de cinq actes, la liaison des scènes*, the quick mounting from a condensed background of exposition to a crisis in the relation between two protagonists, the many *fausses fenêtres* for balancing act and scenes, all this seems almost visually projected onto a plane and thus is explained formally by a contemporary picture like the *Holy Family* by Poussin. In this picture there is the same *beau désordre*, a long suite of figures to fill the foreground, all linked with one another but arranged in pyramid groups, highlighting the main actors before an immense landscape background that seems meaningless in view of the subject in the foreground, where the secondary figures are introduced only for balancing the groups.

The classically austere, although lively, baroque-art principle of a sermon by Bossuet consists of well-delineated, harmonious, and rhythmical sentences. These, however, are enlivened only by a colorful Biblical quotation, or a visualizing epithet, or one of the rare comparisons. The eye receives the very same impression from a baroque chapel such as that of Versailles, austere in its white arches and high columns, the only colorful spots being the vault picture above the main altar, the mosaics of the floor, and the silk and velvet of pews and chairs.

Lamartine's romantic language, having few metaphors and purposely kept pale by traditional metonymies, is generally misunderstood. This liquid coloring and moderation of a century-old classical heritage, however, can be well explained by the same principle as that used by Ingres in his *Apotheosis of Homer*; for here, too, ancient and modern historical figures are grouped around Homer seated in front of a Greek temple. They are dimly rendered in pale colors mitigated by the clear lines of the figures.

In impressionist pictures like *Spring* by Corot, *The Wave* by Courbet, and *Port of Bordeaux* by Manet, one can see clearly that the literary technique of Flaubert, Loti, Verlaine, and Zola, independent of their realistic, naturalistic, or symbolic creeds, corresponds closely to that of the painters, the broad brush strokes corresponding to the *style nominal*, the prevalence of color over form corresponding to the adjective obscuring the substantive.

The technique of disintegrating snatches of a whole in geometrically exact and arranged forms, as can be seen in *The Chessboard* by Juan Gris, is the key to the metaphorically veiled riddles of a ' pure ' poem, which is not comprehended at once in its entirety but in its partly pure, partly occult forms of frozen associations of thought, as represented by the poetry of Paul Valéry in his *Le Cimetière marin*.

## VI. Art Forms Explained by Literary-Stylistic Expressions

Much more delicate is the converse problem, whether literary composition and style forms may be called upon to elucidate formal problems in the arts of design. It is a fact that the art historians who have faced this problem have practically denied this possibility. Nonetheless, this possibility exists to a certain degree. Either the formal implications of a composition like the *History of Saint Honoré*, which is inserted between the Apostles and the Crucified on the tympanum of Amiens, must be denied or it must be conceded that such compositions represent the combination of the tight, biographical type of dramatized gradation story (*Perceval*, Saints' lives) and the loose *exemplum* type (*Lais* of Marie de France, *Mary Legends* of Gautier de Coinci).

An interior architecture of the type of Mansart's *Galerie des glaces* remains confused for the onlookers because of its contradictory principles: classical simplicity of forms and baroque pompousness of decoration. These contrasting tendencies, however, are brought to a greater unity in Pascal's formula of *esprit de géométrie* and *esprit de finesse*. Hence Pascal's philosophy together with Molière's comments on Mignard's ceiling of Val de Grâce reveal what today modern literary historians call *le classicisme baroque*.

## VII. The Constant, Sharp, and Unmistakable Borderlines between Literature and Art

It can be easily understood from the small number of works of art needing a formal interpretation through literature, as compared to the considerable number of literary techniques stemming from art, that the *transposition d'art* is a drive in one direction, but precisely the direction that interests literature as one of its vital factors and that has been, accordingly, the central concern of this study. Nevertheless, even these imitations and transpositions are limited by the laws that Lessing once established in his *Laocoön* about the boundaries between poetry and painting, laws that are still valid. A last comparison of the remainder of our examples illustrates the correctness of Lessing's old but classical contention. His own example of a dressed figure in art, with all details simultaneously shown, and a figure dressing itself successively are also evidenced by the royally dressed statues of the Gothic age and, in narrative or didactic literature, by the contemporary descriptions of ladies preparing to go to church or to a feast.

Nature scenes with mythological subjects are repeated endlessly in art from the Greeks to the French classics. But Nature mythology never has been an adequate symbolic means for the painter. In literature, however, La Fontaine discovered that in a society without Greco-Roman mythological concepts such a thing can be done only if there are ironic sidelights.

Charles Le Brun, the painter, can enhance the mystical meaning of the mystery of Christ dying on the Cross only by replacing the human surroundings with angelical ones. Pascal as a writer can deepen this same mystery much more effectively by a profound meditation that is pure thought, and thought artistically expressed. The same advantage holds true for his dialogue with Christ as compared to the treatment of the same topic, which necessarily had to be confined to a traditional Biblical scene and its ' transitory moment,' by Mignard in *Christ and the Woman of Samaria.*

Girodet-Trioson, illustrating the burial of Atala, reveals exactly what he cannot imitate in Chateaubriand's text: the emotional, historical, and retrospective elements. Conversely, it is seen how little has been achieved by Vigny in his literary portrait of Cinq Mars, because he only added a few details to the portrait of Meissonier's *Cavalier* of the time of Louis XIII.

The symbolic efforts of painting generally lack the convincing, even the persuading, element. *Officer of the Imperial Guard* by Géricault expresses the essence of Napoleonic military glory less well than August Barbier's ' equation ' of France as *une cavale* and Napoleon as her rider. The many *Mazeppa* pictures can depict only choice episodes, while the poem of Victor Hugo can relate the whole story. On the other hand, the detailed *Massacre of Scio* by Delacroix can be rendered by Victor Hugo also in the form of some lyrical reflections. Prud'hon's *Crime Pursued by Justice and Divine Vengeance,* by mixing allegorical and realistic elements, was bound to become an artistic failure, while Hugo, doing exactly the same in his *Conscience,* could produce a chef-d'œuvre, since poetry is able to amalgamate these two formal language elements. Painting, however, can symbolize facts and events also by aggrandized, typical, exaggerated, and even caricatural form elements, as can readily be seen from Daumier's *La République* and *Don Quixote.* The same means used by poets and writers (Hugo, Balzac), on the other hand, result in an involuntary caricature, because literature has more subtle means to make unmistakably clear what its symbolism involves; types such as Balzac's Grandet become more individual than typical. Again, typical patterns with the most modern individual nuances can be kept in the symbolic line by one or two decisive gestures or movements, as in the *Emeute* by Daumier. When painting traditional, religious subjects, the unbeliever discloses his lack of faith only by exaggerated gestures and misplaced accents (Bouguereau, Henner), which make him inefficient; or, if he attempts a reinterpretation of older patterns (Delacroix, *Disciples at Emmaus*), he becomes academic. The writer, when doing the same (Gautier, Hérédia), can express ironic empathy and thus bring home at least the intended meaning to the reader.

The French realists work consciously along the lines of the *Laocoön*. Courbet chooses for description a funeral procession that has reached the cemetery, where the mourners are standing around the grave. Flaubert chooses to describe the successive scenes of a funeral procession as it moves through the streets. Renoir can show only the life of the boulevards as seen from a point that takes in the entire vista; Flaubert can show this life in cinematographic, small pieces, as it would be visible to someone riding in a coach along those streets. Monet, painting the cathedral at different moments of the day, can, at best, array all these atmospheric snapshots as in a museum; Zola, picturing Paris from the same window at morning, noon, evening, and night, can make out of the resultant moods the pivotal elements of the composition of *Une Page d'amour*. The law that art must reproduce the beautiful and literature the characteristic features still comes to the fore, even when art tries to assume the task of literature in naturalistic style: *Les Repasseuses* of Edgar Degas are tired, yawning, hard-working, like those of Zola in *L'Assommoir*, but they are much less vulgar because they do not speak. It was only expressionism that violated the Laocoön laws. For example, Georges Braque tried to paint the *Waltz* by creating tripartite compositions to imitate the rhythm, and Guillaume Apollinaire attacked the necktie in a *calligramme*, the letters of which were arranged in the form of *La Cravate*. Again, however, the literary attempt is acceptable because it is done with ironic empathy; the pictorial one much less so.

The discovery by the painter Pierre Roy of magic and the fairy tale as present even in modern, everyday life is manifested in such elements as a moonlit chamber and a girl playing a cello in the night — an extreme combination of rarely occurring coincidences stressed by rare colors. The same discovery develops in Alain Fournier's *Grand Meaulnes* into a perhaps still stronger coincidence of rare situations, but a running, explicit psychology gives them a verisimilitude that is lacking in the painting.

## Epilogue

With our examples arranged historically as well as phenomenologically, in both cases guided by psychological-aesthetic principles, we have exhausted the possibilities of an objective approach to French literature through art. Furthermore, in the course of this work there was brought home every single methodological problem that, until recently, the historians of art have solved with more convincing means than the historians of literature. Such problems are: cultural psychology, the history of ideas, the network of style elements as individual, epochal, and national, the problem of the generation, the increasingly greater importance of technique in art and its implications of an elaborate, collective mannerism as a normal phenomenon, in contrast to the greater importance of the unique personality in literature and its implications of the lack of creativeness in literary schools and *cercles, chapelles,* and *cénacles,* to which a collective mannerism can never be counted as an achievement.

This study was only possible at a moment when it has been fully recognized that the descriptive and comparative method is necessarily the starting point for any formal understanding of art. We recognized further that this method remains superficial and does not produce deeper insights if there is no way from the outer to the inner form. Interior form means psychological implication of the outer form; that is, psychology changes with the epochs and with individuals, and consequently this psychology itself needs a historical backing. Thus the formal approach must be broadened from the immanently psychological to a strictly historical understanding of the underlying forces responsible for the spirit or meaning of the forms of literature and art at the different moments in history. It seemed to me not only a sound point of view but an absolute principle that the primary and predominantly aesthetic approach in the analysis of any art cannot be replaced by any other, if art is not to be deprived of its very character. But it must be supplemented by what some have called *Geistesgeschichte* or the 'History of Ideas,' if the aesthetic problems are to be understood. This understanding itself is a decisive part in the final enjoyment of art and literature, as formulated by Heinrich Wölfflin:

> He who is accustomed to look at the world as an historian knows the profound feeling of happiness arising when, for the scrutinizing gaze, things take shape clearly, according to origin and evolution and the objects have lost the appearance of accidental phenomena and are understood as something grown by necessity.[1]

It is a process in which the free interplay of the individuals co-exists with the unconscious trends of becoming. Using the famous Saussurian terms, Wölfflin has shown the interplay between synchrony and diachrony in the investigation of art. Precisely this was the purpose of the present book, where these principles are applied to the literary field in its inseparability from art.

# Notes and Bibliography

*Citations in the notes are for specific references. Sources of more general material are found in the bibliography for each chapter. Unless otherwise noted, translations are by the author and make no attempt to reflect the literary quality of the original.*

## Chapter I                                                        Notes

1. *Les Légendes épiques* (Paris: Champion, 1900–1913), 4 vols.
2. Details and description in Meyer Schapiro, 'The Romanesque Sculpture of Moissac,' *Art Bulletin*, XIII (1931), 249–350 and 464–531. For Moissac as the cradle of the medieval drama, see Edith A. Wright, *The Dissemination of the Liturgical Drama in France* (Diss. Bryn Mawr, 1936).
3. Sister Marianna Gildea, *Expression of Religious Thought and Feeling in the Chansons de geste* (Diss. Catholic University, Washington, D.C., 1943), pp. 126ff.
4. Ilona Deak-Ebner, 'The Sickle-Shaped Wing in Ancient Art,' *Gazette des Beaux-Arts*, XXXIV (1948), pp. 65–76.
5. *L'Art d'occident. Le Moyen âge roman et gothique* (Paris: Colin, 1938), pp. 5 and 46.
6. *Le Bestiaire de Philippe de Thaün*, ed. Emmanuel Walberg (Paris: Welter, 1900), lines 27–112 *passim*.
7. 'Zur Interpretation des Alexiusliedes,' *Zeitschrift für Romanische Philologie*, LVI (1936), pp. 113–39.
8. Francis Salet, *La Madeleine de Vézelay* (Melun: D'Argences, 1948), description pp. 174–7, details plates 14–19. See also Arthur Kingsley Porter, *Romanesque Sculpture of the Pilgrimage Roads* (Boston, 1923).
9. *La Sculpture française du moyen âge et de la Renaissance* (Paris et Bruxelles: G. Van Oest, 1926), pp. 17–18.
10. Edmond Faral, 'Une Source latine de l'histoire d'Alexandre. La lettre sur les merveilles de l'Inde,' *Romania*, 43 (1914), pp. 199–215 and 353–76.
11. *The Medieval French Roman d'Alexandre*, ed. Milan S. LaDu (Princeton and Paris, 1937), I, pp. 257ff. See also Rudolf Wittkower, 'Marvels of the East: A Study in the History of Monsters,' *Journal of the Warburg and Courtauld Institutes*, V (1914).
12. *University Prints* (Newton, Mass.), K 73.
13. Emile Mâle, *L'Art religieux du XIIe siècle en France* (Paris: Colin, 1922), pp. 377 and 442.
14. Cf. W. W. Comfort, 'Types in the Chansons de geste,' *PMLA*, XXI (1906), p. 301.
15. Cf. Helmut Hatzfeld, 'Literarisches Hochmittelalter in Frankreich,' *Tijdschrift voor Taal en Letteren* (Tilburg, 1935), p. 114; and Anna Granville Hatcher, 'Epic patterns in Old French,' *Word*, II (1946), pp. 8–24.
16. Op. cit. p. 165.
17. *The Idea of the Holy. An Inquiry into the Non-Rational Factor in the Idea of the Divine and Its Relation to the Rational*. Trans. by J. W. Harvey from the ninth German edition (London, 1936).
18. For the importance of Biblical tropology, see E. Auerbach, *Mimesis* (Bern: Francke, 1946), *passim*.

19. Guernes, *La Vie de Saint Thomas de Cantorbéry*, ed. Walberg (Lund, 1922), 5423–30.
20. Op. cit. p. 34.
21. Ed. J. P. Strachey (Cambridge: University Press, 1942), p. 21, lines 192–6.
22. Ed. A. G. van Hamel (Paris: Vieweg, 1885).
23. Helmut Hatzfeld, 'Einige Stilwesenszüge der altfranzösischen religiösen Reimdichtung,' *Zeitschrift für Romanische Philologie* (1932), especially pp. 701–2 and 706–7; and H. P. I. Ahsmann, *Le Culte de la Vierge et la littérature française profane du moyen âge* (Utrecht-Nimègue, 1929).
24. Guillaume de Lorris, *Le Roman de la Rose*, ed. E. Langlois, Société des anciens textes (Paris, 1920), I, lines 2093–6.
25. See Amédée Boinet, *Les Sculptures de la cathédrale de Bourges* (Paris Champion, 1912), pp. 52–70.
26. Marcel Aubert, op. cit. p. 38.
27. Chrétien de Troyes, *Erec und Ernide*, ed. Wendelin Foerster (Halle: Niemeyer, 1934), 2159–70.
28. Ed. G. A. Crapelet and A. C. M. Robert (Paris: Crapelet, 1834), 2 vols., lines 6931–94; cf. Fay Fisher, *Narrative Art in Medieval Romance* (Diss. Columbia, Cleveland, 1938), p. 51.
29. René Schneider, *L'Art français des origines à la fin du XIIIe siècle* (Paris: Laurens, 1928), p. 201; and Amédée Boinet, op. cit. pp. 53ff.
30. Ed. L. Constans, Société des anciens textes (Paris, 1890), lines 9848–54.
31. Ed. W. Foerster (Halle: Niemeyer, 1888), lines 1392–5.
32. Ed. Karl Warnke (Halle: Niemeyer, 1938), lines 835–42.
33. Ed. Gaston Paris and Gaston Raynaud (Paris: Vieweg, 1878), p. 438.
34. See Louise Lefrançois-Pillion, *La Cathédrale d'Amiens* (Paris: Plon, 1937), p. 46.
35. Focillon, op. cit. p. 169.
36. 'Marie de France – Dichterin von Problem Märchen,' *Romanische Stil-und Literaturstudien* (Marburg: Elwert, 1931), pp. 55–102.
37. On scholastic aesthetics see St. Thomas Aquinas, *Summa Theologiae*: Ia Iae Qu.5,4; Qu.39,8. Ia IIae Qu.21,2; Qu.27,1; Qu.57,3ff. IIa IIae Qu.47,1ff; Qu.49,5; Qu.162,2.
38. *Roman d'Enéas*, ed. Jacques Salverda de Grave (Halle, 1891), lines 7867–82.
39. *Li Contes del graal*, ed. Alfons Hilka (Halle: Niemeyer, 1932), lines 3157–3200 *passim*.
40. For the development of the concept of the Blessed Virgin in art see M. Vloberg, *La Vierge, notre médiatrice* (Grenoble: Arthaud, 1938).
41. Focillon, op. cit. p. 229.
42. Cf. Eunice Rathbone Goddard, *Woman's Costumes in French Texts of the Eleventh and Twelfth Centuries*, Johns Hopkins Studies in Romance Languages (Baltimore, 1927).
43. Quoted in Goddard, op. cit. p. 23.
44. Ed. Foulet in *Classiques français du moyen âge* (Paris: 1925), lines 2013–17.
45. See René Merlet, *La Cathédrale de Chartres* (Paris: Laurens, 1929).
46. *Mystères et Moralités du Ms. 617 de Chantilly*, ed. G. Cohen (Paris: Champion, 1920), pp. 43–9.
47. Bartsch-Wiese, *Chrestomathie* (Leipzig: Vogel, 1913), no. 39, lines 215–30 *passim*.
48. Ed. W. Foerster (Halle: Niemeyer, 1891), lines 288–308.
49. *Alexandre le Grand*, ed. Paul Meyer (Paris: Vieweg, 1886), I, lines 132–8.
50. *Etudes sur le théâtre français du XIVe et XVe siècle* (Paris: Rousseau, 1901); and Manya Lifschitz-Golden, *Les Juifs dans la littérature française du moyen âge* (Mystères, Miracles, Chroniques) (Diss. Columbia University, 1935), p. 11.

## Chapter I                                    Bibliography

Jahn, Johannes, *Kompositionsgesetze französischer Reliefplastik im 12 und 13. Jahrhundert* (Leipzig: Hirsemann, 1922).
Kuhn, Alwin, 'Über Charakter und Ursprung des westromanischen Heldenepos,' *Germanisch-Romanische Monatsschrift* (1935).

Lefrançois-Pillion, Louise, *Les Sculpteurs français du XIIe siècle* (Paris: Plon, 1931).
Michel, André, *Histoire de l'Art* (Paris: Colin, 1922), II.
Weisbach, Werner, *Religiöse Reform und mittelalterliche Kunst* (Einsiedeln-Zürich: Benziger, 1945).

## Chapter II                                                                   Notes

1. Johan Huizinga, *The Waning of the Middle Ages* (London, 1924). Later corrected German edition, *Herbst des Mittelalters*, 5th edition (Stuttgart: Kroner, 1939).
2. Even 'Empress' alone is a very rare epithet of Mary, according to Anselm Salzer, *Die Sinnbilder und Beiworte Mariens in der deutschen Literatur und lateinischen Hymnenpoesie des Mittelalters* (Linz, 1893). It occurs in John Lydgate.
3. *Masterpieces of French Painting from the Primitives to the Sixteenth Century.* Text by E. Tériade (Paris: Skira, 1934).
4. Louis Gillet, *Histoire artistique des ordres mendiants* (Paris: Flammarion, 1939), p. 175. There is another *Vierge protectrice* from the Ecole d'Auvergne (1420) in the Musée du Puy, reproduced in Henri Bouchot, *L'Exposition des primitifs français* (Paris 1904–5), plate 12.
5. Arnold Goffin, *L'Art religieux en Belgique. La peinture des origines à la fin du XVIIIe siècle* (Paris: Van Oest, 1924), p. 54.
6. E. Harris, 'Mary in the Burning Bush: Nicolas Froment's Triptych at Aix en Provence,' *Journal of the Warburg and Courtauld Institutes,* I (1937), facs. 4; and Arthur Watson, 'Mary in the Burning Bush,' ibid. II (1938), facs. 1.
7. Antoine de la Sale, *Le Petit Jehan de Saintré,* ed. J. Marie Guichard (Paris: Gosselin, 1943), ch. 69, p. 226 and ch. 71, p. 233. Translation by Irvine Gray.
8. Cf. Baron Joseph van der Elst, *The Last Flowering of the Middle Ages* (Garden City, N.Y.: Doubleday, 1944), pp. 119–27.
9. *University Prints,* K 103.
10. Goffin, op. cit. p. 23.
11. *Le Petit Jehan de Saintré,* op. cit. ch. 69, pp. 228, 229.
12. Musée Condé, Chantilly.
13. *Les Très Riches Heures du Duc de Berry* (Paris: Laurens, 1933), p. 13ff.
14. *Les Quinze Joies de mariage. Huitième joie,* ed. Ferdinand Heuckenkamp (Halle: Niemeyer, 1901).
15. Paul Durrieu, *Les Très Riches Heures de Jean de France, Duc de Berry* (Paris: Plon, 1904), plate II, p. 137, and description.
16. Edmond Huguet, *Le Langage figuré au seizième siècle* (Paris, 1933).
17. Henri Pirenne, Gustave Cohen, Henri Focillon, *La Civilisation occidentale au moyen-âge du XIe au XVe siècle* (Paris: Presses Universitaires, 1933), p. 408.
18. Martial d'Auvergne, *Les Arrêts d'amour,* ed. Luise Götz (Frankfort, 1932), p. 110.
19. *Les Quinze Joies de mariage,* op. cit. pp. 8 and 27.
20. Friedrich Winkler, *Die flämische Buchmalerei des 15. und 16. Jahrhunderts* (Leipzig: Seemann, 1925); and Georges Lafenestre, *L'Exposition des primitifs français* (Paris, 1904).
21. *Rondeau,* ed. Champion, no. 31 and 30. Translation by Henry Francis Cary, *The Early French Poets* (London, 1923), pp. 179–80.
22. *Ballades amoureuses,* ed. Kervyn de Lettenhove, no. 8.
23. *Oeuvres,* ed. Ernest Hoepffner (Paris: Champion, 1908–21); see René Schneider et Gustave Cohen, *La Formation du génie moderne dans l'art de l'occident* (Paris: Renaissance du Livre, 1936), p. 28.
24. A. G. Canfield and W. F. Patterson, *French Poems* (New York: Holt, 1941), pp. 9, 10 (modernized spelling).
25. 'La Vierge d'Anvers (de Melun?) — Agnès Sorel — couronée d'or et des perles avec sa robe en fourreau, très serré à la taille, et son corsage étroit d'où jaillit le beau sein célèbre à la cour de Chinon.' Georges Lafenestre, p. 74. See note 20.
26. J. Huizinga, *Herbst des Mittelalters,* pp. 225–6.
27. *Les Arts plastiques de 1500–1815* (Paris: de Boccard, 1925), pp. 302ff.
28. See long comment on the passage in E. Auerbach, *Mimesis* (Bern: Francke, 1946), pp. 224ff.

29. J. Nève, *Antoine de la Sale* (Paris et Bruxelles, 1903), pp. 101ff.
30. Johan Huizinga, *Herbst des Mittelalters*, p. 444.
31. Lafenestre, op. cit. plate 1.
32. *University Prints*, ME 55.
33. *Masterpieces of French Painting* . . . op. cit. no. 17. See Otto Pächt, 'Jean Fouquet: A Study of His Style,' *Journal of the Warburg and Courtauld Institutes*, IV (1940), facs. 1–2.
34. Lafenestre, op. cit. p. 76.
35. *Histoire de Saint Louis*, ed. N. de Wailly (Paris: Hachette, 1874), p. 64.
36. *Grammaire historique de la langue française* (Copenhagen, 1930), VI, 283, 284.
37. *Hubert et Jan van Eyck* (Bruxelles, 1910), p. 119.
38. *Masterpieces of French Painting* . . . op. cit. no. 5 in color.
39. *Les Clouet et leurs émules* (Paris: Laurens, 1924), II, 150.
40. Lucien Paul Victor Febvre, *Autour de l'Heptaméron* (Paris: Gallimard, 1944).
41. *University Prints*, E 180. There is no classical pattern for these nymphs. See Albert E. Wier, *Thesaurus of the Arts* (New York: Putnam, n.d.), p. 484.
42. Armand Fourreau, *Les Clouet* (Paris: Rieder, 1929), p. 47.
43. *Catalogue of the New York World's Fair 1940: Masterpieces of Art*, p. 36.
44. *Oeuvres de R. Belleau*, ed. A. Gouverneur (Nogent-le-Rotrou, 1867), I, 149.

## Chapter II                                                            Bibliography

Boethius, Gerda, *Broderna van Eyck* (Stockholm: Norstedt, 1946).
Leroy, Alfred, *Histoire de la peinture française au moyen âge et à la renaissance* (Paris: A. Michel, 1937).
Vloberg, Maurice, *L'Eucharistie dans l'art* (Grenoble: Arthaud, 1946); for Madonna types see M. Vloberg's *La Vierge et l'Enfant dans l'art français* (Grenoble: Arthaud, 1933), 2 vols.

## Chapter III                                                                   Notes

1. *Le Classicisme français* (New York: Editions de la Maison Française, 1942), pp. 113, 114.
2. I, ch. 5, in *Bibliotheca Romanica* (Strasbourg), p. 258.
3. A new interpretation of this picture was given by Erwin Panofsky in a lecture at the National Gallery of Art, Washington, D.C., March 1949.
4. *Oraison funèbre d'Henriette d'Angleterre*, Classiques Larousse, I, pp. 59 and 70.
5. The Metropolitan Museum of Art, New York.
6. *Pensées*, ed. Z. Tourneur (Paris: Bibl. St. Cluny, 1938), II, 263.
7. René Jasinski, 'Trois Sujets raciniens avant Racine,' *Revue d'histoire littéraire de la France*, XLVII (1947), pp. 2–56.
8. *Le Paysage français* (Paris: Payot, 1928), p. 21.
9. Detroit Institute of Arts; *Catalogue of New York World's Fair*, op. cit. p. 46.
10. See Anthony Blunt, 'The Heroic and the Ideal Landscape in the Work of Nicolas Poussin,' *Journal of the Warburg and Courtauld Institutes*, VII (1943), facs. 3 and 4.
11. 'Défense des fables dans la poésie,' *Oeuvres*, ed. M. Ch. Marty-Lavaux (Paris: Hachette, 1862), pp. 238–9, a free translation of a Latin contemporary poem by Jean Baptiste Santeul.
12. *University Prints*, E 10; the original is in the Louvre.
13. Jeanne Magnin, op. cit. p. 48. See note 8.
14. *University Prints*, 1220 in color.
15. Jeanne Magnin, op. cit. pp. 43, 44.
16. Pierre Courthion, *Claude Gellée, dit Le Lorrain* (Paris: Floury, 1932), p. 8.
17. See also color reproduction of several landscapes of this type in Henri Roujon, *Les Peintures illustres. Claude Lorrain* (Paris: Lafitte, n.d.).
18. R. H. Wilenski, *French Painting* (Boston: Hale, Cushman, Flint, 1936), pp. 62, 63; revised edition (Boston: Charles T. Branford Co., 1949).

19. Frank Jewett Mather, Jr., *Western European Painting of the Renaissance* (New York: Holt, 1939), p. 719.
20. *University Prints*, E 8.
21. See also Charles Mitchell, ' Poussin's Flight into Egypt,' *Journal of the Warburg and Courtauld Institutes*, I (1937), facs. 1.
22. *Pensées. Les deux infinis*, Classiques Larousse, 1941, pp. 21, 22.
23. 'Lettre de Guez de Balzac à M. de la Motte-Aigron,' *Princeton Anthology*, p. 43.
24. *Catalogue of New York World's Fair*, op. cit. p. 38.
25. George B. Rose, *Renaissance Masters* (New York: Putnam, 1908), p. 217.
26. R. H. Wilenski, op. cit. plate 38, p. 81.
27. *Journal 1921–1923* (Paris: Corrêa, 1946), p. 383.
28. *University Prints*, E 19.
29. *University Prints*, E 24.
30. Classiques Larousse, I, p. 30.
31. See A. Gazier, *Philippe et Jean-Baptiste de Champaigne* (Paris: Librairie de l'Art, 1893), p. 17.
32. *Lettre à Mme de Grignan*, 31 July 1675.
33. See Luc Benoist, *Coysevox* (Paris: Plon, 1930), ch. IV, pp. 72–104.
34. *Oraison funèbre du prince de Condé*, Classiques Larousse, II, 53–4.
35. See André Mabille de Poncheville, *Philippe de Champaigne* (Paris: Plon, 1938), ch. IV, pp. 42–50.
36. Edition des Grands Ecrivains, XXVIII, p. 87.
37. *Traité de la concupiscence* (Paris: Les textes français, 1930), ch. XVI, p. 51.
38. *Histoire littéraire du sentiment religieux en France*, XI, pp. 200ff.
39. *University Prints*, E 21.
40. *Art in the Western World* (New York: Harper, 1942), p. 746.
41. *Oeuvres choisies* (Paris: Hachette, 1890), vol. II, p. 106.
42. Pierre Kohler, ' Le Classicisme français et le problème du baroque,' in *Lettres de France. Périodes et problèmes* (Lausanne: Payot, 1943), p. 111.
43. *La Gloire du Dôme du Val-de-Grâce, Oeuvres*, ed. Nelson, VI, p. 468.
44. *University Prints*, G 349.
45. *University Prints*, G 348.
46. *University Prints*, G 346.
47. *Théorie des belles lettres* (Paris: Téqui, 1885), pp. 490, 491.
48. See settings of *Pompes funèbres* in the baroque style: Maurice Vloberg, *Notre Dame de Paris et le vœu de Louis XIII* (Paris: L'auteur, 1926), plates XXXII and XLVIII.
49. *The Letters of Mme de Sévigné* (Philadelphia: Horn, 1927), vol. II, pp. 88–90 *passim*.
50. *University Prints*, G 344.
51. *University Prints*, E 181.
52. ' Christus est immutablis,' *Oeuvres de Corneille*, Edition des Grands Ecrivains, IX, p. 33.
53. *University Prints*, E 16.
54. *Manuel de Muséum français* (Paris: Treuttel et Würte, 1805), III, p. 78.
55. Werner Weisbach, *Der Barock als Kunst der Gegenreformation* (Berlin: Cassirer, 1921), p. 149, plate 66.
56. See also Werner Weisbach, *Französische Malerei im siebzehnten Jahrhundert* (Berlin: Keller, 1932), p. 227.
57. Details and genesis of picture in André Gide, *Poussin* (Paris: Au Divan, 1945), p. 24.
58. Marc Antoine Gérard de Saint Amant, *Oeuvres Poétiques* (Paris: Garnier, 1930), pp. 232ff., passim.
59. *Le Mystère de Jésus*, Classiques Larousse, pp. 70, 71.
60. *Catalogue of New York World's Fair*, op. cit. plate 62.
61. *University Prints*, E 17.
62. Cf. Franz Werfel, ' Realism and Inwardness,' *The American Bookman*, I (1944), pp. 5–22.
63. *Les Frères Le Nain* (Paris: Floury, 1933), p. 35.

64. See reproduction in André Lévêque, *Histoire de la civilisation française* (New York: Holt, 1940), p. 217.
65. *Catalogue of New York World's Fair*, op. cit. plate 54.
66. *Catalogue of a Collection of Pictures including examples of the works of the Brothers Le Nain* (London, 1910), p. 39, no. 37.
67. See also Wilenski, op. cit. plate 28a, one of Le Nain's motives: *The Fife Player*.
68. New York Metropolitan Museum of Art.
69. *Oraison funèbre d'Henriette de France*, op. cit. I, p. 28.
70. *Les Caractères* (Paris: Flammarion, n.d.), I, 169.
71. Werner Weisbach, *Französische Malerei des 17. Jahrhunderts* (Berlin: Keller, 1932), plate 47.
72. *Nicolas Poussin* (Paris: Rieder, 1929), p. 31.
73. Werner Weisbach, *Französische Malerei* . . . , op. cit. p. 310.
74. *Terre de France. Poussin* (Paris, Gallimard, 1933), p. 66.
75. Louis Hautecœur, *Littérature et peinture en France du XVIIᵉ au XXᵉ siècle* (Paris: Colin, 1942), p. 18. It is worth while to read the entire discussion for and against the absence of the camels in Poussin's picture. See Guillet de Saint Georges, ' Discussion of Philippe de Champaigne's Lecture on Poussin's Painting, Rebecca and Eleazar,' reprinted in Elizabeth Gilmore Holt, *Literary Sources of Art History* (Princeton University Press, 1947), pp. 388–394.

## Chapter III                                    Bibliography

Caudwell, H., *Introduction to French Classicism* (New York: Macmillan, 1931).
Crump, Phylis E., *Nature in the Age of Louis XIV* (London: Routledge, 1928).
Friedlaender, Walter, *Nicolas Poussin. Die Entwicklung seiner Kunst* (München: Piper, 1914).
Jan, E. von, *Die Landschaft des französischen Menschen* (Weimar: Boehlau, 1935).
Spitzer, Leo, ' Die klassische Dämpfung in Racines Stil,' *Romanische Stil-u. Literaturstudien* (Marburg: Elwert, 1931), pp. 135–268.

## Chapter IV                                         Notes

1. *History of Art. Modern Art* (New York: Garden City Publishing Co., 1937), p. 198.
2. Cf. A. E. Brinckmann, *Watteau* (Wien, 1943), nos. 19, 52.
3. *Der höfische Roman des französischen Rokoko* (Diss. Greifswald, 1936), p. 106.
4. See Fiske Kimball, ' The Creation of the Rococo,' *Journal of the Warburg and Courtauld Institutes*, I (1937), facs. 3 and 4.
5. *Letter to Mariotte*, 28 March 1766.
6. *Les Egarements du cœur et de l'esprit* (Paris: Au Divan, 1929), p. 247.
7. *Le Neveu de Rameau* in O. E. Fellows and N. L. Torrey, *The Age of Enlightenment* (New York: Crofts, 1942), p. 220.
8. Cf. Ruth Kirby Jamieson, *Marivaux. A Study in Sensibility* (Diss. Columbia University, New York, 1941), p. 73.
9. R. H. Wilenski, *French Painting* (Boston: Hale, Cushman, Flint, 1936), p. 122; and University Prints, E 36.
10. Helvétius, *De l'esprit*, in Fellows and Torrey, op cit. p. 350. See other examples in Marie-Louise Duffrenoy, *L'Orient romanesque en France*, 1704–1789 (Montreal: Beauchemin, 1946), p. 61ff.
11. *Histoire de la peinture française au dix-huitième siècle* (Paris: Michel, 1934), p. 235.
12. *Diderot's Imagery. A Study of a Literary Personality* (Diss. Columbia University, New York, 1941), p. 42.
13. *University Prints*, E 29.
14. Brinckmann, op. cit. p. 22.
15. *Pensées détachées sur la peinture*, in Fellows and Torrey, op. cit. p. 294.
16. Helmut Hatzfeld, ' Rokoko als literarischer Epochenstil,' *Studies in Philology*, xxxv (1938), pp. 522–65.
17. *Le Paysage français* (Paris, 1928), p. 105.

18. Louis Dimier, *Les Peintres français du dix-huitième siècle*, vol. 1 (Paris, Bruxelles: Van Oest, 1928), p. 19.
19. M. Petitot, *Répertoire du théâtre français* (Paris: Didot, 1804), pp. 458, 459.
20. *Poésies de Gentil-Bernard*, quoted in Richard Ashley Rice, 'Rousseau and the Poetry of Nature in Eighteenth Century France,' in *Smith College Studies in Modern Languages* (Northampton, Mass., 1925, April and July), p. 41.
21. Cf. Margaret Louise Buchner, 'A Contribution to the Study of the Descriptive Technique of Jean Jacques Rousseau, in *Johns Hopkins Studies in Romance Languages*, vol. 30 (Baltimore, 1937), *passim*, particularly appendix.
22. Fellows and Torrey, op. cit. p. 296.
23. *University Prints*, GM 278. The original is in the Louvre. See also F. Baldensperger, 'Intellectuels français hors de France,' *Revue des Cours et Conférences*, xxxvi (1934-5), p. 77.
24. Ruth Kirby Jamieson, op. cit. p. 71.
25. Buchner, op. cit. p. 109.
26. *University Prints*, E 32.
27. Elie Faure, op. cit. p. 211. See note 1.
28. Louis Dimier, op. cit., vol. 2 (Paris, 1930), p. 103.
29. J. Joubert, *Pensées*, quoted in André Gide et autres, *Tableau de la littérature française de Corneille à Chénier* (Paris: Nouvelle Revue Française, 1939), p. 237.
30. *Poésies mêlées*, no. 276, *Oeuvres complètes* (Paris: Leroi, 1833), vol. 1, p. 1165.
31. 'Lettre à D'Alembert sur les spectacles,' in Fellows and Torrey, op. cit. p. 543.
32. *University Prints*, E 28.
33. *Watteau* (London: Stokes, n.d.), p. 23.
34. *Arlequin comédien aux Champs Elysées* (Paris: Seneuze, 1694).
35. Op. cit. p. 33.
36. Brinckmann, op. cit. plate 45.
37. See also Leo Spitzer, 'Pages from Voltaire,' in *A Method of Interpreting Literature* (Northampton, Mass.: Smith College, 1949), pp. 64-101.
38. Montesquieu, *Lettres persanes*, no. 88 in Fellows and Torrey, op. cit. p. 129.
39. Montesquieu, *Lettres persanes*, no. 24, op. cit. p. 112.
40. Voltaire, *Micromégas*, *Oeuvres complètes* (Paris, 1785), vol. 44, p. 153ff.
41. Voltaire, 'Essai sur les mœurs,' *Oeuvres complètes* (Paris, 1785), vol. 17, p. 466.
42. *Jeannot et Colin*: *Oeuvres complètes* (Paris, 1785), vol. 44, p. 212.
43. Chamfort, quoted in A. H. Fink, *Maxime und Fragment* (München: Hueber, 1934), p. 46.
44. See Felix Vexler, *Studies in Diderot's Esthetic Naturalism* (Diss. Columbia University, New York, 1922); and Armand Behets, *Diderot, critique d'art* (Bruxelles: Lebègue, 1944).
45. Alfred Leroy, op. cit. p. 388.
46. Ibid. p. 390.
47. *Lettre sur les Sourds et Muets*, in Fellows and Torrey, op. cit. p. 272.

## Chapter IV                                                    Bibliography

Chérel, Albert, *De Télémaque à Candide* (Paris: de Gigord, 1933).
Goncourt, Edmond and Jules de, *Fragonard* (Genève: La Palatine, 1946).
Holzbecher, Karl, *Denkart und Denkform von Pierre de Marivaux* (Diss. Berlin, 1936).
Schoolman, Regina, and Charles E. Slatkin, *The Enjoyment of Art in America* (Philadelphia, New York: Lippincott, n.d.).
Wildenstein, Georges, *Lancret* (Paris: Les Beaux Arts, 1924).

## Chapter V                                                          Notes

1. *Oeuvres* (Paris: Michaud, 1824) VII, p. 365.
2. 'Le Chant du départ' in A. G. Canfield and W. F. Patterson, *French Poems* (New York: Holt, 1941), pp. 217-19.
3. See also Agnes Mongan, 'Ingres and the Antique,' *Journal of the Warburg and Courtauld Institutes*, x (1946).

4. 'Le Peintre' in *Oeuvres posthumes*, ed. P. A. Coupin (Paris: Renouard, 1829), I, p. 91.
5. *Ingres* (Paris: Hachette, 1928), p. xii.
6. See Henri Lemmonier, 'L'Atala de Chateaubriand et l'Atala de Girodet,' in *Gazette des beaux arts*, I (1914), pp. 363-71.
7. *Oeuvres complètes* (Paris: Garnier, 1929), III, p. 62.
8. Henri Marcel, *La peinture française* (Paris, 1905), p. 114.
9. *Une Jeune Femme au bain. Pensées d'Août* 1837, quoted in Jacques-Henry Bornecque, *Peintres et écrivains* (Paris: Arts et Métiers graphiques, 1947), p. 34.
10. Op. cit. p. 52. See note 8.
11. *Masterpieces in Art*, Bates and Guild, p. 40.
12. Gustave Lanson, *L'Art de la prose* (Paris, n.d.), p. 294.
13. *University Prints*, E 76.
14. *Gros, ses amis et ses élèves* (Paris: Floury, 1936), p. 12.
15. Musée de Rouen. Reproduction in Victor Hugo, 'Poésie,' *Oeuvres* (Paris: Larousse, n.d.), p. 158.
16. *University Prints*, E 123.
17. In Albert Schinz, *Nineteenth Century French Readings* (New York: Holt, 1939), I, p. 530.
18. Gustave Lanson, *L'Art de la prose*, op. cit., p. 219.
19. Trans. Jessie Haynes (New York: Collier and Son, 1902), pp. 226-8.
20. See Leon Rosenthal, *Géricault* (Paris, 1905).
21. *University Prints*, E 90.
22. *Curiosités esthétiques*, ed. Crépet (Paris, 1868), p. 120.
23. *Carmen*, ed. M. Parturier (Paris: Les textes français, 1930), p. 31.
24. See Marion Elizabeth Carter, *The Role of the Symbol in French Romantic Poetry* (Diss. Catholic University, Washington, D.C., 1946).
25. In *Victor Hugo, Encyclopédie par l'image* (Paris, 1927), p. 49.
26. Oskar Walzel, 'Handbuch der Literaturwissenschaft,' in Hanns Heiss, *Romanische Literaturen des 19. und 20. Jahrhunderts*, I (Berlin, Neubabelsberg, 1923).
27. 'Dieu est toujours là,' *Les Voix intérieures*.
28. *Actualité de Daumier* (Beyrouth, 1942), pp. 34, 35.
29. 'Visionnaires. Balzac et Daumier.' *Essays in honor of Albert Feuillerat* (New Haven: Yale University Press, 1943), p. 201.
30. Quoted in Pierre Abraham, *Créatures chez Balzac* (Paris: Gallimard, 1931), p. 50.
31. Quoted in Helen T. Garrett, *Clothes and character. The function of dress in Balzac* (Philadelphia, 1941), p. 73.
32. Trans. O. W. Wight and F. B. Goodrich (New York: Rudd and Carleton, 1861), pp. 97-9.
33. *University Prints*, E 253.
34. *Law and Justice* (New York: Pantheon, 1944), Introduction.
35. *La Dernière Incarnation de Vautrin, Oeuvres* (Librairie Nouvelle, 1856), p. 115.
36. Julien Maurice Cain, *Millet* (Paris: Librairie centrale, 1913), p. 37.
37. *University Prints*, 1206 in color.
38. Cain, op. cit. p. 53ff.
39. Ibid. p. 55.
40. Henri Guillemin, *Le Jocelyn de Lamartine* (Paris: Boivin, 1936).
41. *University Prints*, 1207 in color.
42. Concerning the importance of the *dessins* and *crayons* in Millet's work, see Louis Souillié, *Peintures, Aquarelles, Pastels, Dessins de Jean François Millet* (Paris: Souillié, 1900).
43. Pierre du Colombier, 'Decamps,' in *Les Peintres illustrés*, ed. P. Lafille (Paris: Rieder, 1928), p. 43.
44. Germaine Maillet, *Peinture religieuse* (Paris: Bloud, 1934), p. 208.
45. L. Hourticq, *Delacroix* (Paris: Hachette, 1930), p. 12.
46. René Ménard *et al.*, *Grands peintres français et étrangers* (Paris: Launette, 1884), p. 7.
47. Perry Pictures, Boston edition, no. 498. Original is in the Louvre.
48. Marthe Kolb, *Ary Scheffer et son temps* (Paris: Boivin, 1937), pp. 391, 392.
49. *Achille et Eugène Dévéria* (Paris: Floury, 1925), p. 10.

50. Jacques G. Clémenceau LeClercq, *L'Inspiration biblique dans l'œuvre poétique d'Alfred de Vigny* (Marseille: Université, 1937), p. 103.
51. *Catalogue of New York World's Fair* 1940, op. cit. p. 170.
52. 'Le Huchier de Nazareth,' *Oeuvres. Les Trophées* (Paris: Lemerre, 1931), p. 93.

## Chapter V                                                Bibliography

Alazard, Jean, *L'Orient et la peinture française au XIX^e siècle* (Paris: Plon, 1930).
Calmette, Joseph, *François Rude* (Paris: Floury, 1920).
Courthion, Pierre, *David, Ingres, Gros, Géricault* (Genève: Skira, 1943); *Eugène Delacroix* (Paris: Skira, 1939).
Guiffrey, Jean, *L'Oeuvre de P. P. Prud'hon* (Paris: Colin, 1924).
Hautecœur, Louis, *Rome et la renaissance de l'antiquité à la fin du XVIII^e siècle* (Paris, 1912).
Lassaigne, Jacques, *Honoré Daumier* (Paris: Hyperion, 1946).
Poirier, Alice, *Les idées artistiques de Chateaubriand* (Paris: Presses Universitaires, 1930).
Thomson, Leslie, *Jean François Millet* (London: Sheldon Press, 1927).
Wilenski, R. H., *French Painting* (Boston, 1949).

## Chapter VI                                                      Notes

1. *Courbet* (Paris: Skira, 1940), p. 4.
2. *Madame Bovary*, trans. Gerard Hopkins (New York: Oxford University Press, 1949), ch. x, p. 388ff.
3. *Extraits d'un journal*, 1908–1928 (Paris: Pléiade, 1929), pp. 43, 44.
4. *Art poétique. Jadis et naguère*, in A. G. Canfield and W. F. Patterson, *French Poems* (New York: Holt, 1941), pp. 407, 408.
5. In H. Bornecque, *Les Chefs d'Oeuvre de la langue française. Prose* (Paris: Larousse, 1924), p. 202.
6. *Catalogue of New York World's Fair*, op. cit. p. 195.
7. 'Le Port de Carquehuit,' in *A l'Ombre des jeunes filles en fleur*, iii, p. 99.
8. *L'Assommoir*, trans. Havelock Ellis (New York: Knopf, 1938), pp. 319–20.
9. D. L. Demorest, *L'Expression figurée et symbolique dans l'œuvre de Gustave Flaubert* (Paris: Les Presses modernes, 1931).
10. *University Prints*, E 166; the original is in The National Art Gallery, Washington, D.C.
11. *University Prints*, E 290.
12. Cf. John Rewald, *Georges Seurat* (New York: Wittenborn, 1946), pp. 57–62.
13. *Manette Salomon*, quoted in François Fosca, *E. et J. de Goncourt* (Paris: A. Michel, 1941), pp. 243, 244.
14. Musée d'art moderne de Moscou.
15. *Du Côté de chez Swann*, trans. C. K. Scott Moncrieff (New York: Random House, 1934), ii, p. 108.
16. Cf. also Maurice E. Chernowitz, *Proust and Painting* (New York: International University Press, 1945), p. 173.
17. Trans. Hugh Craig (New York: Routledge, 1890), p. 171.
18. Paris: Nelson, 1921, pp. 201–37 *passim*.
19. *Father Goriot*, in *The Works of Honoré de Balzac*, trans. Ellen Marriage and James Waring (Philadelphia: Avil, 1901), vol. xxvi, pp. 123–4.
20. Hans Graber, *Edgar Degas* (Basel: Schwage, 1942), p. 83.
21. *Extraits d'un journal* 1908–1928 (Paris: Pléiade, 1929), p. 14.
22. See Camille Mauclair, *Edgar Degas* (New York: Hyperion Press, 1941), p. 40.
23. *University Prints*, E 259; original in Musée de l'Impressionisme, Paris.
24. Variant of the same motif in Hans Graber, op. cit. p. 124.
25. *Littérature et peinture en France* (Paris: Colin, 1942), p. 164.
26. Op. cit., pp. 135–43 *passim*.
27. Manet's portrait of Zola (1888) is described in Theodore Duret, *Manet* (New

York: Crown Publishers, 1932), pp. 52, 53. Manet's *Déjeuner sur l'herbe* is described in Zola, *L'Oeuvre* (Paris: Charpentier, 1931), II, pp. 51–65.
28. *Anthologie de la poésie précieuse de Thibaut de Champagne à Giraudoux* (Paris: Egloff, 1946), p. 221.
29. Charles Leconte de Lisle, 'Midi,' *Poèmes antiques*, in Canfield and Patterson, op. cit., p. 357.
30. *Introduction à la peinture hollandaise* (Paris, 1935).
31. A portrait completely composed of geometrical forms is Juan Gris's *Arlequin à table* (1918), in G. di San Lazzaro, *Painting in France 1895–1949* (New York: Philosophical Library, 1949).
32. Louis Danz, *The Psychologist Looks on Art* (London, New York: Longmans, Green, 1937).
33. *Jacob's Night* (New York: Sheed and Ward, 1947), p. 87.
34. See Stanislas Fumet, *Braque* (Paris: Braun, 1946), Introduction.
35. Régis Michaud, *Vingtième siècle* (New York, London: Harper & Brothers, 1933), p. 11.
36. *Art et Catholicisme* (Montreal: Arbre, 1941), p. 70.
37. For the general principles involved, see F. Jean-Desthieux, *Qu'est-ce que l'art moderne?* (Paris: Plon, 1925), and Jean Cassou, Ernest Ansermet *et al.*, *Débat sur l'art contemporain* (Neuchâtel: La Baconnière, 1948). See also Brancusi, *Maiastra*, in Fernando Puma, *Modern Art Looks Ahead* (New York: The Beechhurst Press, 1947).
38. Charles Maurice, *Paul Gauguin* (Paris: Floury, 1919), p. 168.
39. Pallas Postcard 1023, Artex Prints.
40. See Wallace Fowlie, *Rimbaud* (New York: New Directions, 1946), p. 64ff.
41. See the chapter 'The Prayer' in Paul Gauguin, *Noa Noa. My Voyage to Tahiti* (New York: Lear, 1947), p. 112f.
42. Georges Lemaître, *From Cubism to Surrealism in French Literature* (Cambridge, Mass.: University Press, 1941), p. 54.
43. Roch Grey, *Henri Rousseau* (Paris: Editions 'Tel,' 1943), Introduction and plate 105.
44. Hautecœur, op. cit. p. 276.
45. Julius Meyer-Graefe, *Vincent van Gogh* (New York: Blue Ribbon Books, 1933), p. 121.
46. Ibid. plate 49. See also Carl Nordenfalk, 'Van Gogh and Literature,' *Journal of the Warburg and Courtauld Institutes*, x (1946).
47. Meyer-Graefe, op. cit. plate 39; similar motif, *Street café in Arles at Night*. See also Gisèle d'Assailly, *Avec les peintres de la réalité poétique* (Paris: R. Julliard, 1949).
48. R. Pitrou, 'Rilke and van Gogh,' *Revue de Littérature comparée*, xxi (1947), pp. 70–73.
49. *Le Journal des faux-monnayeurs* (Paris: Ed. Eos, 1926).
50. Philo M. Buck, *Directions in Contemporary Literature* (New York: Oxford University Press, 1942), p. 89.
51. *Modern Masters*, p. 25, no. 16.
52. Paris: Plon, 1926, pp. 210–21 *passim*.
53. T. W. Earp, *The Modern Movement in Painting* (London, New York: The Studio, 1935), plate 16.
54. *Le Grand Meaulnes d'Alain Fournier* (Bruxelles: Editions des Artistes, 1941).
55. Ed. Paul Frères (Paris, 1933), pp. 76–81 *passim*.
56. *Hommes et œuvres du XX^e siècle* (Paris: Corrêa, 1938), p. 204.
57. David G. Larg, *André Maurois* (London: Shaylor, 1931), p. 26; *Meipe*, p. 13.

Chapter VI Bibliography

Colombier, Pierre du, *Jean-Baptiste Corot* (New York, 1940).
Dorival, Bernard, *Images de la peinture française contemporaine* (Paris: Ed. Nomis, 1946).
Hamann, Richard, *Der Impressionismus in Leben und Kunst* (Köln: Dumont, 1907).
Jedlicka, Gotthard, *Edouard Manet* (Erlenbach-Zürich: Rentsch, 1944).

Köhler, Erich, *Edmond und Jules de Goncourt* (Leipzig: Xenien-Verlag, 1912).

Rich, Daniel Catton, *Seurat and the Evolution of 'La Grande Jatte'* (Chicago: University Press, 1935).

Schapiro, Meyer, 'Courbet and Popular Imagery: An Essay on Realism and Naïveté,' *Journal of the Warburg and Courtauld Institutes,* IV (1940), facs. 3–4.

Wilenski, R. H., *French Painting* (Boston: Charles T. Branford Co., 1949).

## Chapter VII                                                    Notes

1. *Das Erklären von Kunstwerken* (Leipzig: Seemann, 1940), p. 16.

# Bibliography of General Works

Blunden, Edmund Charles, *Romantic Poetry and the Fine Arts*. Proceedings of the British Academy, Vol. 28 (1942).

Bowie, Theodore Robert, *Les Rapports entre la littérature et la peinture en France de 1840–1880* (Berkeley, 1935).

Breton, André, *Le Surréalisme et la peinture* (Paris: Gallimard, 1928).

Chernowitz, M. E., *Proust and Painting* (New York: International University Press, 1945).

Crump, Phyllis E., *Nature in the Age of Louis XIV* (London: Routledge, 1928).

David-Sauvageot, A., *Le Réalisme et le naturalisme dans la littérature et dans l'art* (Paris: C. Levy, 1889).

Dorbec, Prosper, *Les Lettres françaises dans leurs contacts avec l'atelier de l'artiste* (Paris: Presses Universitaires, 1929).

Engwer, Theodor, 'Französische Malerei und französische Literatur im 19. Jahrhundert. Eine Parallele,' *Die Neueren Sprachen*, XVI (1908), 449–86.

Fardwell, Virginia, *Landscape in Marcel Proust* (Washington: Catholic University Press, 1948).

Giovanni, G., 'Method in the Study of Literature in Its Relation to the Other Fine Arts,' *The Journal of Aesthetics & Art Criticism*, VIII (March 1950), 185–95.

Greene, Theodore Mayer, *The Arts and the Art of Criticism* (Princeton University Press, 1940).

Grigaut, Paul L., 'Art et littérature,' *The French Review*, XII (1939), 459–68.

Hatzfeld, Helmut, 'Literary Criticism through Art and Art Criticism through Literature,' *The Journal of Aesthetics & Art Criticism*, VI (1947), 1–21.

Hautecœur, Louis, *Littérature et peinture en France du XVIIe au XXe siècle* (Paris: Colin, 1944).

Hoerner, Margarete, 'Sprachstil und Kunststil,' *Idealistische Philologie*, III (1927), 184–8.

Hourticq, Louis, *L'Art et la littérature* (Paris: Flammarion, 1947).

Huizinga, Johan, *The Waning of the Middle Ages* (London, 1924).

Jan, Eduard von, *Die Landschaft des französischen Menschen* (Weimar: Boehlau, 1935).

Lehel, Franz, *Morphologie comparée des arts* (Paris, 1930).

Lemaître, Georges, *Cubism and Surrealism in French Literature* (Cambridge: Harvard University Press, 1941).

Maury, Paul, *Arts et littérature comparés. Etat présent de la question* (Paris: Belles Lettres, 1934).

Munro, Thomas, *The Arts and Their Interrelations* (New York: The Liberal Arts Press, 1949).

Ors, Eugenio d', *Coupole et Monarchie* (Paris: Capitole, 1926).

Rensselaer, Lee, ' "Ut Pictura Poesis." The Humanistic Theory of Painting,' *Art Bulletin*, XXII (1940), 197–269.

Schürr, Friedrich, *Das altfranzösische Epos. Zur inneren Form der Gotik* (München: Hueber, 1926); *Klassizismus, Barock, Rokoko* (Leipzig, 1928).

Souriau, Etienne, *La Correspondance des arts* (Paris: Flammarion, 1947).

Stein, Leo, *Painting, Poetry and Prose* (New York: Crown Publishers, 1947).

Stevens, Wallace, *The Relations between Poetry and Painting* (New York: Museum of Modern Art, 1951).

Taylor, John F. A., ed., *An Introduction to Literature and the Fine Arts* (Michigan State College Press, 1950).

Vossler, Karl, ' Über gegenseitige Erhellung der Künste,' *Festschrift Heinrich Wölfflin zum 70. Geburtstag* (Dresden: Jess, 1935), 160–67.

Wais, Kurt, *Symbiose der Künste* (Stuttgart: Kohlhammer, 1936).

Walzel, Oskar, ' Gehalt und Gestalt im Kunstwerk des Dichters,' *Handbuch der Literaturwissenschaft*, 1 (Wildpark-Potsdam, 1924).

Webster, Thomas Bertram Lonsdale, *Greek Art and Literature 530–400 B.C.* (Oxford: Clarendon Press, 1939).

Weisbach, Werner, *Französische Malerei des siebzehnten Jahrhunderts* (Berlin: Keller, 1932); *Religiose Reform und mittelalterliche Kunst* (Einsiedeln-Zürich: Benziger, 1945).

Wellek, René, ' The Parallelism between Literature and the Arts,' *The English Institute Annual* (New York: Columbia University Press, 1942).

Wessels, P. B., ' Poesie und Malerei,' *Neophilologus*, XXXIII (1949), 216–21.

# Index of Artists and Authors

# Index of Terms and Titles